D1265157

THE EARLY CHRISTIAN FATHERS

The Early Christian Fathers is planned by the author as the first volume of a complete English Patrology in three parts:

THE EARLY CHRISTIAN FATHERS

by
F. L. CROSS
*Lady Margaret Professor of Divinity
in the University of Oxford*

GERALD DUCKWORTH & CO. LTD.
3 Henrietta Street, London, W.C.2

Printed in Great Britain by
The Camelot Press Ltd., London and Southampton

CONTENTS

INTRODUCTION

THIS volume is not a manual of early Church history, nor is it a guide to early Christian doctrine, though both these matters take an important place in the writings of the Fathers. Its main purpose is the more restricted one of offering the student a brief survey of Christian literature from the Apostolic Fathers to the beginning of the 4th century. At the upper limit we shall exclude the literature of the New Testament on the ground that it is well covered in other works and any treatment of it on the slight scale of the rest could not but be jejune and superficial. At the lower end we shall not deal with Eusebius because by temper and range of interest he belongs to the post-Nicene age from which, indeed, his later writings come. Perhaps he will some day find a place in a later volume in this series.

The literary remains which will come within our purview form the basis of every reconstruction of pre-Nicene Christianity and as such they are of perennial interest. They are, indeed, the foundation on which both early Church history and the history of early Christian doctrine have to be built. Since the 17th century they have received an ever increasing measure of attention from historians, and if there have been past generations when Patristic learning has been deeper and more extensive, at no time has the study of the Fathers been more alive than it is to-day. But a preliminary observation should be made. The tyro embarking on the study of the Fathers must be prepared to find that many of the documents he will be studying possess a *prima facie* interest hardly commensurate with that of the story of which they contain the record. In the earlier part of the period especially, the Church had comparatively few writers of literary skill, and her authors wrote not to gratify the literary and historical interests of posterity but to meet as best they could the practical needs of the Church of their own day. The student who knows where to look can find plenty of moving and interesting and fascinating passages even among the pre-Nicene writings. But he will encounter wide tracts which are arid and unrewarding and it will be only as he advances in historical knowledge and understanding that he will begin to grasp their significance. As he re-reads the texts and perseveres, he will find the outline of the early Church and its remarkable medley of figures gradually unfolding before him and taking shape in his mind. But he should realise at the outset that because he is dealing with an epic period in the history of the Church, he will not find all, or even a major part, of the literature inspiring on first acquaintance.

It should be pointed out that this manual is designed not for continuous reading, but for use in conjunction with the texts. For ordinary purposes an English translation of the texts is quite adequate. The Fathers do not lose greatly by being read in translation; and the large majority of the pre-Nicene writings are easily accessible in various collections. Of these the *Ante-Nicene Christian Library* is the most complete, but many individual works are better translated elsewhere. It goes without saying that the best introduction to any ancient writer is to read some of his actual work. In many cases the student will have had his interest aroused by studying two or three pages and will then wish to read carefully through a particular treatise, or even the whole works, of some writers. In others he may find his curiosity satisfied, at any rate for the time being, by reading only a few passages. For general guidance the beginner is recommended to have one of the many *compendia* of passages at hand. The older collections of H. M. Gwatkin[1] and B. J. Kidd[2] are commendable; and even better is the excellently

[1] *Selections from Early Writers, illustrative of Church History to the Time of Constantine* ([revised ed.] 1897).
[2] *Documents illustrative of the History of the Church* (2 vols., London, S.P.C.K., 1920).

edited recent collection of Mr. J. Stevenson.[1] A useful set of extracts selected from a doctrinal angle is that of Mr. H. Bettenson.[2] And needless to say, the student should also have at his side a history of the Church and (if he is interested in the dogmatic aspects of the period) a history of Christian doctrine, not to mention works bearing on the secular history of the time. On this last he can find a valuable guide in the two concluding volumes of the *Cambridge Ancient History*. Everyone is familiar with the way in which from the few fragmentary archaeological and literary remains the character of Roman civilisation in Britain is being brought to light by the labours and skill of scholars and archaeologists. In a similar way the early Patristic period can be reconstructed and made to live by the skilful and judicious use of what is really a strictly limited body of texts. But here, too, the picture is in need of constant revision as new documents come to light and new interpretations are put on others already known.

Most of the ground covered in this volume is necessarily well trodden and there is only limited scope for originality. Moreover, the volume makes no pretence of being complete; an exhaustive survey of the ever growing 'Apocryphal New Testament', for instance, would have been impossible within its limits and we must be content with a selection of the more important writings in this field. On matters on which competing views are possible, I hope that the fact is sufficiently indicated and that the particular view here stated will be understood as not intended to be exclusive of others. Of purpose rather more than their due share of attention has been given to certain recent discoveries or restorations, such as the Toura fragments of Origen, Melito of Sardis' treatise on the Pasch, and the Coptic documents from Nag Hammadi, notably the 'Gospel of Thomas'. Whether or not the interpretation put on Melito's treatise, which as far as I know is not to be found elsewhere, will prove to be the

[1] *A New Eusebius* (London, S.P.C.K., 1957).
[2] *The Early Christian Fathers* (London, 1956).

correct one, only further study of this document can show. I need not say that in compiling this book I have had constantly at my side the larger works of Harnack, Bardenhewer, de Labriolle, Altaner and Quasten, and innumerable other aids.

In most cases the methods of abbreviation should be found self-explanatory. In general, the conventions followed in the *Oxford Dictionary of the Christian Church* have been adopted. The reader is referred to this work for further details.

TABLE OF DATES

211–17	Caracalla, Emperor
c. 215	Death of Clement of Alexandria
217–22	Callistus, Bishop of Rome
218–22	Elagabalus, Emperor
c. 220	Death of Tertullian
222–35	Alexander Severus, Emperor
231	Origen finally leaves Alexandria for Caesarea
232–72	Firmilian, Bishop of Caesarea
235–38	Maximinus Thrax, Emperor
236	Death of St. Hippolytus
245–65	Gregory Thaumaturgus, Bishop of Neo-Caesarea
247–65	Dionysius, Bishop of Alexandria
249–51	Decius, Emperor
250	Fabian, Bishop of Rome, martyred
251–53	Cornelius, Bishop of Rome
c. 253	Death of Origen
253–60	Valerian, Emperor
258	Martyrdom of St. Cyprian (14 September)
260–8	Gallienus, Emperor
c. 269	Dionysius, Bishop of Rome
270–5	Aurelian, Emperor
284–305	Diocletian, Emperor
300–11	Peter, Bishop of Alexandria
305–11	Galerius, Emperor
312	Battle of the Milvian Bridge (28 October)
313	'Edict of Milan'
314	Council of Arles
314–35	Silvester, Bishop of Rome
314–39	Eusebius, Bishop of Caesarea
325	Council of Nicaea

I.—THE APOSTOLIC FATHERS

[The best modern collected editions are those of O. Gebhardt—A. Harnack—T. Zahn (3 vols., Leipzig, 1875-7; ed. minor, ibid., 1877); J. B. Lightfoot—J. R. Harmer (texts, with Eng. tr., in one volume, London, 1891); F. X. Funk (2 vols., Tübingen, 1878-81); and K. Bihlmeyer (Tübingen, 1924). Eng. tr. also in A.N.C.L., and several items in A.C.W. and L.C.C. For vocabulary, E. J. Goodspeed, *Index Patristicus* (Leipzig, 1907). For use of N.T. see *The New Testament in the Apostolic Fathers* (ed. Oxford Society of Historical Theology, 1905). For doctrine, L. J. Tixeront, *Histoire des Dogmes*, i (1905), ch. iii, pp. 115-63 (Eng. tr., 1910, pp. 104-48); J. N. D. Kelly, *Early Christian Doctrines* (1959), pp. 90-5.]

EVER since 1672, when in a famous edition of the writings of Barnabas, Clement of Rome, Hermas, Ignatius and Polycarp, J. B. Cotelier described these primitive Christian authors in his title as 'The Fathers who flourished in the times of the Apostles', these five sub-Apostolic writers have been commonly known as the 'Apostolic Fathers', though by convention the list has been somewhat extended since Cotelier's day. Besides their early date these documents have certain characteristics in common. They are all relatively short; they are preserved for the most part in very few manuscripts; they have strictly limited literary merit; and they tend to raise the same type of problems, since they all belong to a period of Church life of which records are very scanty. Hence the student finds it convenient to treat them together. But for the historian it is only in an accidental sense that the 'Apostolic Fathers' form a unity. They might be compared with the older pieces in an antique shop. Such pieces, not very attractive at first sight, are usually of diverse origin and have little in common, and many of them will generally have lost some of their pristine glory either through the ill advised handling of the repairer or the intentional deceit of

the forger, but yet can be of surpassing interest to those who
have the requisite knowledge to appreciate and understand
them and to appraise them at their true worth.

THE DIDACHE

[Ed. with facsimile by J. R. Harris (Baltimore, Md., and London, 1887).
Other edd. by A. Harnack (T.U. ii, 1-2, 1884) and H. Lietzmann
(Kl. T., 1936). Eng. trr. by C. Bigg (1898; rev. by A. J. Maclean, 1922)
and J. A. Kleist, S.J., in A.C.W. (1948).]

This short manual of moral instruction and Church order,
the most interesting discovery in the field of Patristic
literature in the last hundred years, was first published in
1883 by Philotheos Bryennios, Greek Metropolitan of Nicomedia, who had found it in a MS. written in 1056 in the
library of the Greek Patriarch of Jerusalem at Constant-
inople.[1] The treatise is entitled in the MS. 'The Teaching of
the Lord to the Gentiles through the Twelve Apostles', but
it is more generally known by the abbreviated title in the
index of the MS., 'The Teaching of the Twelve Apostles', or
still more shortly as 'The Didache'.

In the early Church the *Didache* was held in much greater
repute than in later times. It was probably known to Clement
of Alexandria,[2] certainly to the author of the Pseudo-
Cyprianic *De Aleatoribus*,[3] and to several later writers; and
it was incorporated in some important Church Orders.
Eusebius and Athanasius even regarded it as on the fringe of
the Scriptural canon. Further evidence of its popularity is
the existence of widely scattered fragments of the text and
of versions which have recently come to light. Two Greek
fragments from chs. 1-3 have been found in the Oxyrhynchus
papyrus 1782 (late 4th century); a small portion of an early
Latin version of the first six chapters survives in a 9th-10th-
century MS. at Melk in Austria and the whole of these

[1] The MS. also contained the Epistles of Barnabas and of Clement
which Bryennios had published in 1875. Shortly after the publication
of The *Didache* in 1883, the MS. was transferred to the library of the
Greek Patriarchate at Jerusalem, where it now rests (Cod. 54).
[2] *Strom.* 1. 20. 100.   [3] Ch. 4.

chapters in an 11th-century Munich (formerly Freising) MS.;[1] while a considerable section (10. 3b-12. 2a) exists in a 5th-century Coptic papyrus in the British Museum (Or. 9271). There also exist Ethiopic and Georgian fragments.

The *Didache* is in effect a handbook of Church discipline. It falls into three parts: (i) an epitome of the Christian moral code, described under the figure of the Two Ways,—the 'Way of Life' and the 'Way of Death' (1-6). This portion of the work is probably based on a Jewish moral code which the author has worked over and Christianised; (ii) a liturgical section dealing with Baptism (7), Fasting and Prayer (8) and the 'Eucharist' (9f.); (iii) a section concerned with Church order—it deals with apostles and prophets, how true prophets are to be distinguished from false and how these itinerant ministers are to be received by the Christian community (11-13), with the celebration of the Sunday Eucharist which is to be prefaced by a confession of sins (14), and with bishops and deacons and the respect due to them (15). A final section deals with the eschatological setting of the Christian life (16).

What is the origin of this little treatise? It is difficult to relate its enactments with any known historical setting. The community is expressly bidden to fast, not, however, with the Jews on Mondays and Thursdays, but on Wednesdays and Fridays. Baptism is in the Threefold Name (cf. Matt. xxviii. 19), and both the baptizer and baptisand are to fast before the sacrament is administered. In case of need, it can be by affusion and in warm water. The 'Eucharistic' prayers in 9f.,—perhaps intended for the Agape rather than the Eucharist,—are quite unparalleled. Their strong eschatological flavour and phraseology ('the holy vine of David'; 'Hosanna to the God of David'; 'Maranatha') and the description of Christ as 'Thy Servant ($\pi\alpha\tilde{\iota}\varsigma$) Jesus', strike a very primitive note. The faithful are all to say the Lord's Prayer three times daily. Itinerant apostles and prophets still fill an important place in the life of the Church, but their

[1] Edited by J. Schlecht in 1900 and again in 1901.

authority is declining. Much in its pages breathes a very early atmosphere.

But the question arises whether this archaism is genuine or feigned. The issue is complicated by some intricate literary problems. The concluding chapters of the *Epistle of Barnabas* (see below) have such close affinities with the 'Two Ways' in *Did.* 1-6 that the existence of some literary connexion between the two writings is beyond dispute. There are three possible solutions: (1) That *Barnabas* used the *Didache*; (2) That the *Didache* used *Barnabas*; and (3) That both were dependent on a common source. The problem is further complicated by some apparent (though less un-equivocal) literary connexions between the *Didache* and *Hermas*.[1] P. Bryennios and A. Harnack maintained that the *Didache* was dependent on *Barnabas*. But the majority of older scholars (T. Zahn, F. X. Funk, P. Schaff) held the date for the *Didache* is established beyond question.

In 1912 a strong reaction set in in Britain against this early dating. In a paper in the *Journal of Theological Studies*[2] J. A. Robinson argued for the priority of *Barnabas* and a relatively late date for the *Didache*. This thesis found an able champion in R. H. Connolly of Downside Abbey; it was defended by an American scholar, Dr. J. Muilenburg,[3] and it was later upheld by Mr. F. E. Vokes in his book *The Riddle of the Didache* and by Gregory Dix. Though it was challenged by V. Bartlet, B. H. Streeter and J. M. Creed, it came to be widely accepted in the English speaking world. According to this view, the *Didache*, so far from being an actual description of Church life in a remote community, was an imaginative reconstruction, based on fragments skilfully pieced together from various early sources to convey a picture of supposed primitive Church life and practice. There was less agreement

---

[1] See below, pp. 23-7.

[2] xiii (1912), pp. 339-56. Robinson developed this view further in his *Barnabas, Hermas and the Didache* (Donnellan Lectures, 1920).

[3] *The Literary Relations of the Epistle of Barnabas and the Teaching of the Twelve Apostles* (Marburg Diss., 1929).

among these scholars as to the purpose of the author. One view was that his design was to commend Montanism. On a late date, of course, the work loses much of its historic interest.

Recently strong reasons have been adduced against this view of the *Didache*, which, it may be observed, never gained much following outside the Anglo-Saxon world. The literary connexions between the *Didache* and *Barnabas* have been studied afresh and there is a growing consensus of opinion that they presuppose the use of a common source. Indeed it appears that this common source, an independent code of moral instruction (a 'Two Ways' document), is none other than the text actually preserved (in a Latin form) in the Melk and Freising MSS. of *Did.* 1-6 and, further, that this was a Jewish and not a Christian work. If so, the early date of the *Didache* is not compromised by that of *Barnabas* and we may still accept the older view, which is the more readily credible one, that it is a very primitive document. In his recent massive and important commentary Père J. P. Audet, O.P.[1], puts it as early as A.D. 60.

CLEMENT OF ROME

[Much the fullest collection of material, with text, is in J. B. Lightfoot's splendid edition (2 vols., London, 1890; superseding his earlier ed. in one vol., 1877). The *editio princeps* was ed. from the Biblical 'Codex Alexandrinus' by P. Junius [Patrick Young], London, 1633. Ancient Lat. version ed. G. Morin, O.S.B., Maredsous, Belgium, 1894; ancient Syr. version ed. R. L. Bensly—R. H. Kennett, London, 1899. Eng. trr. in edd. of Apostolic Fathers; also useful ed. by W. K. L. Clarke, S.P.C.K., 1937.]

Clement was Bishop of Rome in the last years of the 1st century. According to a tradition widely received in the early Church, he was the immediate successor to St. Peter, who appointed him Bishop. Another, and almost certainly more reliable, tradition makes him the third successor to Peter (or to the Apostles, Peter and Paul), who were immediately followed by Linus or Anencletus (or 'Cletus'). Both Origen

[1] *La Didache*. Instructions des Apôtres (Études Bibliques, Paris, 1958).

B

and Eusebius, probably wrongly, equate him with the Clement mentioned as St. Paul's fellow-labourer in Phil. iv. 3. In more recent times he has sometimes been identified with the consul, Titus Flavius Clemens, one of Domitian's cousins, who was executed in 95 or 96. But this last identification is also improbable. If such a prominent personality had been head of the Church of Rome, the circumstance must have attracted much comment from pagans and Christians alike. Clement was a very common name and the plain fact is that our surest guide to Clement's person is the internal evidence of his Epistle. His intimate familiarity with the Old Testament supports the view that he came of Jewish stock.[1] A 4th-century legend asserts that he at last met his death by being tied to an anchor and cast into the Black Sea; but there is no early evidence for his martyrdom.

Though many writings were current in the early Church under the name of Clement, his only genuine work is his ('First') *Epistle to the Corinthians*. Written in the name of the Church of Rome to the Church of Corinth, it probably dates from the last decade of the 1st century, and is thus earlier than the latest parts of the New Testament. He writes to the Corinthian Church in a state of uproar. Dissensions such as those with which St. Paul had had to deal half a century earlier had again broken out. Certain hasty and self-willed persons (1. 1) had stirred up strife and deposed the lawful leaders in the community from their office; the community was seriously disturbed; and unbelievers were using the occasion to mock at the Christian name.

Clement contrasts the disturbed state of the Corinthian Church with its past glories. He bids his readers put away envy and jealousy and pleads for humility and an obedient and forgiving spirit. He illustrates the evils of dissension at length from the Old Testament. The conflicts which now rend the Church are at variance with the Divine spirit of order

[1] L. Sanders, *L'Hellénisme de Saint Clément de Rome et le Paulinisme* (Louvain, 1943), has argued, however, that the background of I Clement is Greek.

which is manifested in God's mode of action in nature and the spirit reflected by Christ. This order is attested by the whole of creation and the arrangement of the angels in their ranks (chs. 4-36).

In the later chapters Clement deals more directly with the actual situation in Corinth. What is needed is mutual love and forbearance, and submission to those in authority. The Apostles provided for a permanent mode of ordered replacement of the members of the ministry. It is therefore no light sin to depose from the episcopal office its legitimate occupants. Let those who were the cause of the divisions in the Church at Corinth put away their pride and obstinacy and produce the fruits of repentance.

In the concluding chapters Clement summarises his message, asks his readers to welcome the bearer of the letter, and again expresses his hope that peace may soon be restored (62-5).

Clement shews himself to be very familiar with some of St. Paul's Epistles, as well as with the Epistle to the Hebrews; and his *Epistle* is of doctrinal interest as shewing how well and how little St. Paul's theology was understood at Rome at the end of the 1st century. Though he is already a would-be follower of the Pauline teaching on justification, his mention of Rahab the harlot as being justified 'by faith *and hospitality*' (12. 1) shews that he hardly understood it. His use of the Old Testament indicates how readily the Christian Church had taken over the Greek Scriptures from the Jews and understood their relevance to Christianity as the New Israel.

SECOND EPISTLE OF CLEMENT

[Editions and lit. in general as for I Clement. B. H. Streeter, *The Primitive Church* (1929), pp. 238-47.]

The writing which goes by the name of the 'Second Epistle of Clement' is in a less elegant style than the 'First', so much so that it can hardly be by the same author. Moreover, it is clearly not an epistle at all, but a homily. As such it is the oldest surviving Greek sermon.[1] It treats of the moral combat which confronts the Christian as he faces the world. In this spiritual conflict the weapons which the author recommends include penance, fasting, almsgiving and love.

There is very little evidence to set the homily in an historical context. Its traditional association with *I Clement* suggests a Roman origin. On the other hand, as J. B. Lightfoot observed, this association could equally well be explained if it were a product of Corinth where, if it were preserved among the Church archives with the original copy of *I Clement*, it might easily have been ascribed to Clement. Support for this view is found in the imagery in ch. 7, which could well have come from the Isthmian games.[2] On another theory it is a product of Alexandria.[3] This view is supported by the Alexandrian affinities of its theology; also by a possible quotation from the *Gospel of the Egyptians* at 12. 1f.

THE PSEUDO-CLEMENTINE 'TWO LETTERS TO VIRGINS'

There also survive under the name of Clement two letters addressed to ascetics of both sexes ('Ad Virgines'). Both were written in Greek; but, apart from fragments, they survive only in Syriac.[4] They probably date from the 3rd century. The purpose of the work,—it is really a single treatise and the division into two letters is artificial,—is to extol the ascetic state. Those who pursue it have put on Christ and live the life of angels. But over against its great excellence celibacy also has its abundant dangers, especially when not accompanied by works of charity. The author strongly attacks the practice of ascetics of both sexes living together under a common roof.

[1] Harnack's early attempt to identify it with the letter which Pope Soter (*c.* 166-*c.* 174) addressed to the Corinthians (cf. Eusebius *H. E.* IV. xxiii. 10-12; II. xxv. 8) appears to have been universally abandoned.
[2] So F. X. Funk and G. Krüger.
[3] Defended by J. R. Harris and B. H. Streeter.
[4] In a Peshitta MS. of the New Testament. Part of the first letter also survives in Coptic; in this form it is ascribed to Athanasius.

IGNATIUS

[Monumental history of Ignatian question and presentation and discussion of texts in J. B. Lightfoot, *Apostolic Fathers*, Part II (3 vols., 1885). Convenient smaller editions of Eng. text with notes by J. H. Srawley (2 vols., 1900) and by J. A. Kleist, S. J., in A.C.W. [1946]; of Greek text, with Fr. tr., by P. T. Camelot, O.P., in S.C. x (1944; ed. 2, 1951). H. Schlier, *Religionsgeschichtliche Untersuchungen zu den Ignatiusbriefen* (Beihefte zur Z.N.T.W., viii; 1929); C. C. Richardson, *The Christianity of Ignatius of Antioch* (New York, 1935); B. H. Streeter, *The Primitive Church* (1929), pp. 78-81.]

Almost all our knowledge of Ignatius (early 2nd century) is derived from his seven genuine letters. From these we learn that he was Bishop of Antioch;[1] that during a period of persecution he had been condemned to death for his faith; and that at the time of writing he was being taken as a prisoner across Asia Minor, to be thrown to the wild beasts at Rome. As he passed from city to city he was met by representatives of the local Christian communities and at Smyrna by the Bishop, Polycarp. We see him for the last time at Troas, where his escort was under orders to bring him by ship to Neapolis. There is every likelihood that he was taken thence along the Via Egnatia to Dyrrachium (Durazzo) and thence across the Adriatic to Italy. That he did in fact suffer martyrdom when he reached Rome is already asserted by Irenaeus and Origen, though whether in the Flavian Amphitheatre (the 'Colosseum'), as tradition has it, or elsewhere, is less certain. The 'Acts' of his Martyrdom is a relatively late document and historically untrustworthy.

Of the seven genuine letters, the first four were written at Smyrna, three of them letters of thanks to the Christians of Ephesus, Magnesia and Tralles for sending representatives to greet him on his journey. In the fourth, which is addressed to the Church at Rome, his purpose is to dissuade the Roman Church from interfering with his appointed sentence; for he can conceive of no greater happiness than to win a martyr's crown. The other three letters were written from Troas at a later stage in his journey, after he had received the happy

[1] Later tradition would have it the second successor of St. Peter.

news that the persecution at Antioch had ended. Of these two were addressed to the communities at Philadelphia and Smyrna while the third was directed to Polycarp, Bishop of Smyrna.

These seven letters,—*To the Ephesians, the Magnesians, the Trallians, the Romans, the Philadelphians, the Smyrnaeans* and *To Polycarp*,—are of great interest on account of the vivid picture they give of their author. Even St. Paul does not reveal himself more clearly in his writings. A highly strung person, Ignatius is passionately devoted to his faith and eagerly looks forward to his approaching death. He lives in the supernatural world and sees its manifestations everywhere in the daily life of the Church. The bishops, priests and deacons going about their daily tasks can be none other than God or Jesus Christ. He is filled with the mysticism of the Passion, which we see here in all its original freshness. Combined with this is a shrewd sense of the practical. He has an intense concern alike for doctrinal orthodoxy and for the daily life of the Churches. The psychiatrist might be disposed to pronounce him unbalanced or neurotic. But the reader of his letters will soon discover that he falls outside all conventional categories. 'His passionate devotion, his exuberant fancy, his magnificent contempt of the world, his audacious quaintness of style and thought, produce an impression which is unique'.[1]

These letters had a complex literary history. In the later 4th century they underwent drastic interpolation at the hands of a forger who is almost certainly to be identified with the compiler of the *Apostolic Constitutions*. He was possibly an Arian (T. Zahn, C. H. Turner); but more probably (F. X. Funk, Hugo Koch) he belonged to a school of professional Apollinarian forgers. A series of further fabrications followed. A set of six wholly spurious Greek letters was foisted on Ignatius and came into circulation alongside the interpolated seven genuine letters. These six new items were: (1) a letter of a certain 'Mary of Cassobola to Ignatius'; (2) Ignatius'

[1] H. B. Swete, *Patristic Study*, p. 14.

reply to her; and (3)-(6) four letters of Ignatius to the Tarsicians, to the Philippians, to the Antiochenes and to Hero, a deacon of Antioch. It was this extended *corpus* of thirteen letters, known to modern scholars as the 'Long Recension', that circulated widely in later times both in the East and (in a Latin version, probably of the 8th century; but in this form extended by four additional spurious letters, which were original Latin compositions) in the West. But the Greek text of the seven genuine letters in its original form was not wholly lost. It survived in a few MSS., and this text was taken as the basis of a Latin version made in England in the 13th century, probably by Robert Grosseteste, with the six spurious letters attached. The result was that by the beginning of the modern era scholars were confronted with a large and confusing variety of texts.

The first printed edition of the Latin text of the Epistles was issued by J. Faber of Étaples (Stapulensis) at Paris in 1498; it adopted the text of the Long Recension. The first text of the Greek followed at Dillingen nearly sixty years later, in 1557, also in the Long Recension. Early scholars, understandably, were inclined to regard the whole collection as a fabrication. It was not until 1598 that 'Scultetus' (the Reformed theologian, Abraham Schultes) propounded what in the end turned out to be the true view, viz. that while the six later letters were forgeries, the other seven had a genuine basis. A lively controversy ensued. Owing to the early testimony of the letters to episcopacy the tendency was for Catholics to consider the letters to be genuine, while Protestants for the same reason mostly regarded them as spurious. The publication of six of the seven epistles in the Short Recension by J. Ussher in 1644 from two Latin MSS. of English *provenance*,[1] which was followed by the publication of six of the seven letters in the original Greek from the Florentine Laurentian MS. (Plut. lvii. 7) by Isaac Voss at

---

[1] One of these is in the Library of Gonville and Caius College, Cambridge (Caiensis 395); the other, which was formerly in the possession of Richard Montague, is now lost.

Amsterdam in 1646,[1] made it clear that there was a case for the genuineness of the letters in this form. In the ensuing debate a large part was taken by English scholars, notably by John Pearson, Bishop of Chester (1672), and, two hundred years later, by John Barber Lightfoot, Bishop of Durham (1885-9). In 1845 W. Cureton was able to produce a Syriac text of three of the genuine epistles and for a short time the view was defended that these alone were truly Ignatian. The upshot has been that the genuineness of the seven Epistles is now almost universally recognised.

The letters are of very great doctrinal interest. Ignatius had long meditated on the central mysteries of the Christian faith and expressed his beliefs in short and pithy, if occasionally somewhat cryptic, formulae. There are signs that some of these formulae derive from his reflexion on primitive credal and hymnal phrases. He insists on the two-fold element in Christ, at once earthly and heavenly, and sees here the fundamental fact about His Person. 'There is only one physician both carnal and spiritual, born and unborn (γεννητὸς καὶ ἀγέννητος), God become man, true life in death, sprung both from Mary and from God, first subject to suffering and then incapable of it,—Jesus Christ our Lord'.[2] He is 'the Timeless, the Invisible, Who for our sake became visible, the Impassible, Who became subject to suffering on our account, and for our sake endured everything'.[3] He describes the Church as the place of sacrifice (θυσιαστήριον)[4] and is also the first writer to use the phrase 'the Catholic Church'[5] (ἡ καθολικὴ ἐκκλησία). The Eucharist is the 'Flesh of Our Saviour Jesus Christ which suffered for our sins';[6] it is also the 'medicine of immortality' (φάρμακον ἀθανασίας) and the 'antidote against death' (ἀντίδοτος τοῦ μὴ ἀποθανεῖν).[7]

---

[1] All but the Ep. to the Romans were included. The original text of this epistle was first published by the Maurist, T. Ruinart, in 1689 from the 10th-century Codex Colbertinus (Colbert 460, now Par. gr. 1451).

[2] *Eph.* vii. 2.   [3] *Pol.* iii. 2.

[4] *Eph.* v. 2; *Trall.* vii. 2; *Philad.* iv.   [5] *Smyrn.* viii. 2.

[6] *Smyrn.* vii. 1.   [7] *Eph.* xx.

POLYCARP

[The 'Epistle' and 'Martyrdom of Polycarp' are regularly printed in edd. of Apostolic Fathers. See esp. large ed. of Ignatius by J. B. Lightfoot (Part II, 3 vols., 1885). P. N. Harrison, *Polycarp's Two Epistles to the Philippians* (1936).]

Closely linked with Ignatius is Polycarp, Bishop of Smyrna. According to Irenaeus, who had sat at the Bishop of Smyrna's feet in his youth, Polycarp had been personally acquainted with St. John, 'the disciple of the Lord'.[1] Since Polycarp told the Proconsul at his trial that he had served Christ six-and-eighty years and the trial is probably to be dated at 155-6, Polycarp was presumably born at latest in A.D. 70. He was already Bishop of Smyrna by *c.* 110, as we can deduce from Ignatius' letter to him. Many years later we find him a zealous champion of Quartodecimanism, a matter which brought him to Rome to confer with Pope Anicetus (*c.* 154-165). He and the Pope failed, indeed, to reach agreement, but they parted on friendly terms, each being willing to tolerate the practice of the other. It was on this visit to Rome that Polycarp won over many heretics,—Valentinians and Marcionites among them—to the Catholic faith. When Marcion encountered him in person and asked him whether he did not recognise his adversary, Polycarp gave Marcion the uncompromising reply: 'Indeed I do, I recognise you as the first-born of Satan'.[2] A contemporary and vivid record of his martyrdom survives in a letter from the Church of Smyrna to that of Philomelium.[3] It probably took place either on 23 February 155 or on 22 February 156.[4]

[1] Irenaeus, *Adv. Haer.* III. iii. 4.   [2] Ibid.   [3] Cf. below, p. 194.
[4] This is one of the most discussed dates of early Church history. Older scholars, following Eusebius and Jerome, put it at *c.* 167. But since W. H. Waddington's investigations it would appear that the Statius Quadratus of the *Martyrdom of Polycarp* (ch. 21) is to be identified, not with the Proconsul Quadratus mentioned by Aelius Aristides, but with the Quadratus who was consul for 142 and held the Proconsulship of Asia from 151 to 157. These researches of W. H. Waddington, since carried further by C. H. Turner and E. Schwartz, have led to a choice between one or other of the dates in the text. Recently H. Grégoire and P. Orgels have challenged this view, on the basis that the

The only letter of Polycarp to survive is his *Epistle to the Philippians*.[1] This Epistle has close connexions with those of Ignatius with which it (or at least part of it) is contemporary. After thanking the Philippians for their warm reception of Ignatius and his companions Polycarp urges his readers to stand fast in their faith. As the Philippians had been instructed by St. Paul he would not have dared to teach them Christian doctrine had they not pressed this upon him. They had better study St. Paul's letters (2-3). He then addresses himself to various groups in the community, to the women and widows (4), to the deacons and young men and virgins (5), to the presbyters (6). All must beware of being led astray by heretics (7). His readers should look to the martyrs as their models in matters of faith and well-doing (8-10). He is sorry to learn that a presbyter of Philippi named Valens had proved himself unworthy of his office (11-12). Finally he promises to send on the letters he had received from the Philippians to Antioch and adds that he is sending to them with the present letter such letters of Ignatius as he possesses. He also asks the Philippians for any further tidings they have of Ignatius and his companions (13). He concludes with epistolary greetings (14).

Some apparent contradictions in the letter have long been recognised. In ch. 9 Polycarp writes as though Ignatius and his companions were already dead, whereas in ch. 13 he would appear unaware of their state. Chronological difficulties arise from phrases which suggest the writer's acquaintance with the heresies of the middle of the 2nd century. On the other hand, the letter bears too evidently the marks of authenticity

only sure evidence is Eusebius' Chronicle ('La véritable date du Martyre de Polycarpe [23 février 177]' in *Anal. Boll.* lxix (1951), pp. 1-38). Grégoire has been severely handled by the experts and met with little following. As F. Sagnard, O.P., shewed, it makes nonsense of Irenaeus' reference to Polycarp (Irénée de Lyon, *Contre les Hérésies* xii, S.C. 34; 1952), p. 10n.). Cf. also E. Griffe in *Bulletin de Littérature Ecclésiastique* [Toulouse], Juli 1951, pp. 170-7.

[1] The extant Greek text of the Epistle is defective (all the MSS. deriving from an imperfect archetype), but it is complete in a Latin version. Irenaeus mentions other letters which are now lost.

to be dismissed as spurious. Till recently it was generally
supposed that in ch. 9 Polycarp was speaking in general
terms and accepting the view of current gossip though in
fact he had no definite information. In 1936, however, P. N.
Harrison[1] suggested that these difficulties disappear if we
suppose that the present text is a conflation of two of
Polycarp's epistles. The concluding sentences (ch. 13) would
be a brief acknowledgement to the Philippians of the collection of Ignatius' letters and almost contemporary with
Ignatius' visit, while the rest of the text (chs. 1-12) is an
independent letter addressed to the Philippians written much
later in Polycarp's life. Harrison argued that the latter was probably written in the reign of Hadrian, say between 135 and 137.

As this thesis solves a number of problems, among them
the existence of so many quotations from New Testament
books which seem to imply that the Church had advanced
considerably further towards possessing a Scriptural Canon
than was the case at *c.* 110, it has been widely accepted.

THE EPISTLE OF BARNABAS

[For modern texts and translations, see bibl. s.v. 'Apostolic Fathers'.
The Ep. was first printed by Abp. J. Ussher at Oxford in 1642, but the
whole edition was destroyed by fire before publication. It was reissued
three years later from a MS. now at Leningrad by the Maurist, H.
Ménard, at Paris in 1645. The Greek text in its entirety first came to
light in the Codex Sinaiticus of the N.T. and was issued in a sumptuous
ed. by C. Tischendorf (Leipzig, 1863). Modern discussions include A. L.
Williams in *J.T.S.* xxxiv (1933), pp. 337-46 (on date); P. Meinhold in
Z.K.G. lix (1940), pp. 255-303 (on history and exegesis); L. W. Barnard
in *J.E.A.* xlix (1948), pp. 101-7 (on date).]

The tradition which ascribes the so-called *Epistle of
Barnabas* to Barnabas, 'the son of consolation' of Acts iv. 36,
though found already in Clement of Alexandria and Origen,
is certainly mistaken, if only because the *Epistle* implies that
the fall of Jerusalem (A.D. 70) took place in the considerably
distant past. Moreover its attitude to Judaism is so wholly

---

[1] *Polycarp's Two Epistles to the Philippians* (Cambridge, 1936). See,
however, the important review by H. C. Puech in *Revue d'Histoire des
Religions* cxix (1939), pp. 96-102.

negative that the work cannot have emanated from a close associate and disciple of St. Paul. Nor is it really an 'Epistle' at all. Despite its epistolary opening, the writing is in form a theological pamphlet, or, less probably, a homily.

The work falls into two parts. The first seventeen chapters constitute the main part of the treatise. The remainder (chs. 18-21) consists of a series of moral instructions after the pattern of the 'Two Ways' which (as we have already noted) has literary affinities with the corresponding section of the *Didache*.[1]

The chief evidence for the date of *Barnabas* is the reference to the destruction of the Temple at Jerusalem in 16.3f. Here we read: 'Furthermore He says again, Lo, they who destroyed this temple shall themselves build it. That is happening now. For owing to the war it was destroyed by the enemy; at present even the servants of the enemy build it up again'. The fall of the Temple here is most naturally taken of that of A.D. 70, though H. Lietzmann sees a reference to its second destruction in the rising of Bar Cochba (*c*. 135). If the rebuilding mentioned at the end of this passage means an actual rebuilding of the Temple in stones and mortar 'at present', the reference is presumably, as A. Harnack observed, to the building of the shrine of Jupiter Capitolinus at 'Aelia' on the site of the Temple at the end of Hadrian's reign (117-38). This would date the Epistle within narrow limits. But in its context the passage suggests rather that the author had in view no physical reconstruction of the Temple but the spiritual building in the soul which came through the Gospel. If so, these *data* are compatible with any date after A.D. 70. The general tenor of its contents suggests a date in the first half of the 2nd century.

The treatise is marked by strong hostility to Judaism. Though the Jews had received the Divine Scriptures they mistook their character from the first, since they took them to be documents to be interpreted literally. The Mosaic law was never meant to be observed literally and the Jews were

[1] Cf. above, pp. 10f.

wholly misguided in so understanding it. It was not the
circumcision of the flesh that God wanted, but that of the
heart and ears. It was an evil angel who had misled the Jews.
The one and only purpose of the Law was to point forward to
the Christian dispensation. It was to point to the 'glory of
Jesus' and to be interpreted by a form of symbolism known
as γνῶσις. The Cross was already foreshadowed in Moses'
outstretched arms and the lifting up of the Brasen Serpent.
The Parousia was foretold by the Scapegoat of Lev. xvi. 7-10,
the red wool (Barnabas is there elaborating a late Jewish
tradition not found in Scripture) signifying the purple mantle
which Christ will wear at the Parousia. The Crucifixion is
indicated by the 318 (*TIH*) servants who were circumcised
by Abraham; for the Greek T (= 300) indicates by its form
the Cross, while IH (=18) indicates Jesus (*IHσουs*).

HERMAS

[On the state of the text, cf. below. Text, with fullest presentation of
evidence, ed. Molly Whittaker (G.C.S., Berlin, 1956). For other edd. see
s.v. 'Apostolic Fathers'; for further bibl. see *O.D.C.C.*, p. 630.]

Hermas, the author of the *Shepherd*, tells us that he had
been sold into slavery in his early years and then sent to Rome
where he was purchased by a certain Rhoda. From the
Muratorian Fragment on the Canon[1] we learn that the
Shepherd belongs to a 'very recent date, in our own times',
when Pius, the author's brother, was Bishop of Rome
(*c.* 140-150), a statement which, taken by itself, would put
the *Shepherd* well into the 2nd century. A considerably earlier
date is suggested, however, by Hermas' own assertion that he
had been supernaturally instructed to write two books and
send one to 'Clement', 'who shall send to the foreign cities, for
this is his duty' (*Vis.* ii. 4). If, as would seem likely, we are to
identify this Clement with the Bishop of Rome who wrote to
the Corinthians (d. *c.* 96),[2] then the work would have to be

---

[1] Pastorem vero nuperrime temporibus nostris in urbe Roma Herma
conscripsit, sedente cathedram urbis Romae ecclesiae Pio episcopo
fratre eius (Lines 73-7). Cf. below, pp. 68-70.   [2] Cf. above, pp. 11-13.

placed at the end of the 1st century. Scholars have long contended about these conflicting dates. Internal evidence,—the
crude character of Hermas' theology, hints of an undeveloped
Church organisation and the general primitiveness of the
work,—is in favour of the early date. It is also argued that
such a date would best accord with the readiness of Irenaeus,[1]
Clement of Alexandria,[2] Tertullian,[3] and apparently
Athanasius[4] in his earlier years, to regard the work as quasi-
canonical, as well as with the inclusion of the *Shepherd* in the
Codex Sinaiticus in the New Testament.[5] On the other hand
the statement in the Muratorian Fragment is precise and
definite and hardly likely to be an invention, especially as
both Hermas and the Muratorianum are Roman documents.
Hence this date was also widely defended.[6]

These difficulties are lessened if we may suppose that the
treatise was not written all at once. The four opening *Visions*
(which contain the reference to Clement) clearly form a unity
and stand apart from the rest of the book. They also suggest
the work of a much younger writer. There is nothing improbable in a rambling work of this kind covering an interval of
thirty or forty years. The assertion that the author was the
brother of Pope Pius is not likely to have been invented.
Indeed, it may well have been Hermas' distinguished kinship
which saved his work from oblivion.

The *Shepherd* is divided into twenty-seven tractates,—five
'Visions', twelve 'Mandates' and ten 'Similitudes'. But this
grouping is artificial and bears little relation to the contents
of the work, which is of much the same texture throughout.

In the first four 'Visions' the Church is revealed to Hermas
as a matron clothed in white, becoming ever younger. The

[1] *Adv. Haer*. IV. xx. 2.
[2] Passim. See Stählin's index, pp. 108, 167.
[3] *De Orat*. 16; but contrast *De Pudicit*. 10.
[4] *De Inc*. iii. 1.
[5] Actually, owing to the loss of (esp.) its later leaves, only about a
quarter of the work is now extant in this MS.
[6] The proposal of Origen (*De Princ*. iv. 11) to identify the author with
the Hermas of Rom. xv. 4 may be safely dismissed.

matron's first task is to bid him call everyone to repentance, as the final hour is at hand. In *Vision* 3 the Church takes the form of a high tower. The faithful Christians form the building, while the stones which are rejected are the unrepentant Christians who can only be incorporated into the tower after they have repented. The fifth Vision is transitional. In the *Mandates* Hermas receives his teaching from the 'Angel of Penance' who comes before him in the form of a Shepherd. Here, and in the first five of the *Similitudes* which follow, we have a Christianised form and development of the Old Testament moral code. It is the duty of the rich to assist the needy, of the poor to pray for the rich. The interdependence of rich and poor is illustrated by an allegory of the vine and the elm (*Simil.* 2). The world to come is like a forest in summer time when (in contrast to the conditions of winter) the healthy trees can be distinguished from the dead by the leaves on their boughs (*Simil.* 4 and 5). The next four *Similitudes* (6-9) deal in detail with the question of penance. In the last *Similitude* (10) the vision of the tower reappears. The Angel of Penance again instructs Hermas to purge his family of all evil and bids him summon everyone to penance.

For Hermas, who saw his primary mission in the preaching of repentance, a fundamental matter was the forgiveness of post-Baptismal sin. From the first it was agreed among Christians that Baptism washed away all sin. But what of those Christians who fell away from their pristine purity? Could there be another cleansing? There are indications that in early times many believed that the Church could offer no comfort to such sinners; offenders must be left to the mercy of God. With this rigorism Hermas will not agree. In *Mand.* 4. 3. 1-6 the matter is the subject of a colloquy between himself and the Angel of Penance. Hermas here insists that those who have fallen can be granted forgiveness on repentance and received back to grace. 'I tell you, said he [*sc.* the Angel], that after that great and solemn calling [i.e. Baptism], if a man should be tempted by the devil and sin, he has one repentance.' But Hermas carefully points out that this message is directed only to those Christians who have actually sinned. He is not addressing those who are preparing for Baptism, who are warned against attaching less than its full seriousness to the impending washing. Nor is he proclaiming repentance to those who sin frequently. There is only one repentance. If a man 'sin repeatedly (ὑπὸ χεῖρα) and repent, it is unprofitable for such a man, for hardly shall he live' (*Mand.* 4. 3. 6). It is a debatable question how far Hermas is innovating here. But even if he deals with the question in an allusive way, Hermas gives more direct guidance on this pressing practical issue than any Christian writer before him had done.

As we can see, Hermas was a man of no great intelligence, yet possessed of vivid imagination and ability to give a graphic description of his experiences. He must also be recognised as a man of moral courage, who stood firm in persecution, a fact which must be set over against B. H. Streeter's reference to the 'pottering mediocrity of the timid little Greek'.[1] He had been freed from slavery and acquired property, but he had lost his possessions again by the time he wrote his work and was then in a condition of poverty. How far he is to be described as a visionary it is hard to say. His pages certainly do not describe visions such as we have in the canonical Apocalypse. On the other hand he is obviously describing more than mere allegories.

In recent times, our knowledge of the original text of Hermas has much increased. Until the middle of the last century the *Shepherd* was known only in Latin versions. But, as we have mentioned, the Greek text was contained at the end of the 'Codex Sinaiticus' (א) of the Scriptures, though owing to the defective condition of the last pages of the MS., only a quarter of the text (to *Mand.* 4. 3. 6) is here preserved. Shortly before 1855 the notorious forger, Constantine Simonides discovered in the Monastery of St. Gregory on Mount Athos a 15th-century text of Hermas. It now appears that this MS. (of which Simonides brought back the first three

[1] *The Primitive Church* (1929), p. 203.

leaves)[1] contained the whole of Hermas on ten leaves of which the last was missing.[2] The remaining six leaves (i.e. all those known apart from those at Leipzig) are still at Mount Athos. More recently further fragments of the Greek text have been found which include a considerable part of the hitherto missing concluding portions. They include: (1) two papyrus fragments in the University of Michigan and published by Mr. Campbell Bonner; (2) a small vellum fragment at Hamburg; and (3) short papyrus fragments in the Amherst, Oxyrhynchus and Berlin collections. There also survive two Latin versions and an Ethiopic version. On the basis of these a new edition has been recently issued (1956) at the Berlin Academy by Miss Molly Whittaker of Nottingham.

THE EPISTLE TO DIOGNETUS

[*Ed. princeps* by H. Stephanus (Paris, 1592). For edd. see s.v. 'Apostolic Fathers'. Modern edd., with full notes and introdd., by H. G. Meecham (Manchester, 1949) and H. I. Marrou (in *S.C.* xxxiii, 1951).]

It is usual to include among the 'Apostolic Fathers' the 'Epistle to Diognetus', though it perhaps more properly belongs with the Apologists.[3] In this persuasive and attractive apology for the Christian code of life, the unknown author invites a certain Diognetus to consider the superiority of Christianity to the beliefs of the Jews and the heathen. In contrast to the unsatisfying faith of the current Hellenistic religions, with their foolish worship of idols, stands the Christian ideal, with its basis in love and good citizenship. This religion proceeds directly from God, and its intrinsic excellence is proved by its reasonableness and its fruits. The Christians live, indeed, in the setting of contemporary society, but they themselves constitute its essence. Whatever is good in it is properly theirs. The Christian living in the world, therefore, is what the soul is inhabiting its body. If it be

[1] These found their way into the University Library at Leipzig (Cod. gr. 9).
[2] According to the monks it had been abstracted from the MS. by Minas Minoides when he visited Mount Athos in the eighteen forties.
[3] Cf. chapter iii.

C

asked why such an excellent religion was so late in making its appearance in the world, the answer is that God wished to convince the human race of its inability to find true happiness out of its own resources.

The 'Epistle' was evidently intended for a wider circle of readers than the single individual whose name it bears. Its author is unnamed and unknown. Formerly H. Kihn and G. Krüger ascribed it to Aristides; but since the recovery of the genuine *Apology of Aristides*[1] this attribution has become finally untenable. Recently Abbot Paul Andriessen has ascribed it to Quadratus.[2] More recently still, Professor H. I. Marrou has ascribed the work, including the two final chapters, to Pantaenus, the teacher of Clement, but without conclusive arguments.[3]

The two concluding chapters of the Epistle (11 and 12) almost certainly derive from another source. They have often been ascribed to Hippolytus; and the case of Hippolytean authorship has been considerably strengthened in recent times by R. H. Connolly in *J.T.S.* xxxvii (1936), pp. 2-15.[4]

To judge by the MS. tradition, the work can never have circulated widely. It is not known to have ever been quoted; and the one MS. in which it came down to modern times was burnt at Strasbourg in 1870 in the Franco-Prussian War.

[1] See below, pp. 45-7.   [2] Cf. below, p. 45
[3] In a pleasing edition in *Sources Chrétiennes*, xxxiii (1951).
[4] He also argued, less cogently, that the chapters were the concluding passages of Hippolytus' *Philosophumena*.

II.—THE LITERATURE OF GNOSTICISM

[With the increasing tendency of modern students to link up Gnosticism with Oriental cults the large literature has many ramifications. Among the more important items since 1900 are W. Bousset, *Hauptprobleme der Gnosis* (1907); H. Leisegang, *Die Gnosis* (1924); F. C. Burkitt, *Church and Gnosis* (1932); H. Jonas, *Gnosis und spätantiker Geist* (vol. i, 1934; vol. ii(1), 1954; R. McL. Wilson, *The Gnostic Problem* (1958). There is a useful collection of Gnostic texts in W. Völker, *Quellen zur Geschichte der christlichen Gnosis* (1932). L. Bouyer, 'Gnosis: Le sens orthodoxe de l'Expression jusqu'aux Pères Alexandrins' in *J.T.S.* N.S. iv (1953), pp. 188-203. Further items in *O.D.C.C.*, p. 565.

On the new texts from Nag Hammadi, see the summary description by H. C. Puech, 'Les Nouveaux Écrits gnostiques découverts en Haute-Égypte' in *Coptic Studies in Honor of Walter Ewing Crum* (Boston, Mass., 1950), pp. 91-154; F. L. Cross (ed.), *The Jung Codex* (1955); W. C. van Unnik, *Evangelien aus dem Nilsand* (1959).]

THE Hellenistic world was deeply religious. Its denizen was conscious of supernatural powers around him which at once aroused his fears and fascinated his sensibilities. The old confidence in reason which had marked the classical period had disappeared; and its place had been taken by an emotional religiosity. Everywhere the gods were sensed. Yet they did not bring satisfaction. The scene on Areopagus with people standing round in quest of the Unknown God and some new religious experience was a common phenomenon in the cities of the Greek world. But it was not possible to use reason to discriminate between one faith and another. All creeds were equally true,—and equally false. And hence from whatever quarters religious ideas came they could be tried out and if acceptable adopted. The prevailing spirit was one of syncretism.

It is readily explicable that this generous attitude to all faiths, combined with a love of religious speculation for its own sake, should have aroused in many pagans an interest in

Christianity. It presented itself as yet another speculative religious system. Here was a faith making rapid progress, of undoubted moral seriousness, and desperately anxious to win converts. That it owed its effectiveness to a view of history which cut it off from all other Creeds, and that it was by its nature exclusive, would not have been immediately evident to those who approached it by the standards of contemporary religiosity. To the world it was yet one more religion. It was to be explained in terms of the current rationalism and thereby subjected to a process to which all religious systems in the Hellenistic world were submitted. In this way the various forms of 'Gnosis'[1] or 'Gnosticism' came into being.

The Gnostics were prolific writers and their literary productions soon became far more extensive than those of the orthodox. They, too, needed their Scriptures, expressive of their own tenets, and hence brought into existence a large body of Apocryphal literature, written in conscious imitation of the New Testament writings. Moreover, the first 'Synopsis' of the Four Gospels comes from a Gnostic;[2] so does the oldest known 'commentary' on the Fourth Gospel.[3] The Gnostics were also very prolific in writing treatises. For the most part this literature has not survived; but its disappearance need cause no great surprise, nor, indeed, any excessive regret. To

[1] A few remarks may be added about the word 'Gnosis'. By itself it is, of course, just the common Greek word for 'knowledge'. But in relation to what is here in question the word 'Gnostic' is used in three different ways: (1) In Patristic times the word was used for a special group of Gnostics, viz. the Barbelo-Gnostics. This restricted use is no longer current. (2) 'Gnosis' is used, especially by German writers, for the whole range of Hellenistic doctrines in which $\gamma\nu\tilde{\omega}\sigma\iota\varsigma$ plays an important part. (3) In the older and more common English usage, the word is applied to those systems which have definite Christian elements. The Manichaean and Mandaean systems of later times, however, are not ordinarily reckoned as belonging to Gnosticism.

[2] On Tatian's *Diatessaron*, cf. below pp. 66-8.

[3] The $\dot{\upsilon}\pi o\mu\nu\dot{\eta}\mu\alpha\tau\alpha$ of Heracleon. Heracleon was a disciple of Valentinus. According to E. Preuschen (*Der Johanneskommentar des Origenes* (1903), pp. cii ff.), Heracleon's $\dot{\upsilon}\pi o\mu\nu\dot{\eta}\mu\alpha\tau\alpha$ was not a commentary in the ordinary sense, but a collection of concise glosses designed to indicate the chief ideas of the text. On Heracleon, cf. below, p.38.

judge by what has come down to us it was incredibly tedious and repetitive and the modern reader can reconstruct their bizarre and complicated systems only by an expenditure of intellectual energy which they certainly do not merit.

Our knowledge of Gnosticism has recently been much increased by the collection of documents dug up at Nag Hammadi in 1945 or 1946. Other Gnostic items are preserved in the works of their orthodox opponents, either as actual texts, e.g. the 'Hymn of the Naassenes' in Hippolytus, or in epitomes. And many of the orthodox anti-Gnostic writers described their opponents' systems in full, e.g. Irenaeus gives a full account of the system of Valentinus, and Tertullian of that of Marcion. Clement of Alexandria collected a series of extracts from Theodotus, a disciple of Valentinus, apparently for the purpose of refutation, and this collection has come down to us in substantially its original form. And there is a letter on the Christian use of the Old Testament, sent by the Roman Gnostic, Ptolemy, to Flora, which is preserved by Epiphanius.[1] Further, a considerable proportion of the 'Apocryphal New Testament', i.e. writings modelled on the canonical Gospels and Acts and Apocalypses, appears to be of Gnostic *provenance*. Let us first look at the actual Gnostic documents which are available.

THE 'CODEX ASKEWIANUS' AND THE 'CODEX BRUCIANUS'

Two Coptic Gnostic texts from Egypt have long been accessible to scholars, the 'Codex Askewianus' and the 'Codex Brucianus'. The former of these, a vellum MS. once owned by A. Askew and now in the British Museum (Add. 5114), contains in Coptic translation the treatise known as *Pistis Sophia*.[2] This last text, which emanated from Barbelo-Gnostic circles and extends over the first three books, consists of conversations between the Risen Christ and His

---

[1] *Haer.* xxxiii. 3-7.
[2] It was first published by M. G. Schwartze and J. H. Petermann at Berlin in 1851.

disciples, especially John the Apostle and Mary Magdalene. Their subject is the fall and redemption of the aeon *Pistis Sophia*. The fourth book, which appears to be the oldest part of the text, consists of other revelations which Jesus made to His disciples after His resurrection. The other papyrus, which was formerly in the possession of James Bruce and is now in the Bodleian Library, consists of two Coptic texts and dates from the 5th-6th century. The treatises themselves are of much older date. The former consists of two books of the 'Mystery of the Great Logos'; according to C. Schmidt these last are identical with the 'Books of Jeû' referred to in the *Pistis Sophia*. The other appears to be a production of the Sethite Gnostics and was probably composed between 170 and 200. In both these MSS. the treatises appear to be translations from the Greek.

THE NAG HAMMADI TEXTS

These papyri have now been far outstripped in importance by the large collection of Gnostic texts discovered recently at Nag Hammadi on the east bank of the Nile, not far from the ancient Pachomian monastery situated at Chenoboskion. The collection, whose contents are still very imperfectly known, consists in all of thirteen volumes of Coptic texts in the Sub-Akhmimic dialect. The MSS. date from the 4th century and were apparently assembled at a monastic library. Altogether there are a hundred or so short treatises, which cover some 1,000 pages. There is every reason to suppose that here again we have translations from Greek originals, some at any rate of the texts dating from the 2nd century.

Of these thirteen codices, which were discovered by peasants and bought by dealers, twelve were eventually acquired by the Coptic Museum at Old Cairo, where most of them now await publication. Here again many seem to be texts of a form of vulgar Gnosticism (the so-called 'Barbelo-Gnosticism'). But the thirteenth codex stands apart and is at present better known. It made its way to Europe and through the exertions of Professor G. Quispel of Utrecht was acquired in 1952 by the Jung Institute at Zurich. It contains four items: (1) *A Letter of James*, containing revelations made by the Risen Christ to the Apostles before His Ascension; (2) *The Gospel of Truth*, perhaps to be identified by the writing of Valentinus of this name, referred to by Irenaeus;[1] (3) *A Letter to Rheginos*, a work on the Resurrection; and (4) A *Treatise on the Three Natures*. The last three of these appear to emanate from the Valentinian school of Gnostics, (2) and (3) being very probably the work of Valentinus himself and (4) possibly that of Heracleon, Valentinus' disciple. There is insufficient evidence to pronounce a verdict about (1), but the presumption is that it too came from the same school.

The other twelve codices contain a miscellaneous assortment of texts, several of them previously known[2] and in some cases repeated twice, or even three times, in different MSS. Among these writings is a new *Gospel of Thomas*,[3] a work quite independent of a treatise which has hitherto gone under this name, and the *Apocryphon of John*. Other typical titles are *The Epistles of Eugnostos the Blessed, An Exposition on the Soul* and *The Dialogue of the Redeemer*.

THE APOCRYPHON OF JOHN

This text, a MS. of which has been in the Berlin Museum (Pap. Berol. 8502) since 1896,[4] has now at last been made generally available by Dr. W. C. Till in his edition of the papyrus.[5] Its repeated occurrence in the Nag Hammadi collection shews that it was among the most highly prized

[1] *Adv. Haer.* III. xi. 9. On Valentinus, see below, pp. 36f.

[2] A list made by Prof. H. C. Puech, based on a preliminary examination of the MSS. will be found in *Coptic Studies in Honor of Walter Ewing Crum* (Boston, Mass., 1950).

[3] On this treatise see below, pp. 77-9.

[4] There is a description of it by C. Schmidt, 'Irenaeus und seine Quelle in *Adversus Haereses* I 29' in *Philotesia. Paul Kleinert zum LXX. Geburtstage dargebracht von A. Harnack* (1907), pp. 317-36.

[5] *Die gnostischen Schriften des koptischen Papyrus Berolinensis* 8502 in T.U. lx (1955), pp. 33-195.

texts of the Egyptian Gnostics. It is clearly a translation from the Greek and was known to Irenaeus who used it in his *Adversus Haereses*. Hence the original cannot be later than 180.

Like most Gnostic literature, the *Apocryphon of John* is tedious and verbose. Its purpose is to account for the presence of evil in the cosmos and to shew how man, who in his present state is a mixture of good and evil, can be redeemed from it. In a revelation which the Risen Saviour makes to His disciple, John, on the Mount of Olives, He bids the Apostle write down what he hears and disclose it only to those who can understand it. He begins by stressing the absolute contrast between God, the highest being in the world of light, and the material world. The world-process began when God saw His features reflected in pure water of light, whereon the Barbelô, a female being, came into existence as His image. God then created a series of supernatural beings, while the Barbelô, contemplating God, brought forth a divine spark, the Son of God who was the Christ. Further beings were created, the lowest of them being 'Sophia'. Sophia in turn, without God's consent, brought forth a son who on account of his illegal birth was a bad character and was called by his mother Jaldabaôth. Yet Jaldabaôth had inherited from his mother the power of creating and he it was who brought into being the evil material world in which we are living.

An elaborate cosmology follows in which Jaldabaôth is the Creator God and, as he mistakenly conceives himself to be the only God, He says to His creatures 'I am a jealous God' (Deut. v. 9) and 'There is no other God beside Me' (Ex. xx. 3). He is, therefore, the God of the Old Testament. In the created world the planet-kings take a central place. Then followed the creation of Paradise and of Adam and Eve (who is not named). The tree of the knowledge of good and evil was placed by God in Paradise to support man in his conflict with Jaldabaôth, and it was Christ Himself who encouraged man to eat from the tree of knowledge. In this way an unending conflict was brought into the world, and only those who have accepted the knowledge of the truth brought to men by Christ, the Saviour, will be redeemed. Indiscriminate teaching of this doctrine would lead to its corruption. Its knowledge (the Risen Christ warns John) is to be confined to those who are worthy to receive it.[1]

SIMON MAGUS AND EARLY GNOSTICISM

The historical development of Gnosticism, however, is to be far better understood from the polemical references to them in the orthodox Church Fathers than from these obscure and prolix Gnostic texts.

The usual view of the Fathers was that Gnosticism began with Simon Magus whose encounter with St. Peter is recorded in Acts viii. 9-24. Justin Martyr (himself a native of Samaria) names Gitton in Samaria as Simon's birthplace and says that Simon arrived in Rome in the reign of Claudius (A.D. 41-54) where he was venerated as a god. Hippolytus asserts that Simon was the author of a work entitled 'The Great Tidings'.[2]

Even if these details are not all beyond reproach, the fact that primitive tradition traces the Gnostic conflict back to early Apostolic times lends considerable support to the view that Gnosticism is a pre-Christian heresy.

Other Christians of Gnostic or semi-Gnostic views who figure in early Patristic literature are Dositheus, Menander and Cerinthus, though it is doubtful if any of these have any claims to literary productivity. The ascription of the Fourth Gospel and the Apocalypse to Cerinthus by the Alogi in the second century[3] and of the Gospel to Menander by J. Kreyenbühl in the early years of the present century, are aberrations of criticism which have never merited serious attention.

[1] For a fuller account of the treatise, W. C. Till, 'The Gnostic Apocryphon of John' in *Journal of Ecclesiastical History* iii (1952), pp. 14-22, may be consulted.

[2] *Philos.* VI. 7-20.   [3] So Epiphanius, *Haer.* lii. 2f.

SECOND-CENTURY GNOSTICISM

When towards the middle of the 2nd century Gnosticism blossomed in its full strength, it became the most serious threat to Christian orthodoxy that the Church had ever known. By this date, it was of three main types: (1) An Egyptian form, with pantheistic leanings, of which Rome became the centre of propaganda; (2) A Syriac form, of a more dualistic type and less remote from orthodoxy, especially as it developed in the East; (3) The system of Marcion, which should perhaps not be classified among the Gnostic heresies at all.

VALENTINUS

(1) Of the Egyptian Gnostics, the most influential was Valentinus. Valentinus was a native of Alexandria and clearly derived his doctrines from the East. But he taught mainly in Rome whither 'he made his way in the time of Hyginus [136-40], flourished under Pius [150-55] and remained until Anicetus [155-60]'.[1] Here he evidently cut a considerable figure and, if Tertullian is to be believed, even had hopes of becoming Pope.[2] Tertullian tells us that it was only when his ambitions were thwarted that he separated from the Catholic Church.

Apart from the Nag Hammadi documents[3] our principal source for Valentinus' teaching is Irenaeus. It is beyond question that Irenaeus had authoritative Valentinian sources at his disposal; and, as F. M. M. Sagnard has shown recently, there are good grounds for holding that Irenaeus was closely following a single document. From Irenaeus we learn that Valentinus' system was rooted in a Platonic parallelism between the world of ideas ($\pi\lambda\acute{\eta}\rho\omega\mu\alpha$) and the world of phenomena ($\kappa\acute{\epsilon}\nu\omega\mu\alpha$). His principal tenets included an elaborate doctrine of aeons which formed a succession of pairs or 'syzygies'. Their ultimate offspring, which came into being by the fall of Sophia, one of the lowest aeons, was the Demi-

---

[1] Irenaeus, *Adv. Haer*. III. iv. 3.
[2] Tertullian, *Adv. Valentinianos* 4.   [3] Cf. above, p. 32f.

urge. This Demiurge, who created the visible world, was the God of the Old Testament. Redemption was effected by the aeon Christ, who united Himself to the man Jesus at His Baptism to bring men the gnosis. This gnosis, however, is given only to the 'pneumatics', i.e. to the Valentinians, who through it enter into the *pleroma*, whereas the Catholics or 'psychics' by faith and good works attain only to the middle range of the Demiurge, and the 'hylics' (i.e. the rest of mankind), being all engrossed in matter, are given over to eternal perdition. The accounts of Valentinus' teaching in later Patristic writers seem to be almost wholly dependent on Irenaeus.

But it is quite possible that we have a new source for Valentinus' teaching among the Nag Hammadi documents. The longest item in the Jung Codex is dubbed 'The Gospel of Truth'; and the question arises whether this is the actual work of Valentinus referred to under that title by Irenaeus.[1] At one point this text accords with Irenaeus' account of it, namely, in having nothing in common with the canonical Gospels. But the system in the new text differs considerably from the familiar account in Irenaeus. There is no trace of the syzygies of Aeons which fill such a prominent place in the traditional accounts of Valentinus. If we are to accept the Valentinian authorship of this newly recovered work, we may suppose with Dr. Quispel that the 'Evangelium Veritatis' represents an earlier stage of Valentinus' teaching.

PTOLEMY AND HERACLEON

Valentinus had a number of disciples who developed his system, both in Italy and in the East. The two best known of his Italian disciples were Ptolemy and Heracleon. From PTOLEMY there survives a 'Letter to Flora'[2] which deals with the present-day value of the Mosaic Law. He insists that its ordinances are of three kinds. First there is the moral law, epitomised in the Ten Commandments, which is permanent.

---

[1] Veritatis evangelium, in nihilo conveniens apostolorum evangeliis. *Adv. Haer.* III. xi. 9.

[2] Preserved by Epiphanius, *Haer.* xxxiii. 3-7.

It is this which Christ came to fulfil. Next comes the law of retaliation which Christ came to abolish and replace by the higher law of love. And lastly there is the ceremonial law which Christ came to spiritualise. These facts establish, according to Ptolemy, that the Mosaic Law was imperfect and that it was the work of the Demiurge and not of the Supreme God. HERACLEON is known to us from the extracts from his Commentary on St. John's Gospel which are preserved by Origen.[1]

THEODOTUS AND MARK

Of the Eastern school of Valentinus' disciples, we are best acquainted with THEODOTUS, who appears to have taught between 160 and 170. His teachings survive in the so-called 'Excerpta ex Theodoto', a scrap-book which Clement of Alexandria appended to his *Stromateis*. These 'Excerpta' contain not only extracts from Theodotus' writings, but also the summaries which Clement had made in reading Theodotus, as well as Clement's own constructive comments.[2]

MARK, another member of the same school and founder of the 'Marcosians', taught in Proconsular Asia. Irenaeus informs us that he had disciples in Gaul known to him personally, and also that he employed magic and fraud in the Eucharist.

BASILIDES

Basilides, probably a Syrian by birth, taught at Alexandria *c.* 120-140. His writings include a Gospel Commentary in twenty-four books, entitled *Exegetica*, as well as Psalms and Odes; but apart from a few fragments these are lost. A Gospel, which was perhaps not more than a compilation

[1] Cf. below, p. 126.
[2] Cf. R. P. Casey, *The* 'Excerpta ex Theodoto' *of Clement of Alexandria* (1934), p. 4. For further comment on Theodotus, see F. M. M. Sagnard, O.P., *Clément d'Alexandrie: Extraits de Théodote* in S.C. 23 (1948), and A. J. Festugière, O.P., 'Notes sur les Extraits de Théodote de Clément d'Alexandrie et sur les Fragments de Valentin' in *V.C.* iii (1949), pp. 193-207. On Clement's *Stromateis*, cf. below, pp. 120f.

from the canonical Gospels, was also ascribed to him. Both Irenaeus[1] and Hippolytus[2] describe his system in detail, but their accounts are so incompatible that we must either suppose that they present different stages in the development of Basilides' system or, more probably, that Hippolytus was badly misled by his sources.

According to Irenaeus, Basilides held that a succession of spiritual beings issued from the Unborn Father, first 'Nous', then 'Logos', then 'Phronesis', and so on until the total number in the heavens was 365. The function of Nous, the Father's first begotten and the Basilidian Christ, was to bring us salvation. But He never suffered death. Not the redeeming Nous was crucified, but Simon of Cyrene, who bore the cross in his stead. Our redemption, which comes through 'gnosis', is wholly in the sphere of the spirit, since our bodies are material and lie outside the Divine plan. As such they are no concern of the Godhead and the worst sins of lust are of no religious consequence.

BARDESANES

(2) Of the Syrian Gnostics, Bardesanes (Bar Daisan) is the best known. He was born at Edessa on 11 July 154; was converted to Christianity in 179; and soon became a keen missionary for the faith. On the conquest of Edessa by Caracalla in 216-17, he fled to Armenia. Later he returned to his native land where he died c. 222. He was one of the pioneers of the Christian faith in Syria; and the fact that Eusebius speaks of him with respect makes it unlikely that he regarded Bardesanes as a Gnostic.

Bardesanes is the leading interlocutor in a *Dialogue on Fate, or The Book of the Laws of the Lands* which survives in the original Syriac.[3] The Dialogue was put into literary form by his disciple, Philip. It attacked the fatalism of the later Greek philosophers, especially their teaching on the

---

[1] *Adv. Haer.* I. xxiv.   [2] *Philosophumena* VIII. xx-xxvii.
[3] Two long passages from it are quoted by Eusebius, *Praeparatio Evangelica*, vi. 10.

influence of the stars on destiny, but it expressly denied the Divine creation of the world.

Bardesanes was the first Syriac hymnwriter. With the help of his son, Harmonius, he wrote many hymns with a missionary purpose. It is also possible that the 'Acts of Thomas' go back to Bardesanes or his school. He has sometimes been regarded as the author of the *Odes of Solomon*,[1] but on insufficient grounds. Bardesanes also wrote in Syriac a (lost) *Dialogue against Marcion*.

MARCION

(3) Finally, Marcion. He stood apart from other Gnostics, notably in that he had no interest in cosmological speculations and that his purposes were essentially practical.

Marcion was the son of a bishop of Sinope in Pontus where he was born. Before leaving Pontus he amassed a fortune as a ship-owner.[2] In *c.* 138-140 Marcion made his way to Rome and here joined the Roman Church to which he gave a very large sum of money. Before long he met the Gnostic, Cerdo, who sharply distinguished between the God of the Old Testament and the Father of Jesus Christ. Marcion developed similar teaching, left no doubt as to his unorthodoxy, and in July 144 was excommunicated from the Roman Church. He stayed on in Rome where he founded a church of his own, a compact community with its own hierarchy of bishops, priests and deacons. He was a man of outstanding talents and organising gifts and exercised a strict discipline over its members. The sect which he called into being spread rapidly and was the greatest challenge that Catholic Christianity ever had to face. In due course it produced its own martyrs. It was still a flourishing community in the East in the 5th century, and it survived, in declining numbers, down to the Middle Ages. Marcion himself appears later to have sought re-admission to the Catholic Church, but was told that this could

[1] Cf. below, p. 190.
[2] The tradition that he was excommunicated by his father is of doubtful reliability.

not be allowed unless he brought back with him all his perverts.

As far as is known, Marcion was the author of only two literary works, his *Antitheses* and his *New Testament*,[1] neither a treatise in the ordinary sense. But his doctrines were widely propagated and made known through his disciples, and have come down to us through the refutations of the Church Fathers. The fullest account of Marcion is to be found in Tertullian's elaborate refutation of him. But he had already been attacked by his contemporary at Rome, Justin Martyr, and in greater detail by Irenaeus and the other heresiologists. From these writers we learn that Marcion held an extreme anti-Judaism. There was a radical opposition between the Law and the Gospel, so much so that they proclaimed different Gods. Over against the God of love of the New Testament stands the evil God of the Old. The wickedness and incompetence of the God of the latter are revealed on every page of the Old Testament. How could a God who was good have allowed Adam to sin? How could He have ordered the Sabbath rest and yet have required the ark to be carried round Jericho on eight successive days? How could he have forbidden idolatry and yet have ordered representations of the brazen serpent and of the cherubim and seraphim? Over against this ancient God must be set the good God of the New Testament proclaimed by Jesus Christ. This is the God who taught that only a good tree could bring forth good fruit and that by His fruits we should know Him. The leading exponent of this creed was the Apostle, St. Paul. With this dualism Marcion proclaimed a depreciation of the body and the doctrine that marriage was fundamentally evil.

In thus rejecting the 'Old Testament', hitherto the traditional Christian Bible, Marcion had the greater need to have one of his own to replace it. He therefore constructed another Bible, a 'New Testament'. It consisted of a mutilated text of Luke (which constituted Marcion's 'Evangelium') with ten of St. Paul's Epistles, i.e. all except the Pastorals and Heb. (his 'Apostolicon').

[1] On these writings, cf. below, pp. 62-4.

III.—THE APOLOGISTS

[The most detailed collected edition is that of J. C. T. Otto, Corpus Apologetarum (9 vols., Jena, 1847-72; ed. 3 of Justin [vols. 1-5], 1876-81). More recent ed. by E. J. Goodspeed (Göttingen, 1914; does not contain Theophilus, however). Eng. tr. in A.N.C.L. (various editors and dates). For vocabulary, E. J. Goodspeed, *Index Apologeticus* (Leipzig, 1912). Further bibl. in *O.D.C.C.*, p. 72.]

As Christianity spread, it was met by ever growing dislike and hostility. It was an age of syncretism; and though each religion might have its own traditions and rites, it was an accepted premise that everyone might become a member of any religion he chose and this without renouncing any of his previous beliefs. But Christianity knew nothing of such tolerance. Those who entered its fold must break with paganism altogether. And because this paganism was closely linked with the culture of the age, the Church required her members to withdraw from participation in many secular activities and pursuits as well as from most municipal and state offices. She could not but arouse suspicion by demanding this isolation. The misrepresentation, which grew out of ignorance, tended to take on a common pattern in all parts of the Empire. The three charges against the Christians specified by Athenagoras,—Atheism, Thyestian banquets and Oedipodean incest,—were frequently reiterated and presumably seriously believed. To demonstrate their injustice and to refute them was one of the main objects of the 'Apologists'.

But the 'Apologists' had another and more positive aim. At a different level, there were large numbers in the Hellenistic world who aspired after an ethical life. The philosophy on which these aspirations was based was not often very profound, nor were the ethical codes always exacting, but the endeavour to rise above the moral level of worldly self-indulgence was widespread. These contemporary strivings were a challenge to the Church. She had her own way of life, more exacting, indeed, and resting (as she believed) on a far more solid basis but still with the means to satisfy these longings. This situation imposed on the Church the necessity of proclaiming its own moral ideals in language which could be understood. The Apologists thus had the further task of demonstrating the congruity of their principles with those of the highest ethical and philosophical ideals of the secular world. If the Apologists were not thinkers of marked intellectual stature, neither for that matter were many of their opposites in the pagan world.

EARLY OPPONENTS: FRONTO, LUCIAN OF SAMOSATA, CELSUS

The three earliest known attacks on Christianity from writers of repute in the pagan world came from Fronto of Cirta, Lucian of Samosata and Celsus.

FRONTO,[1] an orator held in high repute in the Empire, made the earliest recorded pagan attack on Christianity. Born at Cirta c. 105, he spent most of his life in Rome where he was consul for two months in 143 and became the Latin tutor and close friend of Marcus Aurelius. In his *Octavius*, Minucius Felix twice[2] mentions that Fronto had accused Christians in a public speech of atheism, of indulgence in gross immorality and of partaking in Thyestian banquets. But apart from these two references, we have no knowledge of Fronto's onslaught. There is no reason to suppose that he ever put it into writing.

The satirist, LUCIAN OF SAMOSATA,[3] has a number of

[1] On Fronto, cf. M. Dorothy Brock, *Studies in Fronto and his Age* (Cambridge, 1911).

[2] *Octavius* 9. 6; 31. 2. The suggestion that the Caecilius of the *Dialogue* is Fronto himself is disproved by Caecilius' attitude to philosophy. Fronto was a mere rhetorician and detested philosophy. On Minucius Felix, cf. below, pp. 146-8.

[3] On Lucian, see Marcel Caster, *Lucien et la Pensée religieuse de son Temps* (1937), esp. pp. 346-57.

D

scoffing references to Christianity in his writings. In his *De Morte Peregrini*, he mocks at the folly of Peregrinus (Proteus) of Parium, successively a professed Christian and a Cynic, who won notoriety by burning himself in public. Lucian here scorns Christ as 'the man who was crucified in Palestine because he brought this new cult into the world' (ch. 11) and makes fun of the Christians for their misguided enthusiasm. 'Furthermore, their first lawgiver persuaded them that they are all brothers of one another after they have transgressed once for all by denying the Greek gods and by worshipping that crucified sophist himself and living under his laws. Therefore they despise all things indiscriminately and consider them common property, receiving such doctrines traditionally without any definite evidence. So if any charlatan and trickster, able to profit by occasion, comes among them, he quickly acquires sudden wealth by imposing upon simple folk' (ch. 13). Lucian was widely read. But his attitude was manifestly too superficial to have done the Church much harm.

The earliest serious and considered attack on Christianity came from CELSUS, who in *c.* 177-180 wrote his 'True Word' ('Ἀληθὴς Λόγος). Though this treatise has been lost, a large part of its text, and still more of its subject matter, can be recovered from the extensive quotations in Origen's reply.[1] Celsus went to work seriously, making a first-hand study of Christianity and its Scriptures. He wrote his 'True Word' in four parts. In the first he put his objections into the mouth of a Jew who objects that the Christian Messiah was not that to which the Old Testament looked forward. In the second, a pagan is introduced who from his standpoint argues the absurdity of the Jewish teaching on the Messiah. In the third, Celsus launches out on a frontal attack on Christian faith and morals. In the fourth, Celsus makes his defence of the regnant paganism.

[1] R. Baden, *Der 'Ἀληθὴς λόγος des Kelsos* (Tübinger Beiträge zur Altertumswissenschaft 33, 1940) is less sanguine than older writers were as to the extent of Celsus' text which is recoverable. Cf. H. Chadwick, *Origen; Contra Celsum* (1953), pp. xxii-xxiv.

The work was clearly an able and formidable production, and over half a century had to elapse before it found in Origen a critic competent, and more than competent, to reply to it. As Dr. H. Chadwick remarks, 'Whereas to Celsus, writing about seventy years earlier, the majority of Christians seemed to be stupid and uneducated fools, if they were not knaves, with Origen Christians and pagans met intellectually on equal terms'.[1]

QUADRATUS

Of the Christian Apologists the earliest was Quadratus. About the year 124 he addressed to Hadrian (117-138) an *Apology* for the Christian faith, but apart from a single fragment preserved in Eusebius[2] it has been lost. From the time of Jerome Quadratus has often been identified with an early Bishop of Athens of the same name. The recent contention of Abbot P. Andriessen[3] that the *Epistle to Diognetus*[4] is none other than Quadratus' Apology to Hadrian (the Emperor's identity being concealed under the name of 'Diognetus') and that it was written shortly after the Emperor's initiation at Eleusis in the spring of 126 has met with little favour.

ARISTIDES

[Syr. text ed. J. R. Harris in J. A. Robinson, Cambr. *Texts and Studies* I(i), 1891; with Gk. text in Appendix, pp. 100-12. Other attempted reconstructions of Gk. text by J. Geffcken, *Zwei griechischen Apologeten* (1907), pp. 1-96, and E. J. Goodspeed, *Die ältesten Apologeten* (1914), pp. 2-23. Eng. tr. by D. M. Kay in A.N.C.L., Additional Volume, 1897.]

Eusebius[5] records that Aristides, like Quadratus, left an Apology for the faith dedicated to Hadrian, adding that 'his writing also has been kept by many, even to these times'.

---

[1] H. Chadwick, op. cit., p. xiii. On Origen's reply, see below, pp. 130f.
[2] *Hist. Eccl.* IV. iii. 2.
[3] 'The Authorship of the *Epistula ad Diognetum*' in *Vigiliae Christianae* i (1947), pp. 129-36.
[4] Cf. above pp. 27f..   [5] *Hist. Eccl.* IV. iii. 3.

From this passage, in conjunction with a reference to Aristides in Eusebius' *Chronicle* (ad ann. Abr. 2140), we can infer that Eusebius did not have access to the document himself. Indeed the *Apology* was long lost and has only been recovered in quite recent times.

The history of its recovery is a remarkable story. In 1878, the Mechitarists[1] published at Venice what they believed to be part of the *Apology* in an Armenian text. The authenticity of this text was at first questioned,—by E. Renan among others. But in 1889 their contention received confirmation when J. R. Harris announced his discovery in the Monastery of St. Catherine on Mt. Sinai of a MS. containing the Syriac text of the whole *Apology*. Shortly afterwards J. A. Robinson made an astonishing observation. He found that the same text, but apart from a few variations and changes of expression in the original Greek, had been taken over bodily, with no hint of its true authorship, into the work known as *Barlaam and Josaphat*. This entertaining document, traditionally and apparently correctly[2] ascribed to St. John of Damascus, is a Christian adaptation of the life of the Buddha. The story is pure fiction but the author puts an apology for the Christian faith into the mouth of one of its characters, and this apology turns out to be none other than a somewhat abbreviated text of the 'Apology of Aristides'. The Church had thus been for centuries unwittingly in possession of the substance of Aristides' treatise. Such are the surprises which await the student of early Christian literature.

In the *Apology* Aristides describes himself as an 'Athenian philosopher'. The truth of the Christian creed, he would have his readers believe, follows from the very idea of God, whose existence is sufficiently demonstrated by His orderly

[1] The Uniat Armenian monks who possess houses at Venice and Vienna. See *O.D.C.C.*, p. 881, s. v.

[2] Its claim to be a genuine work of St. John of Damascus has recently been upheld, apparently with success, in F. Dölger, *Der griechische Barlaam-Roman, ein Werk des h. Johannes von Damaskos* (Ettal, 1953).

disposition of the world (ch. 1). Of the four classes into which mankind can be divided,—Barbarians, Greeks (with whom Aristides associated the Egyptians and the Chaldeans), Jews and Christians,—the Christians alone have a right notion of God. The Barbarians worship material bodies such as the earth, fire, water, the winds or the sun (3-7). The Greeks worship gods who are all subject to human weaknesses and passions (8-13). The Jews are far nearer the truth in that they at least believe in a single God. But they have often directed their worship to angels, sabbaths and moons. And they observe such customs as eating unleavened bread, circumcision and discriminating clean from unclean foods (14). The Christians alone, the 'Third Race', have possession of the full truth and because of the fundamentally moral character of their teaching they alone adore God in a worthy manner (15-16). The Apology concludes with an appeal to all those without the knowledge of God to draw near to the Christian creed so that they may be ready to appear before the judgement of God (17).

The treatise was addressed apparently not, as Eusebius[1] asserts, to the Emperor Hadrian (117-138), but to his successor, Antoninus Pius (138-161), and probably dates from c. 140. Nothing further is known of its author. His literary capacities are too limited to allow us to identify him with the author of *Ad Diognetum*.[2] It is hard to think that he can have made any appreciable impact on the public to which he addressed his treatise.

ARISTO OF PELLA

Aristo of Pella is the first known apologist for the Christian faith against the Jews. His Apology took the form of a dialogue between Jason, a Judaeo-Christian, and Papiscus, an Alexandrian Jew; it is not known whether they were real persons. This *Dialogue of Jason and Papiscus concerning Christ* was known to Celsus, who despised it for its absurdities,

---

[1] *Hist. Eccl.* IV. iii. 3.   [2] Cf. above, pp. 27f.

and also to Origen and Jerome; but John of Scythopolis[1] (6th century) is the first writer who records its author's name. The text is now lost, apart from a fragment preserved by Jerome. It probably dates from *c.* 140. Eusebius[2] tells us that it was from Aristo that he learnt that Hadrian excluded all Jews from Jerusalem after the rising of Bar Cochba (132-135). Nothing is known of Aristo's life.

JUSTIN MARTYR

[Most elaborate ed. of Justin's works (incl. dubia and spuria) by J. C. T. Otto in *Corpus Apologetarum* (3 vols., Jena, 1842-8; much extended ed. 3, 5 vols., 1876-81). J. P. Migne, P.G. vi (1857). Convenient modern ed. of *Apologies* with notes by A. W. F. Blunt (Cambr. Patr. Texts, 1911). Further bibl. in *O.D.C.C.*, p. 757.]

Justin, traditionally known as 'the Martyr' or alternatively as 'the Philosopher', is the most considerable of the Apologists. He was born of pagan parents at Sichem[3] in Samaria, probably in the first decade of the 2nd century. As a young man in his search for truth he had eagerly made the round of the philosophical schools,—the Stoics, the Peripatetics and the Pythagoreans,—but without success. For a time, indeed, he believed he had found his goal with the Platonists. But what at last opened his spiritual eyes, he tells us, was a casual meeting with an aged man on the sea-shore. He then learnt why even the Platonist philosophy could not satisfy the human heart and that inner peace could be gained only by leaving the philosophers behind and turning to the Hebrew Prophets, from whose writings and the Christ whom they foretold the true doctrine was to be learned. Such is the story of his conversion, perhaps somewhat idealised, as Justin

[1] Not Maximus Confessor, as currently supposed. Cf. Urs von Balthasar, 'Das Scholienwerk des Johannes von Skythopolis' in *Scholastik* xv (1940), p. 27. Cf. E. Peterson's informative article in *E.C.* i. 1911f., s.v. 'Aristone di Pella'. According to the extant text of John of Scythopolis Clement of Alexandria here attributed the *Dialogue* to St. Luke. More probably the text should be emended to make Clement really say that he identified the Jason of the *Dialogue* with Luke's Jason in Acts xvii. 5ff.

[2] *Hist. Eccl.* IV. vi. 3.

[3] The Greek Flavia Neapolis and the modern Nablus.

recounts it himself in the opening pages of the *Dialogue with Trypho*.

The date of Justin's conversion to Christianity is not recorded. But the fact that he puts the scene of his *Dialogue* in the time of the 'Jewish War',[1] i.e. in the revolt of Bar Cochba (132-135), gives a *terminus ad quem*. It probably took place at Ephesus. Later Justin made at least two visits of considerable length to Rome, where he founded a school. Here he met the Cynic philosopher, Crescens, who, having been convicted by Justin of ignorance, became his sworn enemy. Finally, Justin suffered death for his faith at Rome when Junius Rusticus was Prefect of the City, i.e. between 163 and 167. Eusebius deduced from the passages he cites from Justin and his pupil, Tatian, that his death was compassed by the machinations of the Crescens just mentioned; but the passages to which he refers hardly warrant this deduction.

We have two *Apologies* from Justin; and though there are reasons for thinking that the two *Apologies* are really two parts of a single treatise, it is convenient to follow the traditional practice of treating them separately.

In the *First Apology* Justin begins by seeking to exonerate Christians from the charges laid against them. A Christian (χριστιανός) is not only a follower of Christ (χριστός) but also, he says almost playfully, one who is by nature honest (χρηστός). The accusations of atheism will not stand. It is the pagans with their idol-worship who are to be condemned on this charge. As those who follow the ethical teaching of Christ, Christians are by their very profession loyal citizens of the State. If they teach the resurrection of the dead, this is a doctrine not impossible of belief even by pagans.

Paganism, on the other hand, is full of debased practices. It indulges in magic and its religion is essentially corrupt. Christianity centres its faith in the Divinity of the Messiah. This is proved by the Messianic prophecies of the Hebrew Scriptures. Whatever is good in paganism has been taken

---

[1] *Dial. c. Tryph.* 1 and 9.

over from the Hebrew Scriptures, not least the doctrines of
the 'Divine Plato'.

In a concluding section of this *Apology*, Justin seeks to
shew that the charge that Christian worship is immoral is
wholly groundless. This leads him to give an account of the
Christian Sacraments which is of exceptional value to the
student of early liturgy. Those who are to be baptized are
'brought to the place where there is water', where they are
regenerated. This washing is in the Name of the Three
Persons of the Trinity. From being children of necessity and
ignorance they become children of freedom and knowledge
and obtain in the water the remission of all their past sins.
To this Sacrament Justin applies the word 'illumination'
($\phi\omega\tau\iota\sigma\mu\sigma$), 'because those who learn these things are
illuminated spiritually'. There are also clear signs of the use
of a Baptismal creed.

In the two accounts of the Eucharist which follow, we
have the fullest known description of the 2nd-century rite.
Indeed, apart from the recently recovered *Apostolic Tradition*
of Hippolytus, it is the most detailed account of the
Eucharistic rite from pre-Nicene times. Ch. 65 contains the
rite for the newly baptized; ch. 67 gives the normal Sunday
Eucharist. In the regular Eucharist, after a reading from the
'Memoirs of the Apostles' or the prophets, intercession is
made for the Church and those in the world. The kiss of
peace is then exchanged, and bread, wine and water are
brought up to the 'President' (δ $\pi\rho\omega\epsilon\sigma\tau\omega\varsigma$).[1] The President
then prays extemporarily ('according as he is able') over the
elements, the people say 'Amen' at the end, and then the
deacons distribute the Eucharistic gifts to those present. The
gifts are then taken by the deacons to the absent. Justin
points out that none but the baptized are allowed to take
part in the rite.

The *Apology* concludes (ch. 68) by citing the rescript
(*c.* A.D. 125) of Hadrian to Minucius Fundanus, the Proconsul of Asia, prohibiting the punishment of Christians

[1] Cf. T. G. Jalland in forthcoming *Studia Patristica* (1961).

except on specific charges. Its authenticity is made virtually
certain by the fact that it was added by Justin himself.[1]
Justin inserted it in its original Latin which is preserved by
Rufinus in his version of Eusebius, *H.E.* IV. ix. On the other
hand the version which Eusebius made for inclusion in his
Ecclesiastical History at this point has replaced the original
Latin in the MS. tradition of Justin.

Justin's *Second Apology* is much shorter. Justin opens with
an attack on the injustice of Urbicus, the City Prefect, who
had had three Christians put to death on the sole ground of
their confession. He also denounces the calumnies of the
Cynic, Crescens. To the satirical question of the heathen why
the Christians do not kill themselves that they may go to
God more quickly, Justin replies that suicide is forbidden by
their faith (ch. 4). He then gives reasons why God does not
deliver his followers from their persecutors. In the last resort,
persecutions arise from the hatred of the demons against
truth and virtue (ch. 5). Justin next defends the superiority
of the Christian moral teaching to that of the pagans, including even that of the Stoics. It is the realisation on earth of
what for Socrates had been only an ideal (ch. 10). Whatever
of Christian truth has been proclaimed by the philosophers
is due to their partaking of the 'Seminal Logos' (λόγος
σπερματικός). Finally he begs the Emperor to publish his
book, to treat the Christians with justice and to see to it that
all proceedings against the Christians are for real offences and
in the regular courts.

Besides his *Apologies* there also survives from Justin a
defence of Christianity against the Jews, the *Dialogue with
Trypho*. The work, which is in the form of a discussion at
Ephesus between Justin and a Jew, Trypho, is later than the
Apologies. It may be dated at *c.* 160. Much of the dialogue
rings sufficiently true to reality to make it probable that it is
based on one or more actual discussions, even if they were
considerably adapted before publication. It is possible that

---

[1] This was established by Dom B. Capelle, O.S.B., 'Le Rescrit
d'Hadrien et S. Justin' in *Rev. Bén.* xxxix (1927), pp. 365-8.

'Trypho' indicates the Rabbi Tarphon, one of the leading Palestine Jews of the period who figures in the Mishna. But, if so, he can hardly be the real subject of the *Dialogue*, for Justin's opponent appears to have been a layman and shews no sign of being versed in the Jewish law. It is notable, however, that 'Trypho' seems to ascribe authority only to the Hebrew books of the Biblical canon and makes no reference to the Deutero-canonical books.

The discussion is too discursive to lend itself to a summary exposition. After an introduction in which Justin describes his conversion,[1] Trypho states some difficulties which prevent his acceptance of the Gospel, namely that the Christians break the Law and put their trust in a crucified man. In reply Justin disputes Trypho's conception of the permanent obligation of the Law (1-47). He defends the Divinity of Christ as foretold by the Prophets. He insists that it was His unique position which entitled Him to abrogate the Law. In trying to resist this conclusion, the Jews had mutilated the original Scriptures (48-108). Moreover, Justin maintains that a true interpretation of the Scriptures justifies the admission of the Gentiles to the Christian Church without requiring them to keep the Law (109-36). There is an Epilogue in which, *inter alia*, Justin expresses his longing for the conversion of Trypho and his friends.

The *Apology* and the *Dialogue with Trypho* are the only genuine works of Justin which survive. His lost writings include a 'Book against All Heresies', a 'Treatise against Marcion', a 'Discourse against the Greeks', and works on 'The Sovereignty of God' and the 'Soul'. The considerable bulk of 'Justin' in the earlier printed editions has no claim to be considered genuine. The practice developed of ascribing to 'the Philosopher' and the prince among the Apologists apologetic writings by unknown authors, just as laws were ascribed to Moses and psalms to David. It is possible to assign at least one of these to their rightful owner. The *Expositio de Recta Fidei* has been proved to be the work of

[1] Cf. above pp. 48f.

Theodoret.[1] Titles of other works in the pseudo-Justinian *corpus* of which the authorship is still unknown are the *Cohortatio ad Graecos*, the much briefer *Oratio ad Graecos*, the *De Monarchia*, a series of *Quaestiones* and the *Epistula ad Zenam et Serenum*.

TATIAN

[Best edd. of Tatian's 'Oratio ad Graecos' by J. C. T. Otto (1851), E. Schwartz (T.U. iv(1), 1888), and E. J. Goodspeed (Göttingen, 1914). Eng. tr. by B. P. Pratten in A.N.C.L. (1867). For literature on the *Diatessaron* see below, p. 66.]

Tatian was a native of Syria. The son of pagan parents, he was educated in Greek rhetoric and philosophy and travelled widely in search of truth. Shortly after the middle of the 2nd century he found himself at Rome, where he became a Christian and a pupil of Justin Martyr. After Justin's martyrdom (*c.* 165), Tatian opened a school at Rome of his own. In 172-173 he returned to the East, where he was drawn to Gnostic opinions and founded a sect ('Encratites'). This sect professed extreme asceticism, condemned marriage altogether (not only second marriages), and disallowed the use of wine, which it replaced by water, in the Eucharist. He was a devoted missionary, and seems to have been mainly active in Syria, Cilicia and Pisidia.

Apart from his *Diatessaron*,[2] Tatian's one surviving literary work is his *Discourse to the Greeks* ('Oratio ad Graecos'). Like the other Apologists, he defended the Logos doctrine. Christianity, he argued, with its roots in the Hebrew faith, was prior to that of the Greeks. But the work was conceived less as a positive defence of Christianity than as a fierce attack on paganism. In the surrounding Greco-Roman civilisation he can see nothing but evil. Its ethics, its philosophy, its art, its religion all come under the lash of

[1] This was shewn independently by J. Lebon, 'Restitutions à Théodoret de Cyr II' in *R.H.E.* xxvi (1930), pp. 536-50, and R. V. Sellers, 'Pseudo-Justin's Expositio Rectae Fidei' in *J.T.S.* xlvi (1945), pp. 145-50.

[2] On this cf. below, p. 66.

Tatian's attack, and in places his wrath approaches that of Tertullian. For the historian of contemporary paganism the *Discourse* is a useful source book. It contains, e.g., a list of the statues which Tatian had come across at Rome to demonstrate the immorality of the Roman artists. Tatian was also the author of a number of other writings, but all these have been lost.

MILTIADES

Miltiades, a contemporary of Tatian and perhaps, like him, one of Justin's pupils, almost certainly belonged to Asia Minor. He was the author of a number of apologetic writings, —one directed against the Greeks, another against the Jews, and a third 'to the Ruling Powers in defence of the philosophy which he followed'. These 'ruling powers' (οἱ κοσμικοὶ ἄρχοντες) are probably not the provincial governors, but the Emperors, i.e. Marcus Aurelius (161-180) and his brother, Lucius Verus (161-169). He wrote further treatises against the Gnostics and the Montanists. Unfortunately all his works are lost.

APOLLINARIS OF HIERAPOLIS

Claudius Apollinaris was Bishop of Hierapolis in Phrygia in the reign of Marcus Aurelius (161-180). From Eusebius[1] we learn that he wrote a long series of apologetic writings, but all have been lost. One of these dated from *c.* 172 and was addressed to the Emperor. His other writings include five books against the Greeks and a work against the Montanists. According to the 'Paschal Chronicle' (7th century)[2] Apollinaris was also the author of a work on the Pasch (Περὶ τοῦ Πάσχα). Though this work was not known to Eusebius and Jerome, there is no reason to doubt its genuineness. The Chronicle cites two brief passages which are of interest because they suggest that Apollinaris was opposed to Quartodeciman practice. If so he was at variance with the usual Asia Minor tradition.

[1] *Hist. Eccl.* **IV.** xxvii.   [2] Ed. W. Dindorf, 13-14; *P.G.* xcii. 80-1.

ATHENAGORAS

[Edd. of Gk. text by E. Schwartz (T.U., iv(2), 1891) and P. Ubaldi—
M. Pellegrino (Turin, 1947, with tr.). Best Eng. tr., with annotations,
by J. H. Crehan, S.J., in A.C.W. (1956). Studies by A. J. Festugière,
O.P., in *R.E.G.* lvi (1943), pp. 367-75, and R. M. Grant in *H.T.R.* xlvii
(1954), pp. 121-9.]

Of Athenagoras almost nothing is known beyond what can
be deduced from his two writings, the *Supplication for the
Christians*, which is an apologetic treatise, and his book *On
the Resurrection*. Both survive only in the so-called Arethas
Codex of the year 914 (now in the Bibl. Nat.; Par. gr. 451)
where Athenagoras is described as 'the Christian philosopher,
Athenagoras of Athens'; he lived in the second half of the
2nd century.

The *Supplication* was a defence of Christianity addressed
to the Emperors 'Marcus Aurelius Antoninus and Lucius
Aurelius Commodus'. It is clear from its contents that the
second Emperor mentioned was Commodus, the son, not the
brother, of Marcus Aurelius, and hence the *Supplication* must
be dated between 27 November 176 when Commodus was
granted the title of Emperor ($αὐτοκράτωρ$) and 17 March 180
when Marcus Aurelius died. The most probable date is 177.

Athenagoras' purpose, he tells us, is to rebut the three
charges made against the Christians,—atheism, Thyestian
feasts and Oedipodean intercourse (ch. 3). Much the greater
part of the work (chs. 4-30) is concerned with the first of
these charges. The Greeks have themselves widely abandoned
their traditional polytheism (5-6). The Christians, on the
other hand, derive their teaching from the Prophets, the
messengers of God through whom the Holy Ghost spoke (7).
They are convinced that the unity of God can be established
on rational grounds (ch. 8). Yet for them God is more than
a Unity. They hold that there is the Son of God, the Father's
Logos, and the Holy Ghost, an effluence ($ἀπόρροια$) of God.
Beyond these they also believe in a large body of ministering
angels (ch. 10). The charge of Atheism is refuted by the moral
teaching of Christ with its insistence on God's rewards and

punishments in the next life (11-12). Holding such beliefs, Christians can have no lot in idolatry, nor share in heathen worship, even if the pagan gods are reinterpreted as poetical personifications (22). The miracles which the pagans claim for their gods are really performed by the demons, beings who came into existence through the intercourse of fallen angels with the daughters of men (26). The other charges against the Christians can be more briefly disposed of. That of organised debauchery is absurd, for Christians regard even the unclean thought as sinful and many, both men and women, spend their lives dedicated to chastity (32-4). Nor can they be charged with murder, for they abhor the gladiatorial shows and condemn abortion and the exposure of children with abhorrence.

Athenagoras' attitude to Greek culture and philosophy is that of Justin and contrasts with the hostility of Tatian. In style he seeks to achieve 'Atticism', but without much success.

Athenagoras' treatise *On the Resurrection* is in two parts. In the former he attacks those who reject the resurrection of the body as impossible. It is absurd to say that God could not cause the body to live again. His power is demonstrated by the fact of His Creation of the Universe. Nor is there any real objection in the fact that the individual particles of one man's body may pass into another man's body; for the essence of a man's body is what he integrates into himself. Further, it is just as absurd to say that God would be *unwilling* to raise it. If it is said that such an act would be unworthy of God, the same objection could be made against the Creation.

In the second part of the treatise, Athenagoras seeks to prove the reality and, indeed, the necessity of the Resurrection. It accords with man's destiny for eternity (12f.), with the fact that he is by nature compact of body and soul (14-17), with the Divine Justice with which it would be in accord that the body, as well as the soul, should receive the rewards and punishments due to it (18-23), and lastly with the nature of man's final destiny in contrast with the present life which is only a beginning (24-5).

THEOPHILUS OF ANTIOCH

[Ed. princeps by J. Frisius—C. Gesner, Zürich, 1546. Crit. Edd. by J. C. T. Otto, Jena, 1861; G. Bardy, S.C. xx, 1948. Eng. tr. in A.N.C.L. iii (1867), pp. 49-133.]

According to Eusebius,[1] Theophilus was the sixth Bishop of Antioch in Syria. In his early years he had been a pagan. Of his extensive writings, his only surviving treatise is an *Apology* for the Christian faith written *c.* A.D. 180, and addressed to his pagan friend, Autolycus. He was a writer of little ability. A. Puech described him as 'a Tatian without talent'.[2] His work, which was in three books, expounded the Christian teaching about God, defending the superiority of the doctrine of creation over the immoral myths of the Olympian religion. An exponent of the Logos doctrine, Theophilus carried it a stage further than any of his predecessors in distinguishing between the λόγος ἐνδιάθετος, the intelligence of the Father (2.10), and the λόγος προφορικός, the Word brought forth externally in order to create (2.22). He is also the first theologian to use the word 'Triad' (τριάς) of the Godhead. Among Theophilus' other (lost) writings are (according to Eusebius) works against Hermogenes and Marcion; and (according to Jerome) works on the *Gospels* and on the *Proverbs of Solomon*. He also issued a Gospel Harmony, perhaps an orthodox counterpart to that of Tatian. F. Loofs' attempt to discover considerable portions of Theophilus' treatise against Marcion in Irenaeus' *Against Heresies*[3] has found little following. It should be noted that, though all Theophilus' connexions were with Antioch, his theological outlook was far removed from that of the 'Antiochene School' and fundamentally Alexandrian.

[1] *Hist. Eccl.* IV. xx.
[2] A. Puech, *Les Apologistes Grecs*, p. 227.
[3] F. Loofs, *Theophilus von Antiochien Adversus Marcionem und die andern theologischen Quellen bei Irenaeus* in T.U. xlvi. 2 (1930).

HERMIAS

[Ed. princeps by J. Oporinus, Basle, 1553. Modern ed. by J. C. T. Otto in *Corpus Apologetarum Christianorum* ix (1872), pp. 1-31. See also *O.D.C.C.*, p. 631.]

Hermias is known to us solely as the author of a short treatise, the 'Irrisio' or 'Mockery of the Heathen Philosophers' (Διασυρμὸς τῶν ἔξω φιλοσόφων), which satirises the conflicting opinions of pagan writers on the human soul (cc. 1-2) and the fundamental principles of the universe (cc. 3-10). Its unknown author was a man of very modest capacities. He appears to have derived his knowledge of his pagan opponents not from their writings but from current handbooks of philosophy. Absence of any reference to Neo-Platonism may perhaps indicate that Hermias is not later than the 3rd century; but his date is very uncertain and modern scholars have assigned him to various dates between the 2nd and the 6th centuries.

SEXTUS

[For bibl., see Dr. H. Chadwick's edition (1959) mentioned below.]

One further item may be mentioned, the 451 'Sayings' which go under the name of Sextus. The work is a collection of ethical aphorisms, apparently of pagan origin, which were put into circulation in a Christian form round about the year A.D. 200. Origen twice[1] quotes them, expressly ascribing them to Sextus and also makes use of them in a number of other places. About 200 years later they were rendered into Latin by Rufinus (d. 410). They were also translated into Syriac (twice) and into Armenian (directly, not *via* the Syriac). Rufinus was of the opinion that they were composed by Pope Sixtus II (257-8), a view which became very general, but which was properly rejected already by Jerome.[2] These 'Sayings' teach in the main the Hellenistic ethics of austerity, moderation in food, drink and sleep, and an ascetic attitude to sex. They have recently been reissued in an excellent edition, with discussion, by Dr. H. Chadwick.[3]

[1] *Contra Celsum* viii. 30 and *Comm. in Matt.* xv. 3.   [2] *Ep.* 132. 3.
[3] 'Texts and Studies, Second Series, V', ed. C. H. Dodd, Cambridge, 1959.

IV.—THE SCRIPTURAL CANON

[A full bibl. on the growth of the New Testament Canon cannot be given here. A valuable guide will be found in A. Souter—C. S. C. Williams, *The Text and Canon of the New Testament* (1954) in this Series. For more detailed work, T. Zahn, *Geschichte des neutestamentliche Kanons* (2 vols., 1888-92), remains indispensable, which can be supplemented by his *Forschungen zur Geschichte des neutestamentlichen Kanons* (10 parts, 1881-1929).]

THE Christian Church was never without a Bible. From the first she possessed a collection of sacred Books to which she attached a high, if varying, degree of authority. This body of 'canonical' literature comprised the Law, the Prophets and the Writings. Its contents differed widely in date and character. At the beginning of the Christian era it was not possible to draw a hard and fast line between those books which belonged to this sacred *corpus* and those which lay outside it. Additions to the canon were still being made. But in so far as any particular writing was recognised as within the *corpus*, it was regarded as Divine Revelation and accepted as an authoritative norm in matters of doctrine and conduct. Such was the 'Old Testament'.

This Scripture contained the record of God's self-disclosure to the people of Israel. Its Books were the work of inspired writers who all belonged to Israel; and from the day when Moses received the Law, the Jews had been its appointed custodians and interpreters. Yet, with the appearance of the Messiah the whole situation had changed. Those who accepted Him held that no longer were God's ancient people the sole guardians of these writings. The Church now put forward the astonishing claim that they were hers in a way that they no longer belonged even to the Jews. Henceforward it was

E

the Christian Church which possessed the key to their message and interpretation.

In her earliest years the Church apparently had no expectation that this original canon of Scripture would be extended. Any such expectation would be ruled out by the belief that the end of the world was at hand. In the new covenant the sole complement to the Word in the Torah was the Word made flesh in Christ. The first Christian writings were essentially occasional products, arising out of concrete needs. And there is nothing to suggest that the writers of what we have come to know as the 'New Testament' had any idea that their writings would later receive canonical status. They wrote *in medias res* and they were concerned with the issues and circumstances of their day.

It was only as time went on that a group of early Christian writings began to acquire an authority of their own. They owed this in the first instance to their use in the liturgy. From the outset it had been the custom for the local communities founded by St. Paul, as they gathered together for worship week by week, to read the Apostle's writings.[1] After his martyrdom the respect felt for the letters of St. Paul would have been still further enhanced. And from the middle of the first century onwards the Church began to produce also its primitive Gospels. Accounts of the Lord's life, and particularly of the Passion and of the Resurrection appearances, were written down and circulated; and as the generation of those who remembered the Lord in the flesh passed away, the Church became ever more dependent for her witness to His redeeming work on such written records. And more than this, the tendency for the Church to attach authority to a group of primitive writings of her own was furthered by the demands of controversy. The Gnostics were putting out a body of scriptures of their own whose teachings were in conflict with the main stream of Christian tradition.

[1] This is clear from St. Paul's request that his Ep. to the Colossians should also be read in the Church of the Laodiceans and that the Colossians should also read his letter to the Laodiceans (Col. iv. 16).

When the Gnostics claimed that these scriptures incorporated
genuine, but secret, traditions, the Church found it impera-
tive to counter these claims by ascribing authority to her
own documents which she could rightly assert were of
indubitably greater historical worth.

PAPIAS

[Texts, with Eng. tr., conveniently repr. in J. B. Lightfoot—J. R.
Harmer (edd.), *Apostolic Fathers* (1891), pp. 514-35. Discussions of the
texts in nearly all considerable commentaries on the Gospels. Further
bibl. in B. Altaner, *Patrologie* (ed. 1958), p. 90.]

Among the first of those known to be directly interested
in the early Christian writings as such was Papias, Bishop of
Hierapolis in Phrygia in the earlier 2nd century. The great
interest that he arouses comes from a few fragments which
provide early testimony to the origins of the Gospels.
According to Irenaeus, Papias had heard St. John preach
and was also a friend of Polycarp, Bishop of Smyrna.[1]
Whether Irenaeus himself had known Papias is uncertain;
he may have derived his knowledge of him from books. We
have further details about Papias from Eusebius, whose
evidence, however, does not wholly accord with that of
Irenaeus. But Eusebius was prejudiced against Papias on
account of his Chiliasm,[2] and it was probably for this reason
that he pronounced him 'a man of very limited intelligence'
($\sigma\phi\acute{o}\delta\rho\alpha$ $\sigma\mu\iota\kappa\rho\grave{o}s$ $\mathring{\omega}\nu$ $\tau\grave{o}\nu$ $\nu o\widehat{\upsilon}\nu$).

Papias was the author of a treatise in five books, 'Explana-
tions of the Sayings of the Lord', which probably dates from
c. 130. Unfortunately only a few fragments have survived,
notably in Eusebius. But these have deservedly received the
closest attention of New Testament scholars on account of
what they tell us about the Evangelists and the Gospels.
Papias belonged to the days when it was still possible to
learn details of the life of Christ from living tradition. Indeed, he says, he held that 'what was to be derived from

[1] Irenaeus, *Adv. Haer.* V. xxxiii. 4. On Polycarp, cf. above, pp. 19-21.
[2] I.e., the belief in a literal reign of Christ with his saints on the
earth for a thousand years.

books would not profit [him] as much as what came from the living and abiding voice'.[1]

One of Papias' primary sources of information was 'the Presbyter'. This Presbyter told him that 'Mark had been the interpreter of Peter and had committed to writing what was said or done by Christ, so far as he remembered it, not however in [chronological or factual?] order'. Papias then added on his own account: '[Mark himself] had neither heard nor accompanied the Lord, but had later . . . accompanied Peter, who adapted his discourses in accordance with their needs. . . . For Mark had only one care, namely not to leave out any of the things he had heard or to record any of the things falsely'. As regards the First Gospel, he tells us that '[Matthew] compiled the sayings (τὰ λόγια) in the Hebrew tongue and everyone interpreted them as he was able'. In a fragment containing a list of the early disciples which includes several of the Apostles, Papias twice mentions 'John', and Eusebius read the passage as though Papias here distinguished two Johns, John the Apostle and another 'John, the Presbyter'. This interpretation of the passage has been widely accepted,—until recently, rather uncritically,—and has brought into being a whole literature on John the Presbyter in connexion with the Fourth Gospel. There is a growing tendency among scholars to deny that Papias countenances any second John at all other than John the Apostle.

MARCION'S INSTRUMENTUM

Shortly before the middle of the 2nd century a decisive influence on the construction of a canon of the New Testament was exercised by Marcion[2] We have already drawn attention to Marcion's radicalism. Whereas the main stream of Christian tradition had taken over the 'Old Testament' from Judaism, Marcion was asserting that its tenets were fundamentally at variance with the truth proclaimed by

---

[1] Ap. Eusebius, *Hist. Eccl.* III. xxxix. 4.
[2] On Marcion, cf. above, pp. 40f.

Jesus. Where, then, precisely, was truth embodied? To no one could this problem have presented itself with greater urgency than to Marcion; for he of all theologians was a dogmatist for whom everything must be in sharp definition. There must be no doubt as to which writings lay within and which without the sacred *corpus*. To this end he needed an 'instrument',[1] which would express this distinction. In this way Marcion became the author of the first canon of Christian Scriptures.

Marcion was an avowed Paulinist, and the core of Marcion's Canon was taken from the Pauline writings. As we have remarked it consisted of ten of the Pauline Epistles, i.e. all but the Pastorals, together with a truncated and edited text of St. Luke's Gospel. The Gospel of Luke was selected perhaps because of the evangelist's intimate relation with St. Paul, perhaps as the Gospel best known in Marcion's native Pontus. This *corpus* of writings embodied the whole of Christian truth. It possessed an absolute authority comparable to that which had hitherto attached to the 'Old Testament' which (according to Marcion) was now wholly superseded. Marcion named it, after its two component parts, the 'Evangelion' and the 'Apostolicon'.

Though Marcion's New Testament has not survived, it can be partially reconstructed from Tertullian's *Treatise against Marcion*, as Tertullian quoted it extensively and commonly made a point of answering Marcion out of his own text. The arbitrary treatment to which Marcion subjected the traditional texts is shewn by his omission of the whole of Luke 1 and 2 on the ground that the Infancy stories were derogatory to Christ. For Marcion, the antithesis between flesh and spirit was absolute and he found a real incarnation repugnant. Bethlehem was incredible. Historically his position was impossible. But the indirect effect of Marcion's radical treatment of the Christian writings was to be immense. For it compelled the orthodox Church to settle by contrast what

[1] Lat. 'instrumentum', the name Marcion gave to his Canon. Cf. Tertullian, *Adversus Marcionem* i, 19.

were its own accredited Scriptures and to compile its own Canon. The authority attaching to the incipient 'New Testament' Scriptures which had long been increasing was now finally sealed by the Church. The remarkable fact is that this came about not by any formal act of 'Canonisation' (in any case the Church was too loosely organised in the 2nd century to allow of any such process), but by the general *consensus* of orthodox opinion.

LATIN GOSPEL AND EPISTLE PROLOGUES

Before going further, we may take note of some of the 'Prologues' found in many early manuscripts of the New Testament, for here too Marcion seems to have played a decisive part. These Prologues (*praefationes* or *argumenta*) are prefixed to the several Books of the Bible and provide the reader in brief compass with information about their author and composition. There are three groups which call for notice here:

(1) The 'Marcionite Prologues' to St. Paul's Epistles;
(2) The 'Anti-Marcionite Prologues' to the Gospels;
(3) The 'Monarchian Prologues' to the Gospels.

(1) There can be little doubt that Marcion was intimately connected with the composition of a complete set of thirteen prologues found in 'Codex Fuldensis' and some thirteen other MSS. One of their leading themes is that the recipients of the Epistles had received from Paul the word of truth (*verbum veritatis*) and had been led astray by false apostles (*falsis apostolis*)[1] This strongly suggests a Marcionite origin for the Prologues since for Marcion Paul was the Apostle *par excellence* and the other Apostles were 'false'. This hypothesis is confirmed by the fact that though this characteristic language is found in ten of the thirteen Prologues, in the case of the

[1] E.g. the Prologue to Gal. reads: Galatae sunt Graeci. Hi verbum veritatis primum ab apostolo acceperunt, sed post discessum eius temptati sunt a falsis apostolis, ut in legem et circumcisionem verterentur. Hos apostolus revocet ad fidem veritatis, scribens eis ab Ephesis.

three Pastoral Epistles, i.e. of those Epistles not acknowledged by Marcion, it is modified or wanting: this difference could be readily explained by supposing they were added later to complete a *corpus* of Pauline Epistles which now included them. Their Marcionite origin is further borne out by (1) That they are translations of a Greek original; (2) That they follow the Marcionite order of the Epistles (Gal. at the outset); and (3) That they are evidently of great antiquity. Indeed they lend countenance to the suggestion that we owe to Marcion the first Latin translation of the Pauline Epistles at Rome and that this translation with the Prologues was taken over bodily into Catholic Bibles.

(2) The 'Anti-Marcionite Prologues' are a collection of three Latin Prologues to the Gospels of Mark, Luke and John, contained in some forty MSS. of the Vulgate. They differ considerably in form, but in 1928 Dom D. de Bruyne, O.S.B., argued that they had a common ancestry and that they were completed with a fourth prologue to Matthew now missing.[1] The prologue to Luke survives also in Greek (of which the Latin Luke is a translation); hence the presumption is that all were originally written in Greek. The prologue to John is directed against Marcion. De Bruyne argued that the same could also be proved of that to Luke. De Bruyne argued, and he gained the support of Harnack, that the prologues were composed for a Catholic edition of the Gospel text, drawn up against Marcion probably at Rome, at *c.* 170-180. If this early date could be sustained, the Prologues would be early evidence for historical traditions about the Evangelists.

Further study, however, has thrown a good deal of doubt on the matter.[2] There are serious grounds for questioning whether the three prologues ever formed part of a single series. It is objected that the reference to Acts and other Biblical books at the end of the Lucan prologue would be out

[1] 'Des plus anciens prologues latins des Évangiles' in *Rev. Bén.* xl (1928), pp. 193-214.
[2] Cf. the important paper by R. G. Heard in *J.T.S.* N.S. v. (1955), pp. 1-16.

of place if the prologue formed part of a series. Also, the prologue to John departs widely in form from the other two and appears to embody late traditions. And the supposed reference to Marcion in the Lucan prologue is doubtful. It appears, then, that these prologues have now lost much of their importance. On the other hand certain of their *data* about the Evangelists, e.g. Mark's short fingers or Luke's death in old age in Boeotia, may well preserve authentic traditions.

(3) The so-called Monarchian Prologues to the Gospels[1] are of later date. They are somewhat longer compilations than those we have just considered and were clearly composed of set theological purpose. They appear to have been originally written in Latin. According to P. Corssen, they were put together at Rome early in the 3rd century, apparently to rebut the prevalent Monarchianism. Later scholars (J. Chapman, E. L. Babut, G. Morin) have come to hold that they are of Spanish origin and are probably not older than the 4th century. According to Morin they are the work of Instantius, who defended the Priscillianist party at the Council of Bordeaux (384).

TATIAN'S DIATESSARON

[Arabic text ed. P. A. Ciasca (Rome, 1888; ed. 2, 1934); also by A. S. Marmardji, O.P. (Beyrouth, 1935); Med. Dutch version ed. D. Plooij, C. A. Phillips, etc. (Amsterdam, 1929ff.). C. H. Kraeling, *A Greek Fragment of Tatian's Diatessaron from Dura* (Studies and Documents 3, 1935). T. Zahn, 'Tatian's Diatessaron' in his *Forschungen zur Geschichte des neutestamentlichen Kanons und der altkirchlichen Literatur* i (Erlangen, 1881). Further bibl. in A. Souter—C. S. C. Williams, *The Text and Canon of the New Testament* (1954), p. 227.]

Important evidence of the Scriptural authority attaching to the Gospels, at some date after the middle of the 2nd century, is afforded by Tatian's 'Diatessaron' (διὰ τεσσάρων).[2] This work was a compilation from the four Gospels of

[1] The text is to be found in H. Lietzmann's *Kleine Texte* No. 1 (1908; ed. 4, 1933). Cf. also J. Chapman, O.S.B., *Notes on the Early History of the Vulgate Gospels* (1908), pp. 217-28 (text on pp. 217-20).

[2] On Tatian, cf. above, pp. 53f.

Matthew, Mark, Luke and John into a single continuous narrative. Its purpose was to combine the texts to avoid overlap. As T. Zahn recognised, the 'Diatessaron' used the Gospel of John as its framework.[1] It appears to belong to Tatian's heretical years, i.e. after 172-3.

The original text of the *Diatessaron* has been lost, but it is possible to reconstruct it from various sources, viz.: (1) A commentary on the text made by the 4th-century writer, Ephraem Syrus. This commentary, however, does not survive in the original Syriac, but it has come down in an Armenian version; (2) A 10th-century Arabic version which survives in two MSS.; (3) The Latin 'Codex Fuldensis' of the Gospels, written in 541-6. It was compiled under the immediate direction of Victor, Bishop of Capua. Though the Biblical text is of the Vulgate form, it is a harmony and based on the arrangement of Tatian's *Diatessaron*; (4) A medieval Dutch Harmony of the Scriptures, discovered by D. Plooij at Liége in 1923; (5) To these must be added a short papyrus fragment of fourteen lines of the Greek text, discovered at Dura Europos and published by C. H. Kraeling in 1935.

The language in which the *Diatessaron* was written is disputed. Was it made originally in Greek?[2] Or did Tatian originally compile it in his native Syriac? And, if the latter, did Tatian work with the separate Syriac versions of the Gospels before him? Or was it an original Syriac composition, made directly from the Greek texts, and designed to present in the easiest and most practical way the substance of the Greek Gospels to a Syriac speaking Church? Or was it possibly (a view held by F. C. Burkitt) put together by Tatian in Latin when he was in Rome, as the earliest form of the Latin Gospels, and only later translated from this Latin version into Syriac? And how did it come about that a document compiled by a heretic should have found such wide

---

[1] *Forschungen* i, 112ff.
[2] It is sometimes said, though without any justification, that this view has received additional support from the recovery of the Dura Europos fragment.

acceptance in orthodox circles? To all these perplexing
questions a variety of answers have been given. We must refer
the reader to books expressly devoted to the Canon for
discussion of them.

In the present connexion the construction of the *Diatessaron* is significant. For on the one hand it shews that at the
time that the *Diatessaron* was compiled, there were four
Gospels which had already received a certain authority, and
that this had been acknowledged in Gnostic circles such
as that represented by Tatian. But on the other hand, it shews
that their authority was not so great that there was felt
impropriety in replacing the four individual texts by a single
narrative. Such treatment of the Scriptures would have been
impossible fifty years earlier or fifty years later, when Origen
could comment on the New Testament and Old Testament
texts as alike sacred.

MURATORIAN FRAGMENT

[Text conveniently accessible in A. Souter—C. S. C. Williams, *The Text
and Canon of the New Testament* (1954), in this Series, pp. 191-3, with
notes, p. 193f. For photographic reproductions and full bibl. see
H. Leclercq, O.S.B., in *D.A.C.L.* xii (pt. 1; 1934), cols. 543-60, s. v.
'Muratorianum'.]

Of early canonical lists the most celebrated is the so-called
'Muratorian Fragment on the Canon'. This list, preserved in
an 8th-century MS. from Bobbio in the Ambrosiana (J. 101
sup.), at Milan, was published by L. A. Muratori (1672-1750)
in 1740. It has come down to us in a barbarous Latin, partly
due to the very circumscribed ability of its original compiler
and perhaps even more to the corruptions of its copyist who
belonged to a very uncultured age (8th century). The extant
MS. is of eighty-five lines and is defective at both ends. The
text, possibly a translation from a Greek original,[1] is more
probably a Latin composition. As the author in referring to
Hermas, the author of the *Shepherd*, describes him as the

---

[1] Among recent defenders of a Latin original was A. Harnack,
Z.N.T.W. xxiv (1925), pp. 1-16. The apparent pun ('fel', 'mel') in the
line cited below, p. 70, note 3, is perhaps not decisive.

brother of Pope Pius (*c.* 140-155) and as of 'our own times',[1] he presumably lived in the latter part of the 2nd century, a date which accords with the fact that the teachings of Marcion, Basilides, Valentinus and the Montanists are all living issues. Its author is unknown. Hippolytus has often been suggested;[2] but this proposal, apart from its presupposing a lost Greek original, is also improbable owing to the date. There is no evidence that Hippolytus began to write until after 200 and a work of this kind would more naturally belong to the time of his life when he filled a position of authority. On the other hand, the view once defended by Harnack that it was a canonical list of the New Testament Scriptures put forward officially by the Roman Church is unlikely. We cannot say more of its author than that he was some (probably unknown) Roman Christian.

The list begins abruptly, owing to the loss of the opening lines. The account of Matthew and most of that of Mark are wanting. 'Luke the Physician', we read, wrote his Gospel 'in his own name' on Paul's authority; he, 'too' (i.e., doubtless, 'like Mark'), did not see the Lord in the flesh. There is a strange account of the origin of 'the Fourth of the Gospels'. John, we are told, when pressed to set to work by his fellow disciples and bishops, ordered a three days' fast and decided that 'what may be revealed to any of us let us relate it to one another'. In the same night 'it was revealed to Andrew, one of the apostles, that John was to write all these things in his own name, and they were all to certify'. As B. H. Streeter commented,[3] this 'account of the origin of the Fourth Gospel can only be styled "a cock and bull story" '. After a notice of the four-fold nature of the Gospel and its compatibility with the unity of the faith of believers and a passing reference to John's 'Epistles', there follows the comment on Acts. Luke, we are told, records events which took place 'in his

---

[1] *nuperrime temporibus nostris . . . sedente cathedram urbis Romae ecclesiae Pio episcopo fratre eius.*

[2] E.g. by J. B. Lightfoot, T. Zahn, and more recently by M. J. Lagrange.

[3] *The Primitive Church*, p. 205.

presence' and so omits 'the passion of Peter and also the departure of Paul from the City[1] on his journey to Spain'.

Next comes a long continuous passage on Paul's Epistles. The thirteen Epistles of the traditional canon, including Philemon and the Pastorals (i.e. all except Heb.), are listed. The compiler makes the curious comment that Paul, following his predecessor John',[2] wrote by name to '*seven* churches', viz. to the Corinthians, the Ephesians, the Philippians, the Colossians, the Galatians, the Thessalonians and the Romans, adding that 'for the sake of admonition' he wrote second epistles to the Corinthians and the Thessalonians. The list is then completed with the four addressed to individuals (Philemon, Titus, 1 and 2 Timothy). The Epistles in Paul's name to the Laodiceans and the Alexandrians are rejected as Marcionite forgeries; they cannot be received in the Catholic Church 'for it is not fitting that gall be mixed with honey'.[3]

The list concludes with a collection of miscellaneous items. The Epistles of Jude, 'two of the above named John' (apparently 2 and 3 John; 1 John had already been mentioned with the Gospel), the Wisdom of Solomon (oddly placed here), the Apocalypse of John and the Apocalypse of Peter are all accounted canonical. There is no mention of either of the Petrine Epistles; but the omission of 1 Peter was probably accidental. In the final lines several rejected items are listed including the *Shepherd* of Hermas and various Gnostic and Montanist writings.

---

[1] *Ab urbe.* The word is another indication of the Roman origin of the Muratorian fragment.
[2] I.e. with reference to his Epistles to the Churches of Asia in Rev. iif.
[3] fel enim cum melle misceri non congruit.

V.—THE APOCRYPHAL SCRIPTURES

[The best handbook in English is M. R. James, *The Apocryphal New Testament* (1924), which contains a great deal of information and the principal texts in Eng. trans.; with recent discoveries, however, it is rapidly getting out of date. Far superior is the German handbook of E. Hennecke (ed.), *Neutestamentliche Aprokryphen . . . in deutscher Übersetzung* (ed. 2, 2 vols., 1923-4; new and improved ed. by W. Schnee-melcher, i 1959 [ii forthcoming], with good introductions by J. Jeremias, H. C. Puech, O. Cullmann, W. Schneemelcher, and other competent scholars). Original texts in C. Tischendorf (ed.), *Evangelia Apocrypha* (Leipzig, 1853; ed. 2, 1876); R. A. Lipsius—M. Bonnet (edd.), *Acta Apostolorum Apocrypha* (Leipzig, 1891-1903). See also Patrologies of B. Altaner, O. Bardenhewer and J. Quasten; also art. by E. Amann on 'Apocryphes du Nouveau Testament' in *Dict. de la Bible*, Suppl. i (1928), cols. 460-533. Further reff. under separate items.]

OVER against the Canonical Scriptures, there arose in the early Church a large body of 'Apocryphal' Scriptures of very diverse character, *provenance* and date.[1] As far as the 'New Testament' group is concerned, they are akin in literary form to the Canonical Books, and like them are for the most part associated with the name of one or other of the Apostles (including St. Paul). But here the resemblance ends. They are nearly all by writers of little spiritual power. Many of them are imaginative, indeed almost fantastic, and issue from minds which would regard truth as secondary to edification;

[1] The term 'Apocrypha' is apt to be misleading. Literally it means 'things hidden'. In the Churches which fell under the influence of the Reformation (including the Church of England) it came to be applied especially to the Deutero-canonical Books of the Old Testament, i.e. in general those found only in the Greek Bible but wanting in the Hebrew. The 'Apocrypha' of the traditional English Bible thus comprises books of widely different character, e.g. some which contain some of the best history in the Old Testament, such as 1 Maccabees, or such irreproachable instructions and reflections on life as Ecclesiasticus and Wisdom. On the other hand in the Hebrew Canon there are Books of an imaginative kind such as Daniel which heralded those of the N.T. Apocrypha.

and one may wonder how far their authors themselves conceived they were writing history. It has been widely supposed that much of this literature issued from circles of uncertain orthodoxy. But how far this 'unorthodoxy' reflects anything more than the readiness with which the simple and undisciplined mind falls into 'heresy' may be questioned. Modern teaching in the Sunday School, or even in the pulpit, does not invariably conform to the standards of Chalcedon, to say nothing of those of Geneva or Trent.

These Scriptures were for the most part frowned on by the orthodox, where not officially condemned, and hence circulated in underground channels. They are nearly all pseudonymous and the real names of their authors have rarely survived. Nevertheless they won great popularity. The texts exist in a great variety of languages (among them Greek, Latin, Syriac, Coptic, Ethiopic, Arabic, Armenian), and it is often difficult to determine their original language. Still less is known of their original date and place of writing. Many were probably fabricated in the Egyptian monasteries of the 4th and 5th centuries. They continued to circulate widely in medieval times and their composition continued into the Middle Ages. The so-called *Gospel of Barnabas*[1] appears to be an Italian fabrication of the early 14th century.

A comprehensive survey of this literature would be a large undertaking, partly because of its extent, partly on account of the range and obscurity of the problems involved. Here we must be content with a brief account of some of the more interesting works. There is the less reason for regretting this limitation, for though some areas in the field are of much interest, there are others which are extremely arid. Each text has its own historical and literary problems. For a handy collection of the texts in English, the reader may be referred to M. R. James' *Apocryphal New Testament* (1924), already mentioned. It is convenient, as there, to classify this literature as 'Gospels', 'Acts', and 'Apocalypses', after the New Testament forms on which it is modelled. But these divisions

[1] Ed. by Lonsdale and Laura Ragg, Oxford 1907.

do not always reflect the real connexions.[1] There are also a few apocryphal 'Epistles'. But compositions in this form were far less frequent, doubtless because if the New Testament models were to be followed it gave less scope to the imagination.[2]

APOCRYPHAL INFANCY GOSPELS

These include: (1) The Book of James, or the Protevangelium; (2) The Syriac Gospel of Thomas; (3) The History of Joseph the Carpenter; and (4) The Transition of the Blessed Virgin.

(1) THE BOOK OF JAMES, OR THE PROTEVANGELIUM. This probably late 2nd-century work narrates the miraculous birth and the infancy of the Blessed Virgin. It describes the perplexities and faith of her parents, who are here for the first time named Anne and Joachim, and the Virgin's Presentation in the Temple at the age of three. In general, it is a more sober work than most of the Apocryphal writings. It professes to have been written in Jerusalem by James, the Lord's Brother.

The book survives in its original Greek, and also in Syriac and other Oriental versions; but it appears to be interpolated in all its forms. It was probably known to Clement of Alexandria and was expressly referred to by Origen. The title, *The Protevangelium*, is modern (16th century).

(2) THE SYRIAC GOSPEL OF THOMAS. This work, which must be carefully distinguished from the newly recovered *Coptic Gospel of Thomas* from Nag Hammadi[3] as well as from the lost Naassene 'Gospel of Thomas', mentioned by Hippolytus at *Philos.* v. 7, survives in a longer and a shorter recension,

---

[1] Thus one of the most important apocrypha is known both as the 'Acts of Pilate' and the 'Gospel of Nicodemus'.

[2] Cf. the apocryphal 'Epistle of St. Paul to the Laodiceans', briefly described below, p. 86.

[3] Cf. p. 77f.

as well as in Latin, Syriac, Armenian and Old Slavonic. It consists of a series of trivial stories about the childhood of Jesus, perhaps designed with no more exalted destiny than the nursery. Jesus, once playing with other children on the Sabbath day and having modelled a group of twelve birds out of clay, is reproached before St. Joseph by a Jew for breaking the law. When Joseph reproves him, Jesus claps with his hands and the birds fly away. On another occasion, Jesus goes with his father sowing. The single corn which he sows provides three hundred measures (*cors*) of wheat, enough to satisfy all the poor of the village. The work is headed in its longer Greek text: 'The Stories of Thomas the Israelite, the Philosopher, concerning the works of the Childhood of the Lord'.

(3) THE HISTORY OF JOSEPH THE CARPENTER. The bulk of the book was probably written in Egypt and in Greek in the 4th-5th century, though some passages may be later additions; it survives in Coptic, Arabic and Latin. Jesus is on the Mount of Olives giving the Apostles an account of the life of Joseph, a carpenter of Bethlehem who had had four sons by a former wife. Mary, his future spouse, was brought up in the Temple until she was twelve years old. The priests then decided to give her in marriage; and it was settled by lot that she should marry Joseph. When Joseph was perplexed at the miraculous conception of the Lord and His impending Birth he was reassured by Gabriel. After the Birth and Flight into Egypt, there is a description of Joseph's return to Nazareth with Mother and Child. At length, at the age of 111, Joseph fell ill and realised that his death was approaching; Jesus confirmed Mary in their common forebodings. The book contains a graphic description of Joseph's end. His soul was put in a silken napkin by Michael and Gabriel, and transported by the angels, singing. After mourning, the angels put his body in a shroud and Jesus blessed it to preserve it from corruption. The book concludes with a doxology of the Apostles.

Though the writer drew extensively on the Canonical Gospels and the Gospel of James, he was mainly dependent on his imagination. In the account of the death and burial he was influenced by the traditional myths and customs of Egypt. The book was designed to spread the cultus of St. Joseph, which became very popular in Egypt in later Patristic times.

(4) THE TRANSITION OF THE BLESSED VIRGIN. An apocryphal work known as the *Transitus Mariae* exists in several recensions, Greek, Syriac, Coptic, Armenian, Arabic, and Latin. The original was probably a Greek composition of the 4th-5th century. It recounts how the Blessed Virgin, told by the Angel Gabriel of her approaching death, goes into retirement at Bethlehem whither the Apostles, now dispersed over the world, were brought back. Soon afterwards her death takes place (at Jerusalem) to the accompaniment of miracles; and the Apostles perform the funeral rites. Three days later her body is miraculously transported to Heaven or, according to other forms of the story, to the Garden of Eden, the earthly paradise.

The *Transition* is among the earliest accounts of the Assumption of the Blessed Virgin. In some of its Latin forms it is ascribed to Melito of Sardis. According to M. R. James,[1] all the traditions of the Assumption were probably elaborated in Egypt.

OTHER APOCRYPHAL GOSPELS

Besides the Infancy Gospels there were several other Gospels in circulation in the early Church. Three may be mentioned: (1) The Gospel of Peter; (2) the Gospel of Nicodemus; (3) The Coptic Gospel of Thomas.

(1) THE GOSPEL OF PETER. A fragment of this Gospel on vellum was discovered in 1886-7 by U. Bouriant in a grave at Akhmîm in Upper Egypt and published in 1892. The fragment contains the greater part of a Passion Narrative of

[1] *The Apocryphal New Testament* (1924), p. 194.

F

Christ and also a Resurrection Narrative, decked out with many miracles. The Gospel seems to have been a free working over of the Canonical Gospels, mainly legendary. It ends abruptly with the words: 'But I, Simon Peter, and Andrew, my brother, took our nets and went forth to the sea, and with us was Levi, the son of Alphaeus, whom the Lord . . .', apparently the beginning of an account of the appearance of the Risen Lord on the Sea of Galilee.

The work was known to Sarapion of Antioch[1] (c. 190), who found it in use at Rhossus and attacked it, and to Origen[2] in the next century. The author was strongly anti-Jewish in outlook and docetic in theology. It was included by Eusebius among the apocryphal writings.[3]

(2) THE GOSPEL OF NICODEMUS. This book has circulated under this title since the Middle Ages, but it was known earlier as the *Acts of Pilate* on the ground that it incorporated 'Acta' of the Lord's trial emanating from Pilate. Such 'Acts' were known already to Justin,[4] and in this form they were probably Christian productions. On the other hand in the persecution under Maximin Daza (311-12), the Imperial authorities fabricated pagan 'Acts of Pilate' to discredit the Christian cause.[5] Further evidence of Christian 'Acts of Pilate' is to be found in Epiphanius.[6]

The surviving *Acts of Pilate* or *Gospel of Nicodemus* are apparently later still. They purport to derive from documents written in Hebrew, which had been communicated to the author by Nicodemus. They included accounts of the trial before Pilate, the Crucifixion and Burial (1-11), disputations in the Sanhedrim defending the reality of the Resurrection (12-16) and statements by two disciples whom Jesus had awakened from the dead, Leucius and Charinos, about Our Lord's descent into hell and His deeds in the next world

---

[1] Ap. Eusebius, *Hist. Eccl.* VI. xii. 4, 6.
[2] *In Matt.* X. 17.
[3] *Hist. Eccl.* III. xxv. 6f.; cf. III. iii. 2.
[4] *Apology* i. 35. 9; 48. 3; cf. Tertullian, *Apologeticum* xxi. 24.
[5] Eusebius, *Hist. Eccl.* IX. v. 1.   [6] *Haer.* L. i. 5 and 8.

(17-27). The responsibility for the death of Christ rests entirely with the Jews, while Pilate is acquitted.

It seems certain that the work is wholly a Greek composition of the 5th century (the idea of Hebrew papers is a fiction). It may, however, draw on some older Greek material.

(3) THE COPTIC GOSPEL OF THOMAS. This Gospel, which has recently attracted considerable attention in the secular press, has been recovered among the texts from Nag Hammadi.[1] Like the other documents in this collection, it is in Coptic; but the text is undoubtedly a translation from the Greek. The Coptic (Sahidic) version may be dated at about 400;[2] the original Greek work probably at about the middle of the 2nd century, with some later additions. Hitherto there has been considerable obscurity about the 'Gospel of Thomas' as more than one treatise under the name circulated in the early Church.[3] Now that the full text of this treatise has come to light, many riddles have been solved.

The new Gospel is not an 'historical' book in the sense of giving, like the Canonical Gospels, an account of the Lord's life. It has no narrative portions, but consists of a series of pithy Sayings and parabolic discussions of Jesus. These have many points of contact with the presumed (lost) 'Q source' of the canonical Matthew and Luke. The Gospel is headed: 'These are the secret words which the living Jesus spake and they were written down by Didymus Judas Thomas and he said: "Whoever shall find the interpretation (hermēneia) of these words will not taste of death".' The treatise which follows consists of 114 items, the great majority of them Sayings of Jesus. At the end, there is simply 'The Gospel (euangelion) according to (kata) Thomas.' As Dr. Puech has

[1] Cf. pp. 32f. According to Puech's enumeration of the codices ('Les Nouveaux Écrits Gnostiques découverts en Haute-Egypte' in *Coptic Studies in Honor of Walter Ewing Crum*, Boston, Mass., 1950, pp. 91-157), it is contained in Codex III.

[2] W. C. Till, 'New Sayings of Jesus in the recently discovered Coptic "Gospel of Thomas" ' in *Bulletin of the John Rylands Library* xli (1959), p. 451; J. Leipoldt puts it at about 500, *T.L.Z.* 1958, cols. 481-2.

[3] Cf. above, pp. 73f.

pointed out the treatise must have been known by this name at least since the beginning of the 3rd century. The Coptic text was originally published in the photographic edition of Dr. Pahor Lahib, Director of the Coptic Museum at Old Cairo.[1] It was issued in the last weeks of 1959 from a projected annotated edition by A. Guillaumont and others.[2]

Most of its Sayings are put into the mouth of Jesus with no further context. Here are some examples. Saying 1 is 'Jesus said: Let not the seeker, if he seeks, cease until he finds; and when he finds he will be led astray, and when he is led astray he will wonder and he will become king over the universe'. Saying 9: 'Jesus said: I cast a fire over the world and behold I keep it safe until it burns'. Saying 32: 'Jesus said: No prophet is acceptable in his own city. No physician heals those who are known to him.' Saying 49: 'When two persons make peace with each other in the same house, they will say to the mountain "Turn round" and it will turn round'. Saying 77: 'Jesus said, I am the Light which is over them all. I am the Whole. From Me has the whole come forth and to Me the whole has come. Cleave the wood and I am there. Throw the stone upwards and there you will find Me.' Occasionally the Saying is prompted by some other speaker. Thus, Saying 79: 'A woman from the multitude said to Him: Blessed is the body which bare you and the paps which nourished you. He said to her: Blessed are they who heard the word of the Father and preserved it in truth. For the days will come that you say: Blessed is the body that did not conceive and the breasts that gave no milk!' These instances may give some idea of the contents.[3] About half the Sayings have fairly close Synoptic parallels.

What is the relation of these Sayings to the Lord's Sayings in the Canonical Gospels? Where the texts can be closely paralleled, in most cases there can be no doubt that the

---

[1] *Coptic Gnostic Papyri in the Coptic Museum of Old Cairo,* vol. i, plates 80-99 (Cairo, 1956).

[2] Leiden and London, 1959.

[3] The *average* length of the sayings, which include some parables, is longer. Shorter ones have been given here to save space.

Thomas form is secondary. But in some cases comparison suggests that the Thomas logia do not derive directly from the Synoptists. Indeed there is much to suggest that some came from a common source. It would appear that the Gospel of Thomas also used the 'Gospel according to the Hebrews'. Moreover, Dr. G. Quispel[1] thinks that sometimes the Sayings preserve such an early Judaeo-Christian form of the Scriptural text as to be of use for the textual criticism of the New Testament. He maintains that the Thomas text has affinities with the Bezan text, that it was at the basis of the various forms of the *Diatessaron* text and that it was used for the Pseudo-Clementines.

APOCRYPHAL ACTS

There are five principal sets of Apocryphal Acts: (1) The Acts of John; (2) The Acts of Paul; (3) The Acts of Peter; (4) The Acts of Andrew; and (5) The Acts of Thomas.

(1) THE ACTS OF JOHN. These Acts, which were apparently put together in their original form in Greek in Asia Minor between 150 and 180, describe the missionary travels of John in Asia Minor, professedly by an eye-witness. A considerable number of Greek extracts survive, as well as parts of a Latin version, but all are fragmentary. The work appears to have begun with a description of St. John's travels to Asia. At Miletum, where he landed, he had a vision bidding him go to Ephesus, which he made the centre of much missionary travelling. He was then sent for a time to Patmos into exile. The narratives are highly imaginative and erotic; their standpoint is certainly Gnostic. The Acts have considerable liturgical interest, e.g. they contain the earliest record of a celebration of the Eucharist for the Departed (ch. 72), together with the text of the prayer used in

---

[1] 'The Gospel of Thomas and the New Testament' in *Vigiliae Christianae* xi (1957), pp. 189-207.

this rite (ch. 85). The acts are ascribed to a certain Leucius.[1]

(2) THE ACTS OF PAUL. In 1904 C. Schmidt pieced together and published some 2,000 fragments of the 'Acts of Paul' (Πράξεις Παύλου) from a Heidelberg Coptic papyrus, and thereby established that three items which had hitherto been known independently,—viz. (i) The Acts of Paul and Thecla; (ii) The Correspondence of St. Paul with the Corinthians; and (iii) the Martyrdom of St. Paul,—were in fact all component parts of a single work. This must be the work mentioned by Tertullian in his *De Baptismo* 17, where he says that a presbyter from Asia Minor put the work together (*eam scripturam construxit*) out of his devotion to St. Paul, but that he was deposed from his office on being convicted of his falsification, albeit out of love of St. Paul.

In 1936 a considerable portion of the whole work in Greek was recovered from a Hamburg Papyrus, a striking confirmation of Schmidt's contention.

(2.i) *The Acts of Paul and Thecla.* Thecla is a Greek girl from Iconium who has been won over to the faith by St. Paul's preaching. She accompanies the Apostle in his missionary journeys, has many miraculous escapes and finally returns to Seleucia. It is uncertain what basis of sober history, if any, underlies the narrative.

The story became exceedingly popular. There exist no less than five Latin versions, besides several others in Oriental languages. A passage in ch. 3 describing St. Paul's features had a decisive influence on Christian art: 'a man little of stature, with bald head and bent legs, strong, with eyebrows joining and nose somewhat hooked, full of charm; sometimes he appeared like a man and at others he had the face of an angel'. The treatise was known to Jerome[2] who termed it the 'Peregrinations of Paul and Thecla' (*Periodi Pauli et Theclae*).

(2.ii) *The Apocryphal Correspondence of St. Paul with the Corinthians.* This consists of a short answer of the Corinthian

---

[1] Photius (*Bibl. Cod.* 114) mistakenly ascribed the Apocryphal Acts of the other Apostles, as well as those of John, to Leucius.

[2] *De Vir. Ill.*, 7.

clergy to St. Paul's Second Epistle, and a 'Third Letter of St. Paul to the Corinthians'. It was translated into Latin as early as the 3rd century, and for a time the Syriac and Armenian speaking Churches included it in their New Testament Canon. It treats of several important doctrinal subjects (the status of the Old Testament Prophets, creation, the Virgin Birth and the Incarnation, the resurrection of the body).

(2.iii) *The Martyrdom, or Passion, of St. Paul.* These pages, which narrate St. Paul's missionary activities at Rome, the Neronian Persecution and St. Paul's execution, are wholly legendary. They describe how milk spurted out on the executioner's cloak when the Apostle's head was struck off.

(3) THE ACTS OF PETER. This work was written in Greek in the later 2nd century, perhaps in Asia Minor or Palestine.[1] The original text is mostly lost, apart from its later portion, the 'Martyrdom of Peter'. For the rest, the greater part survives in a Latin version preserved in a single Vercelli MS. (the so-called 'Actus Vercellenses'). These Vercelli Acts narrate, *inter alia*, St. Paul's departure from Rome for Spain, the consternation which Simon Magus caused to Christians at Rome by his miracles in the forum, St. Peter's journey to Rome in the course of which he baptized a certain Theon on a calm night in the Adriatic, and Peter's triumph over Simon Magus who was deprived of his power in an attempt to fly from the Roman forum to heaven. The 'Martyrdom' at the end of the document records two well-known traditions about St. Peter,—the 'Quo Vadis' incident in his attempt to flee from Rome when faced with the prospect of martyrdom, and his crucifixion head downwards. A Coptic fragment survives which describes St. Peter's miraculous treatment of his paralytic daughter.

(4) THE ACTS OF ANDREW. This was apparently the longest of the Apocryphal Acts of the Apostles, though much of the original text is lost. The most considerable of the surviving parts are preserved in Vat. gr. 808 (10th-11th century). The

[1] The writer was poorly informed about Rome.

'Martyrdom of Andrew' with which the work concluded stands on a different footing from the rest. This exists independently in several variant texts. The general nature of the whole treatise can be gathered from a Latin Epitome, which is due to Gregory of Tours. There are also Greek *Encomia* on the Apostle which drew extensively on the Acts.

The Acts depict the Apostle as imprisoned in Patras, where he is charged especially with recommending wives to practice an ascetic life and abandon their husbands. The 'Martyrdom' contains a striking passage in which Andrew addresses his Cross. The standpoint of the work is Gnostic.

(5) THE ACTS OF THOMAS. Of the five sets of Acts listed above, the Acts of Thomas alone survive in their entirety. They were probably composed in Syriac at Edessa and belong to the School of Bardesanes, though they incorporated some older items, notably the 'Hymn of the Soul'. They survive in several versions,—Greek, Armenian, Ethiopic and two different Latin versions.

Their subject is St. Thomas' missionary activities. The fortunes of the apostle, here 'Judas-Thomas', who makes his way to India as a carpenter, are described in fourteen 'Acts', leading up to the Apostle's martyrdom. The story records the conversion of King Gundaphorus (an historical person, who figures on coins under the Greek name Gyndopheres), who, with his brother Gad, is baptized by unction. The story culminates in the martyrdom of St. Thomas by spears. The *Acts* are the basis of the constantly renewed attempts to prove that St. Thomas the Apostle did in fact carry the Gospel to the Malabar coast.

Embodied in the text at ch. 108 is a poetic composition, formerly known as the 'Hymn of the Soul', and now known as the 'Hymn of the Redeemer' or the 'Song of the Pearl'. This noble poem, with its striking and obscure imagery, appears to be a hymn addressed to Christ. It is probably a Syriac composition which had originally no connexion with the Acts. It describes Christ as the son of a King, who was sent from

His native land in the East to defeat the dragon in Egypt and gain possession of the Pearl. Under this imagery it depicts the Lord's descent into the sinful world in order to redeem the soul.[1]

APOCRYPHAL APOCALYPSES

We can refer here only to (1) The Apocalypse of Peter; and (2) The Apocalypse of Paul.

(1) THE APOCALYPSE OF PETER. This work, which probably dates from the first half of the 2nd century, enjoyed great popularity in the early Church. It found a place, as we have seen, in the Muratorian Canon[2] and Clement of Alexandria wrote a commentary on it. It appears from various sticho-metries that it was quite a short work (acc. to Nicephorus 300 lines), and an excerpt rather less than half this size survives in the fragment from Akhmîm which contains the *Gospel of Peter*.[3] This excerpt records several visions in which the Lord appears to the Apostles. Those who saw Him were dazzled by the brilliance of His countenance, which shone like the sun, and could not accurately describe it. In another section the fragment gives a graphic account of the terrors of hell in which every sin has its own form of dreadful punishment. The author is not actually named in the Akhmîm fragment, but he can be identified from Clement of Alexandria's *Eclogae Propheticae* 41, where Clement intro-duces a passage from the Apocalypse with the words: 'Peter says in the Apocalypse'.

(2) THE APOCALYPSE OF PAUL. The original Greek text of this work, which was probably put together in Egypt *c.* 250 and known to Origen, is no longer extant and the Greek treatise which now passes under that name was apparently a recasting of it with many miraculous elements which purports to have been found in the house of St. Paul at

---

[1] For further details see A. A. Bevan in Cambridge Texts and Studies V. 3, 1897.

[2] Cf. above, p. 70.

[3] Cf. above, pp. 75f.

Tarsus between 380 and 388. There also exist revisions of the original Apocalypse in Latin, Syriac and Coptic, all nearer to the original than the extant Greek text.

The Apocalypse is based on St. Paul's assertion in 2 Cor. xii. 2ff. that he had been lifted into the third heaven. Its theme is Christ's supposed commission to the Apostle to denounce sin and preach repentance. The heavenly and terrestrial bodies alike cry out for vengeance against human wickedness. At sunset the angels make their daily report to God on men's deeds. St. Paul is then shewn the destinies which lie before man immediately after death. On the one hand there is the New Jerusalem with the patriarchs and prophets and David and the Holy Innocents. On the other hand there are the pains of the damned, which tell especially heavily on teachers of false doctrine. On Sundays at the Apostle's intercession the Lord grants the damned a day of respite from their torments. Finally the Apostle is allowed to visit Paradise where Adam and Eve committed the first sin. In ch. 14, Michael is depicted as the protector and leader of souls who ascend from earth to heaven, as in the familiar Offertory of the Mass for the Dead in the *Roman Missal*.[1] The work was known to Dante, who refers to it at *Inferno* ii. 28.

OTHER APOCRYPHA

(1) CORRESPONDENCE BETWEEN ABGAR AND CHRIST. Of Apocryphal Epistles, the boldest in conception is the reputed correspondence between King Abgar and Christ. The Greek text in its earliest form is incorporated by Eusebius in his *Ecclesiastical History* (i.13) who asserts that he derived it from the Edessene archives and himself translated it into Greek. King Abgar,—a figure known to history as the King of Edessa from 4 B.C. to A.D. 50,—had fallen ill and sent a letter to Christ asking Him to come and heal him. He had heard that in His own land the Jews were hostile to Him; but Abgar told Him that if He would come to Edessa, He would

---

[1] *Domine Jesu Christe, Rex gloriae, . . . sed signifer sanctus Michaël repraesentet eas in lucem sanctam.*

find that though it was only a very little city, it would be sufficient for them both. In His reply Christ says that, though He cannot come in person, after His Ascension He will send a disciple to cure the King and preach the Gospel to the people.

This correspondence, which formed part of the Edessene tradition, was later considerably embellished and extended. It has had its defenders, Protestant and Catholic, until recent times, but there is now almost universal agreement that it is spurious. The story is preserved in a highly coloured form in the Syriac apocryphal writing known as the *Doctrine of Addai* (*c.* A.D. 400).

(2) THE CORRESPONDENCE OF ST. PAUL WITH SENECA.[1] This apocryphal correspondence consists of fourteen letters, eight by Seneca and six by St. Paul. They are far too commonplace both in style and subject-matter to allow us to suppose them to be the genuine work of either correspondent. They were partly intended to exonerate Paul for clothing his noble thoughts in such a poor style. The correspondence was apparently known to Jerome[2] and Augustine[3] and was perhaps fabricated at Rome in the later 4th century. The oldest MSS. date from the 9th century and the text has reached us in a very corrupt state.

(3) EPISTULA APOSTOLORUM. This work, which appears to date from the middle of the 2nd century (C. Schmidt, 160-170; A. Ehrhard, 130-140), was originally written in Greek, perhaps in Asia Minor; but the Greek text has been lost and it survives complete in a (worked over) Ethiopic version and for the most part also in Coptic. There also survives a single leaf of a Latin version in Vienna. The first edition based on all these authorities was that of C. Schmidt in 1919.[4] The orthodoxy of the treatise has been challenged, but according to M. R. James[5] unsuccessfully.

[1] See M. R. James, op. cit., pp. 480-4.
[2] *De viris illustribus* 12.   [3] *Ep.* cliii. 14.
[4] *Gespräche Jesu mit seinen Jüngern nach der Auferstehung* (Texte und Untersuchungen xliii; 1919).
[5] *The Apocryphal New Testament* (1924), p. 485: M. R. James supplies an English translation.

The 'Epistle' consists of a series of revelations which the Risen Lord made to His Apostles, concluding with an account of the Ascension. The compiler seems to have used all four canonical gospels as well as the *Apocalypse of Peter*, the *Epistle of Barnabas* and the *Shepherd* of Hermas. In the account of the Annunciation, Gabriel appears before Mary as a personification of the Divine Word and says: 'I appeared unto Mary and spake with her. Her heart accepted and she believed, and I formed myself and entered into her body. I became flesh for I alone was a minister unto myself in that which concerned Mary in the appearance in the shape of an angel' (ch. 14). The Epistle also contains an interesting account of the Paschal feast to take part in which one of the Apostles was released from prison. In this passage the Agape is still closely associated, if not actually identical, with Eucharist.

(4) ST. PAUL'S EPISTLE TO THE LAODICEANS is a fabrication prompted by Col. iv. 16. It is only a patchwork of texts derived from St. Paul's canonical Epistles, especially Philippians, and wholly uninspired, and perhaps belongs to the 4th century. It is probably to be distinguished from the Marcionite production of the same name referred to in the Muratorian Canon. The oldest text is contained in the 'Codex Fuldensis' (A.D. 546). It is mentioned by St. Gregory the Great, and its widespread occurrence in English medieval Bibles may be due to Gregory's influence.

(5) THE PREACHING OF PETER. Our chief sources of knowledge of this work, which probably dates from the earlier 2nd century, are some references in Clement of Alexandria and Origen. The work enjoyed great popularity in the early Church, being intended for missionary purposes and designed to shew the superiority of Christian monotheism to the current Jewish and pagan beliefs. It contained a collection of Peter's sermons (κήρυγμα in the title must be understood collectively) and apparently professed to be the work of Peter himself, not of a disciple who took down Peter's preaching.

VI.—THE LITERATURE OF TRADITION

It is natural to every institution to interest itself in its past history. But in the case of the Christian Church there were special reasons for such interest. For the Christian Church claimed to be historical in a unique way. Certain events which took place at a particular time in history were not only the source of her being, but pivotal in God's relations with man. To these events Christian theology must needs always look back. The Christian creed was not a system whose truth, if lost, could be recovered by rational argument in the way that a schoolboy who had forgotten Pythagoras' theorem might deduce it afresh by abstract argument. Her system was rooted in a group of empirical facts in the past, and with these crucial facts contact could be maintained only by an historic continuity of life. If the Church was conscious on the one hand of a Divine commission to preach the Gospel to all the world and as such to direct her vision to the future, on the other she could never cease to look backwards to the Incarnate Life which entrusted her, as she believed, with her supernatural mission. Tradition, therefore, was integral to the structure of the Church.

This sense of tradition developed in new forms in the 2nd century. On the one hand, as we have seen, the integrity of Christian belief was threatened by a form of religion which, sheltering under the name of Christianity, had sought to cut it adrift from its historical roots. Gnosticism had shown the variety of beliefs which could pass under the Christian name. In the face of such absurdities, it was essential for the Church to stress the links which bound it to its foundations. After a period of much fluidity consolidation set in about the middle of the 2nd century. The generation of those who could remember the Lord and His disciples had long since passed away, and what was 'Apostolic' came to assume a new importance. Notably the 'Apostolic Succession' of the Bishops in their sees, reaching back to their first holders, now became a guarantee against the latter-day doctrines of the Gnostics.

In this matter the chief texts were the Canon of Scripture, the body of documents of Apostolic authority; the Creeds, which epitomised the Apostolic doctrine; and a considerable number of other writings which were dubbed 'Apostolic' in the pious hope that they were, or would be believed to be, products of the Apostolic age, though they were in fact of much later date than Apostolic times. In the later books of the New Testament the Apostles were already regarded as Divinely appointed guardians of the Christian faith.[1]

THE CREEDS

[The best single book on the whole subject is J. N. D. Kelly, *Early Christian Creeds* (1950). Much the fullest collection of texts is A. Hahn, *Bibliothek der Symbole und Glaubensregeln der alten Kirche* (ed. 3, revised by G. L. Hahn, 1897). Other manuals are those of A. E. Burn (London, 1899; also three separate volumes on the several creeds by the same author, 'Oxford Church Text Books', 1906-12), E. C. S. Gibson ('Oxford Library of Practical Theology', 1908) and F. J. Badcock (London, 1930; ed. 2, 1938). For further bibl. see J. N. D. Kelly, op. cit., and *O.D.C.C.*, p. 354.]

From a very early date the Church made use of brief formulae to embody the substance of her faith, both for apologetic and didactic purposes. We find traces of such credal formulae in the New Testament. One such is the affirmation 'Jesus is the Lord' ('Kurios Christos'), in which over against the 'Lords many' of the heathen world St. Paul professed that for him there was one Lord, the Incarnate Jesus. Another such formula was 'Maran atha', 'The Lord cometh', which summarised the Christian's hopes for the future. In Acts viii. 37 (but not in the earlier texts) there is the profession of the Ethiopian eunuch: 'I believe that Jesus Christ is the Son of God'. Traces of a longer profession of

[1] Cf. Jude 17, Rev. xxi. 14.

faith are found in St. Paul's statement of belief in 1 Cor. xv. 3ff. and in 1 Pet. iii. 18-22, which sets forth the fundamental elements of Christian belief. The latter formula is almost certainly based on a baptismal profession of faith. The word $IX\Theta Y\Sigma$ (fish) from an early date became a Christian symbol understood as an acrostic of 'Jesus Christ the Son of God, Saviour' ($I\eta\sigma o\tilde{\upsilon}s$ $X\rho\iota\sigma\tau\grave{o}s$ $\Theta\epsilon o\tilde{\upsilon}$ $Y\grave{\iota}\grave{o}s$ $\Sigma\omega\tau\acute{\eta}\rho$) and hence arose the use of the fish symbol in early Christian art. More developed formulae of the same general type can be traced in the post-Apostolic writings.

As time went on these credal formulae assumed an increasingly stereotyped form through their use in the Baptismal rite, where they were regularly employed to delineate the substance of the faith. They thus served as epitomes of the belief which the Christian convert professed and pledged himself to uphold over against the pagan world.[1] Only in later times did the practice arise of ecclesiastical Councils using professions of faith in credal form, e.g. the 'Nicene Creed' at Nicaea (325) and the 'Niceno-Constantinopolitan Creed' at Chalcedon (451), as means of discriminating orthodoxy from heresy.

THE APOSTLES' CREED

Out of these early formularies developed the Apostles' Creed. Though it is much later than the Apostolic age, it can so far claim to be Apostolic that its articles one and all express the faith of apostolic times. Its early history is obscure. The very fact that it was never formally promulgated, but developed in obscurity out of the practical needs of the Church and came to be universally accepted in the West, is significant of its importance. Creeds closely similar to the Apostles' Creed as we know it are found in various places in Western Christendom from the 5th century onwards,

[1] The theory of A. C. McGiffert and others that the Old Roman Creed was drawn up as a formula of orthodoxy over against the heretical teaching of Marcion is without solid foundation. If Marcionism were really in view, we should have expected much clearer references to it in the Creed. McGiffert expounds his view in *The Apostles' Creed* (1902).

but, very surprisingly, it is not until the 8th century that we find the creed precisely in its present form. The earliest writer who cites it *verbatim* is Pirminius, first Abbot of Reichenau (d. 753).

Several hundred years before Pirminius a shorter form of the Apostles' Creed had taken definite shape as the 'Old Roman Creed'. This Old Roman Creed, which was in use at Rome from the 2nd century, ran as follows:

Credo in deum patrem omnipotentem;	I believe in God the Father almighty;
et in Christum Iesum filium eius unicum, dominum nostrum,	and in Christ Jesus His only Son, our Lord,
qui natus est de Spiritu sancto et Maria virgine,	Who was born from the Holy Spirit and the Virgin Mary,
qui sub Pontio Pilato crucifixus est et sepultus,	Who under Pontius Pilate was crucified and buried,
tertia die resurrexit a mortuis	on the third day rose again from the dead,
ascendit in caelos	ascended to heaven,
sedet ad dexteram patris	sits at the right hand of the Father,
unde venturus est iudicare vivos et mortuos;	whence He will come to judge the living and the dead;
et in Spiritum sanctum	and in the Holy Spirit,
sanctam ecclesiam,	the holy Church,
remissionem peccatorum	the remission of sins,
carnis resurrectionem,	the resurrection of the flesh.

Until the present century, satisfactory evidence for the existence of this Creed at Rome could not be traced further back than the 4th century. When, in the year 340, Marcellus of Ancyra,[1] whose orthodoxy had been challenged, made a

---

[1] Epiphanius, *Haer*. lxxii. 3.

profession of faith to a synod at Rome under Pope Julius I
(337-352), he did so in the very terms of this creed. At
about the end of the century, Rufinus of Aquileia, Jerome's
one-time friend and later fierce opponent, wrote a commentary of the credal formulary used in his own church
of Aquileia. Rufinus was fully aware that this local creed,
which he took as the basis of his commentary, differed
somewhat from the Creed of Rome, but he commonly
noted these differences and in this way it is possible to
reconstruct from his commentary the text of the Roman
Creed. This Creed was found to accord almost exactly
with that professed by Marcellus. That it went back in fact
to a date far earlier than the 4th century was indicated by
the occurrence of phrases which seemed to presuppose it in
earlier Roman writers.

But much earlier evidence for the Old Roman Creed is
now provided by the *Apostolic Tradition* of Hippolytus.[1]
This work contains in its Baptismal Rite a form of Creed
which is almost verbally identical with the Roman Creed
as attested by Marcellus and Rufinus. As the conservatism
of Hippolytus makes him a witness to usages far earlier
than his own day, we are taken back to within measurable
distance of A. Harnack's date of *c.* A.D. 100 for the 'Old
Roman Creed'.

For further discussion of the Old Roman Creed, the reader
should consult books expressly devoted to the Creeds. It
may, however, be worth raising briefly here the question of
its earlier history. The most obvious fact about the Old
Roman (and Apostles') Creed is the disproportionate length
of the second article. This suggests that the Creed may have
developed out of the fusion of a short Trinitarian formula
with an independent expression of faith in the Person of
Christ. In support of this is the fact, already mentioned, that
the earliest Christian professions of faith were affirmations

[1] On this treatise, cf. below, pp. 94-96. Owing to a defect in the Verona
manuscript, the opening words in the Latin text of the Creed are missing: but this lacuna is obviously accidental.

G

about the Lordship of Christ and the content of the earliest
Christian preaching was akin to the short statements in Acts.
Thus Professor C. H. Dodd in his classical study of the
primitive Kerygma[1] argues that its original outline, as found
in St. Paul's Epistles, was roughly as follows:

'The prophecies are fulfilled, and the New Age is inaugurated by the coming of Christ.

'He was born of the seed of David.

'He died according to the Scriptures, to deliver us out of
the present evil age.

'He was buried.

'He rose on the third day according to the Scriptures.

'He is exalted at the right hand of God, as Son of God and
Lord of quick and dead.

'He will come again as Judge and Saviour of men.'

This reconstruction of the early Christian preaching has such
striking affinities, verbal and substantial, with the statement
of Christian faith contained in the second article of the Old
Roman Creed that we are left in little doubt as to its origin.[2]

The transformation of the Old Roman Creed into the
Apostles' Creed in its present form came about mainly by
accretion. The chief alterations to the original form of the
Old Roman Creed are:

(1) Addition of the words 'Maker of heaven and earth'
(*creatorem coeli et terrae*);

(2) Change of the characteristic 'Christ Jesus' of the Old
Roman Creed to 'Jesus Christ';

(3) 'Born from the Holy Ghost and the Virgin Mary'
expanded to 'Conceived by the Holy Ghost, born of the
Virgin Mary';

(4) 'Suffered' (*passus*) added;

---

[1] *The Apostolic Preaching and its Development* (ed. 1944), p. 17.
[2] For other attempts to discover the pre-history of the Old Roman
Creed by Holl, Harnack and Lietzmann, we must refer to their original
papers.

(5) 'Dead' (*mortuus*) added;

(6) 'Descended into hell' (*descendit ad infernos*) added;

(7) 'At the Right Hand of God the Father Almighty' (*ad dexteram Dei Patris omnipotentis*) for 'At the Right Hand of the Father';

(8) 'Thence' (*inde*) for 'whence' (*unde*).

(9) 'Catholic' added;

(10) 'Communion of Saints' (*sanctorum communionem*)[1] added;

(11) 'The Life Everlasting' (*vitam aeternam*) added.

HEGESIPPUS

[Collections of fragments in M. J. Routh, *Reliquiae Sacrae* i (ed. 2, Oxford, 1846), pp. 207-19 (annott. 220-84) and T. Zahn, *Forschungen zur Geschichte des neutestamentlichen Kanons* vi (1900), pp. 228-73. For further bibl. see B. Altaner, *Patrologie* (ed. 1958), p. 118.]

This may be the most convenient place to make brief reference to Hegesippus. He was born in the East, perhaps of Jewish parents. In middle life, during the pontificate of Anicetus (155-166), he made his way to Rome where he remained, he tells us, until the time of Eleutherus (174-189). After returning to the East, he wrote his *Memoirs* (ὑπομνή-ματα) in five Books. Unfortunately, though copies of the treatise survived in libraries down to the 16th and 17th centuries, the work is now lost; our knowledge of it comes mainly from Eusebius. It seems to have been designed as a polemical work against Gnosticism; but quite naturally Eusebius was interested only in its historical assertions and it would seem that the history was assembled in the fifth book. In a fragment preserved in Eusebius[2] Hegesippus asserted: διαδοχὴν ἐποιησάμην μέχρι 'Ανικήτου. This has often been taken to mean that Hegesippus compiled a succession-list (διαδοχή) of the Bishops of Rome from the earliest times down to Anicetus; but against this view is the fact that Eusebius, who took a special interest in the episcopal successions in the great

[1] On the various meanings of this phrase, see *O.D.C.C.*, p. 319f.
[2] *Hist. Eccl.* IV. xxii. 3.

sees, records no such list. One way out of the difficulty has been to conjecture διατριβήν for διαδοχήν (so P. Halloix, H. Savile), and the passage would then assert that Hegesippus 'stayed at Rome until the time of Anicetus'. Against this conjecture is the absence of any textual evidence and (we are told) its palaeographical improbability. More likely is the view of C. H. Turner[1] that Hegesippus used the word διαδοχή in much the same sense as παράδοσις and that what he described was the 'tradition' of true doctrine at Rome (not that he drew up an episcopal list) down to the middle of the 2nd century.

THE 'APOSTOLIC TRADITION' OF HIPPOLYTUS

[English edd. by B. S. Easton (Cambridge, 1934) and by G. Dix, O.S.B. (London, S.P.C.K., 1937; with much fuller presentation of textual evidence). H. Elfers, *Die Kirchenordnung Hippolyts von Rom* (1938). A fundamental recent study is J. M. Hanssens, S.J., *La Liturgie d'Hippolyte* (Rome, 1959). For further bibl. see *O.D.C.C.*, p. 74.]

The eagerness felt by the Church at Rome in the early 3rd century to assert its Apostolic basis in matters of discipline and faith is shewn by the famous document which describes itself at the outset as 'The Tradition' (1.2), and which is probably in its present form mainly the work of Hippolytus.[2]

This document, which has had a very strange history, first appeared in print in 1691 when Job Ludolf published it in an Ethiopic version as an appendix to his *Ad suam Historiam Aethiopicam Commentarius*. A Bohairic version of the text was edited, with an English translation, by Archdeacon H. Tattam in 1848, and a Sahidic version, thirty-five years later, by P. A. de Lagarde in his *Aegyptiaca*. About the turn of the last century, E. Hauler discovered a very ancient Latin version of the same text in a MS. belonging to the Cathedral Chapter Library of Verona[3] and published it in 1900 in his *Didascalia Apostolorum Fragmenta Ueronensia Latina*.

---

[1] In H. B. Swete (ed.), *Essays on the Early History of the Church and Ministry* (1918), pp. 197ff.

[2] On Hippolytus see pp. 155-67.   [3] *Codex Veronensis* lv (53).

Accedit Canonum qui dicuntur Apostolorum et Aegyptiorum Reliquiae.[1] Further matter bearing on the text of the 'Apostolic Tradition', including an Arabic version, was issued by G. Horner in 1904 in his *Statutes of the Apostles*. All these versions shewed by their variations that the text had been subjected to considerable re-handling and modification in the course of its history.

This work, which came to be known to older scholars as 'The Egyptian Church Order' (E.C.O.),[2] was observed in its various texts to have literary connexions with several of the other early Church Orders, notably with the *Didascalia Apostolorum* and with a work which has survived in Arabic and was known as the *Canons of Hippolytus*. This last work, which was published in 1870, was soon seen to contain certain primitive elements, and in the last years of the 19th century there arose a tendency to attach increasing historical importance to it, and even to suppose it to be of genuinely Hippolytean authorship. As such the *Canons* were regarded as the earliest of these related documents and the ultimate source of much of the common material found in the others. But a closer study of the relations between these documents, both as regards the text and subject matter, by E. Schwarz and independently by R. H. Connolly, shewed that that view was indefensible. It was the 'Egyptian Church Order' which was really the primary document, and upon this the *Canons of Hippolytus*, as well as other connected documents, depended. And since, as we have seen, this work described itself as 'The Tradition' and in the list of works on the Lateran statue,[3] Hippolytus is expressly credited with a treatise on 'The Apostolic Tradition', it seemed reasonable to identify it, at least provisionally, with the work which Hippolytus was known to have produced. This conjecture has received remarkable confirmation from the language and theology of the 'Tradition', for it was found at many points to agree closely with those of Hippolytus in his other writings.

[1] Leipzig, 1900.   [2] This name was given to it by H. Achelis in 1891.
[3] Now at the Vatican Library. Cf. p. 156 n. 1.

The 'Apostolic Tradition', which covers the equivalent of some twenty or thirty octavo printed pages, may be divided into four parts: (1) The Bishops and other ministers and their mode or appointment; (2) Baptism including the requirements from Catechumens before admission to the rite; (3) Ecclesiastical laws, on such subjects as Fasting, First-fruits, visiting the sick, daily assembly of the clergy, burial charges; and (4) The daily prayers of the laity. Assuming we are right in thinking the document to be genuinely Hippolytean, the information given under each of these headings is of extraordinary interest. It tells us a large number of details on primitive Church life and liturgy at Rome in the early 3rd century. Indeed, it can be said to have revolutionised much in the conventional pictures of Church life whether 'Catholic' or 'Protestant'.

DIDASCALIA APOSTOLORUM

[The most scholarly ed. is by R. H. Connolly, O.S.B., *Didascalia Apostolorum*. The Syriac version translated and accompanied by the Verona Latin fragments (Oxford, 1929), Syr. text ed. P. de Lagarde, Leipzig, 1854. Further bibl. in B. Altaner, *Patrologie* (ed. 1958), p. 48f.]

The 'Catholic Didascalia, that is, The Teaching of the Twelve Holy Apostles and Disciples of Our Saviour', is another collection of miscellaneous precepts of professedly Apostlic origin. It dates from the 3rd century, probably its earlier half. Its compiler was a Bishop possessed, indeed, of unusual medical knowledge, but of strictly limited literary gifts. He was apparently a Jew by birth who compiled his work for a Gentile Christian community in the North of Syria. He drew extensively on other documents, among them the *Didache*, Hermas, the *Gospel of Peter*, the *Acts of Paul* and Irenaeus. That his treatise was held in high and undeserved estimation is illustrated by the incorporation of large parts of it into the *Apostolic Constitutions* (later 4th century).

Apart from a few fragments the original Greek text has been lost. The primary source is an ancient Syriac version, first published anonymously by P. A. de Lagarde from the Paris Codex Syr. 62 in 1854.[1] Considerable sections of a very old Latin version are contained in the *Codex Veronensis* lv (53), i.e. the palimpsest codex of the Verona Chapter Library which contains the 'Apostolic Tradition' of Hippolytus. A careful and exact rendering of the text into English with the Latin version where it survives is conveniently accessible in the edition of R. H. Connolly.[2]

The *Didascalia* is an ill-arranged and diffuse document and passes from subject to subject in no apparent order. It is frequently expanded with long and apparently not very relevant extracts from Scripture. Among the subjects considered are the duties and rights of bishops (4-9), the duty of the Christian not to settle disputes with his brethren in the secular court (11), widows (14f.), deacons and deaconesses (16) and the care of the poor (17f.). Fasting is to be observed on Wednesdays and Fridays throughout the year and with special strictness on the six days before Easter (21). Heresy is strongly condemned (22f.). Special emphasis is laid on Jewish Christians abandoning their former ceremonial practices (26). The author has little interest in doctrinal matters. He is evidently out of sympathy with all rigoristic tendencies. He assumes that the married state is normal for Christians and nowhere praises celibacy or virginity. He shews considerable interest in the ecclesiastical remission of sins and here again he is less rigorist than his Western contemporaries (Tertullian, Hippolytus, Cyprian), holding that all sins can be remitted except that expressly mentioned in the Gospels, the sin against the Holy Ghost. The work purports to embody the teaching which the Apostles gave at the Council of Jerusalem of Acts xv. Though the compiler does not take this claim seriously, it may indicate that the work goes back to canons of one or more (probably the latter) early Councils. A composite origin such as this would explain the rather miscellaneous character of the work.

---

[1] *Didascalia Apostolorum Syriace* (Leipzig, 1854).
[2] *Didascalia Apostolorum* (Oxford, 1929).

PSEUDO-CLEMENTINES

[Ed. princeps of *Homilies* (1-19a only) by J. B. Cotelier in his 'Apostolic Fathers' (1672) from Par. gr. 930; of *Recognitions* by J. Faber Stapulensis (Paris, 1504). Crit. ed. of *Homilies* by B. Rehm in G.C.S. (1953). Eng. trr. in A.N.C.L. O. Cullmann, *Le Problème littéraire et historique du roman pseudoclémentin* (1930). For further bibl. see *O.D.C.C.*, p. 301.]

Traditionalism of a more picturesque and entertaining kind is to be found in the *Clementines Homilies* and the *Clementine Recognitions*. These writings, which purport to be the work of Clement of Rome,[1] retail the adventures of their author who was a member of a Roman Imperial family. In his search for truth about such matters as the immortality of the soul and the origin of the world, Clement heard at last of the appearance of the Son of God in Judea and decided to make the long journey from Rome to the East to see and hear for himself. When he reached Caesarea, he met Peter who, convinced of his good faith, invited him, though still a pagan, to accompany him on his missionary travels. The account of these travels, with their graphic and diverting descriptions, is manifestly fiction. But their author clearly had a serious purpose, namely to commend to the reader a particular form of Judaeo-Christianity.

The twenty so-called *Homilies* (these survive in the original Greek) are prefaced by two introductory letters addressed to James, the Lord's Brother and now Bishop of Jerusalem ('Bishop of Bishops'), by Peter and Clement. The Judaic character of Christianity is emphasised throughout. Christ is a Divine Aeon, who had formerly revealed Himself in Adam and Moses. Though He alone is described as 'Son of God', He is only a prophet and in no sense our redeemer.

The *Recognitions*, on the other hand, have come down to us only in a Latin version due to Rufinus (d. 410). They are in ten Books and so named from the graphic descriptions of the way in which Clement, with Peter's assistance, finds and

---

[1] Cf. above pp. 11-13.

'recognises' his lost relatives (father; mother; brothers) in the East. The Judaic element is less pronounced than in the *Homilies* and there are passages which indicate a more orthodox view of the Godhead. The uniqueness of Christ is again stressed. He is *solus fidelis ac verus propheta*. There is also found an orthodox statement about the Trinity: 'We speak of the Only-begotten Son of God. He took His origin not from some other source, but was ineffably self-originated. And we speak in like manner of the Paraclete'.[1] But in view of the liberties which Rufinus is known to have allowed himself in his translations it is possible that these and similar passages are due to him and do not come from the original writer. *94880*

No agreed solution has so far been reached of the long debated problem of the relation between the *Homilies* and the *Recognitions*, though there is manifestly some literary connexion between them. It is now generally held that both works depend on a common source ('Grundschrift'). As to the character and sources of the 'Grundschrift' itself widely divergent views have been held. Did it emanate from Syria or perhaps Transjordania in the first decades of the 3rd century? And was its theology orthodox or Jewish-Christian? And was it dependent on the *Kerygma Petri* or other known documents? Recently Professor H. J. Schoeps[2] has defended the view in a number of writings that the 'Grundschrift' underlying both works was an Ebionite document to be dated between 160 and 190, and that this work is a primary witness to Jewish Christianity.

[1] Filium Dei unigenitum dicimus; non ex alio initio, sed ex ipso ineffabiliter natum; similiter etiam de paracleto dicimus (*Recog.* i. 69).
[2] *Theologie und Geschichte des Judenchristentums* (1949).

VII.—THE ASIA MINOR SCHOOL

It is clear from the New Testament that Christianity soon gained a very strong and extended foothold in Asia Minor. Prosperous Christian communities sprang up here with remarkable rapidity and at close range.[1] By the 2nd century these communities were already bound together by many links in theology and Church practice. From an early date they expounded a Christian mysticism and doctrine of redemption such as later found expression in Irenaeus and the Cappadocians. This theological mysticism has many affinities with the thought of the Fourth Gospel. There is a strong tradition that St. John the Apostle, or some other John who has been confused with him, settled in Ephesus in his later years, and if the tradition that the Fourth Gospel came from Ephesus is correct, it was doubtless directly shaped under the influence of the Johannine writings.[2] Of the Apostolic Fathers, Ignatius who, as we have seen, had contacts with Asia Minor, had close kinship in outlook to this type of theology; his associate, Polycarp, belonged to Smyrna; Melito of Sardis, one of the most prolific and enterprising theologians of the middle of the 2nd century, of whose abundant writings, alas! too little has survived, was an outstanding representative of this current of thought;

[1] This is vividly shewn by the maps in Dr. F. van der Meer and Miss Christine Mohrmann's splendid *Atlas of the Early Christian World* (1958).

[2] There have been many attempts in recent times to put the Fourth Gospel into another setting. Some have looked to Antioch in view of its Semitic language; others to Mesopotamia; others to Alexandria; and more recently others to Palestine, in view of its supposed Qumran connexions. But the Ephesine tradition is probably still the majority view.

while the tradition reached its full development in Irenaeus.

QUARTODECIMANISM

A characteristic of early Christianity in Asia Minor was Quartodeciman practice in the matter of Easter observance. The feast, which was kept in the Christian Church from the outset, was the annual continuation of the Jewish Passover.[1] But before long the question arose as to the precise day on which the Pasch should be observed. The feast looked back to the redemptive work of Christ which had been completed at the Paschal Season. But from the very early times the Church had also observed a weekly commemoration of the Resurrection on Sundays, and a difference of opinion sprang up as to whether Christians should observe the annual feast of Easter on the precise day on which the Jews kept it, i.e. on whatever day of the week Nisan 14 fell, or whether the Church should strike out on its own and observe the Pasch on the following Sunday, the regular day for communal worship. We may suspect that this difference in practice in different parts of the Church arose merely through 'accident'. There is no record of any early ecclesiastical legislation on the matter, when there was no means of securing such. But gradually the differences became stereotyped and then a matter of controversy. Whereas the rest of the Church observed the Sunday following Nisan 14, the Christians of Asia Minor adopted the Quartodeciman practice of which, from the middle of the 2nd century, they became staunch defenders. It is possible that this is to be connected with the Johannine identification of Christ with the Paschal Lamb in Jn. i. 29.[2] It also accords with the chronology of the Passion in St. John's Gospel which makes the death of Christ on the Cross correspond in time with the slaying of the Passover Lambs on the afternoon of Nisan 14.

[1] Cf. below, pp. 107f.
[2] Dr. C. H. Dodd, indeed, contests this identification; but he has had many critics.

MONTANISM

About the middle of the 2nd century, what professed to be a new form of Christianity arose in Asia Minor under the name of 'Montanism'.[1] It claimed to be a religion of the Holy Spirit and was marked by ecstatic outbursts which it regarded as prophetic manifestations and utterances of the Paraclete. The view once popular, that Montanism set out to be a reversion to the purity of primitive Christianity against the growing institutionalisation of the Orthodox Church, is a misconception. So far from looking to the past, Montanism had its eye on the present and the future. It was 'modernistic' and looked forward to the time when the Christianity of the present age would be transcended by an epoch of the Holy Spirit. With this stress on prophecy it combined a strong emphasis on asceticism.

The Montanists maintained that this new age had recently been inaugurated by happenings in Asia Minor. About the year 157 Montanus, a native of Phrygia, announced himself as one who had been divinely filled by the Holy Spirit and charged to preach a new Gospel. His own function was only passive. He was proclaiming not his own teaching but that which God had imparted to him. 'I am come neither as an angel nor as an ambassador, but I have come as Lord, as God the Father'.[2] He very soon attached himself to two women, Prisca and Maximilla, who professed to be prophetesses; and all three fell into ecstasies and settled in two villages in Phrygia, Pepuza and Timion, which they called the 'New Jerusalem'. The movement quickly spread, apparently among small but widely scattered groups of enthusiasts, and soon secured a footing at Rome and elsewhere; but before long it spent itself in Asia Minor. In the person of Tertullian it won its most notable convert in Africa.

[1] For a recent study, cf. K. Aland, 'Der Montanismus und die kleinasiatische Theologie' in *Z.N.T.W.* xlvi (1955), pp. 109-16.
[2] Epiphanius, *Adv. Haer.* xlviii. 11

MELITO OF SARDIS

[Collection of fragments in M. J. Routh, *Reliquiae Sacrae* i (ed. 2, 1846), pp. 113-53; and J. C. T. Otto, *Corpus Apologetarum* ix (Jena, 1872), pp. 374-478 and 497-512. C. Bonner (ed.), *The Homily on the Passion by Melito* (Studies and Documents xii; 1940). For further bibl. see *O.D.C.C.*, p. 884.]

A much more prolific writer of the Asia Minor school than those already examined was Melito, Bishop of Sardis in Lydia, who was one of the most widely respected figures in the Christian Church of his time. Polycrates, Bishop of Ephesus, in a letter to Pope Victor (189-198), includes him among the departed great lights (μεγάλα στοιχεῖα) of the Church of Asia.[1] But apart from the sparse details in Eusebius, very little is known of him. He is described as a 'eunuch'; by this probably no more is meant than that he was unmarried. We are also told that he made a journey to Palestine to review the holy places, the earliest such pilgrimage known to history. His dates are sufficiently indicated by Eusebius' statement that Melito occupied a prominent position in the Church under Antoninus Pius (138-161) and reached the height of his fame under Marcus Aurelius (161-180).

Eusebius and Anastasius of Sinai record long lists of Melito's works but until recently only fragments were known to survive. Their titles,—among them *On the Church*, *On the Lord's Day*, *On the Faith of Man*, *On Soul and Body*, *On Hospitality*, *On Baptism*, *On Truth*, *On Prophecy*, *The Key*, *On the Devil*, *On the Apocalypse of John*, *On the Corporeality of God* (or perhaps *On God Incarnate*), *Two books on the Pasch*,[2]—give an indication of the range of his interests. He was also the author of an Apology addressed to Marcus Aurelius, fragments of which are preserved by Eusebius and the *Paschal Chronicle*. The surviving fragments have been collected by M. J. Routh and J. C. T. Otto. According to Jerome, Tertullian spoke in a disparaging way (*cavillatur*) of

[1] Ap. Eusebius, *Hist. Eccl.* V. xxiv. 2, 5.
[2] These books must be carefully distinguished from the newly recovered *Treatise on the Pasch* to be discussed at greater length below.

Melito's 'elegant and pompous manner' (*elegans et declamatorium ingenium*); that his style was fulsome is borne out by the fragments, to say nothing of the work to be considered immediately.

Recently our knowledge of Melito has been greatly increased by the recovery of a tract he wrote on the Pasch. It has been preserved in a (prob. 4th century) papyrus which is shared between the Chester Beatty collection[1] and the University of Michigan. This text, first published by Mr. Campbell Bonner in 'Studies and Documents' in 1940, must be regarded as the most important addition to Patristic literature in the present century. Owing to the comparative scarcity of Dr. Bonner's text, this very important document has hardly received the attention it deserves. But it has recently been made easily accessible in Dr. Bernhard Lohse's students' edition in *Textus Minores XXIV* (Leiden, 1958) and there can be little doubt that it will be closely studied in the next few years.

The genuineness of the work cannot be doubted. Not only does it share the highly characteristic style of the fragments of Melito, but a short passage of the work is expressly ascribed to Melito by Anastasius of Sinai.[2] The nature of the treatise is less evident.

In the original edition the work was described by Mr. Campbell Bonner as a 'Good Friday Sermon'. This title, however, arouses considerable misgivings. In the first place if 'Good Friday' is to be understood as opposed to 'Easter Day',—an annual commemoration of the crucifixion two days before the Resurrection,—it is anachronistic because nowhere, at this early date, were the two commemorations distinguished. There was only the single feast of the 'Pasch'.

---

[1] This magnificent collection is now splendidly housed at 20, Shrewsbury Road, Dublin.

[2] Hodegos [Viae Dux], P. G. lxxxix. 197A. (=Otto, frg. 7.) Dr. P. Nautin's attack on its genuineness in 'L'Homélie de "Meliton" sur la Passion' in *R.H.E.* xliv (1949), pp. 429-38, has apparently had no following; cf. W. Schneemelcher in *Festschrift für Günther Dehn* (1957), 119ff.

And secondly, its style is not that of a 'sermon'. Its temper and ethos are declamatory, not persuasive.

The treatise opens with the words:

> Ἡ μὲν γραφὴ τῆς Ἑβραϊκῆς Ἐξόδου ἀνέγνωσται
> καὶ τὰ ῥήματα τοῦ μυστηρίου διασεσάφηται,
>   πῶς τὸ πρόβατον θύεται
>   καὶ πῶς ὁ λαὸς σώζεται.

These sentences, on whose interpretation the purpose of the tract largely hangs, are very ambiguous. First, διασαφέω has been variously understood. Do the first words mean that after the 'reading of the Hebrew Exodus' there had followed a διασάφησις, i.e. some kind of interpretative explanation of the events described, particularised as the slaying of the Lamb and the salvation of the people? The difficulty in accepting this view is that any such διασάφησις would seem redundant. As the whole body of Melito's tract is taken up with expounding the Exodus text, it would have appeared gratuitous to interpose between the Scriptural reading and the tract itself another explanation. It might be replied, however, that such an understanding of διασάφησις would be defensible if it were taken to refer to some mode of explanation of another kind, e.g. as a 'line by line' elucidation of the Scriptural text as in a running paraphrase or again as in a Biblical commentary, sufficiently different from Melito's summary explanation of the whole text not to duplicate it. But it is also possible that διασαφέω is to be understood quite differently. One view, held by certain of Mr. Campbell Bonner's original critics,[1] is that the verb means just 'read' and that what is described in line 2 only expresses in other terms the action described in line 1. But another and more likely explanation is that διασαφέω refers to a translation into another language. In this connexion we should observe that the phrase, 'the Hebrew Exodus', does not necessarily mean, as Bonner supposes, 'the Exodus of the Hebrew people'; but it may also be rendered 'the account of the

---

[1] *Melito of Sardis*, p. 35.

Exodus in the Hebrew tongue'. If so, we must translate the
first seven Greek words not, with Bonner, as: 'The Scripture
of the Hebrew Exodus has been read', as though they meant
'What has been read is the Scriptural narrative of the Cross-
ing of the Red Sea by the Hebrews and its attendant circumstances (including, as the sequel shews, the account of the
Passover Meal)', but simply as 'The passage from the book
of Exodus in Hebrew has been read'.

To understand the force of this rendering we must recall
that the practice of reading the Scriptures in Hebrew
survived to a late date in Jewish and Christian worship. It
is true that after the Exile Hebrew as a living language
gradually went out of use, but its continued use in worship
was made possible by the provision of a targum, i.e. a
paraphrastic rendering into Aramaic. With such assistance
Hebrew went on being read in the Synagogue services, and
there are reasons for thinking that this practice was taken
over into the Christian Church.[1] Here we have the natural
interpretation of the opening sentences of our document.
The passage from the Book of Exodus dealing with the
Passover had been read in Hebrew and it was then 'explained', i.e. gone over line by line, either by a verbal
translation or in paraphrase, in the vernacular.

But over and above this $\delta\iota\alpha\sigma\acute{\alpha}\phi\eta\sigma\iota\varsigma$, there was for the
Christian another interpretation of the passage of much
deeper import and it is this exegesis which is the substance of
Melito's tract. Just as the slaying of the Paschal lamb was
the means of the Hebrews' salvation from the Egyptian
bondage, so the Lord's death on Calvary ensures our own
escape from the bondage of sin and death. In relation to the
latter, the Jews of history were traitors and murderers. They
delivered up Christ to the Cross and will receive their condemnation and punishment. By contrast the faithful are
redeemed by the Pasch from the bondage of hell and share
in the Lord's Resurrection. The Jewish Passover and the

----

[1] This was the *raison d'être* of the second column in Origen's *Hexapla*.
Cf. p. 125.

Exodus are understood as pointing forward to the sacrificial sufferings and death of Christ. This theme is defined by Melito in the recurring phrase: 'the Mystery of the Pasch', and this he seeks to unravel in the tract. In this explanation Melito makes use of the false etymology which connects the Hebrew Pasch with the Greek πάσχω and links it up with the Redemptive Sufferings of the Passion.

As we have already pointed out, the tract is certainly not a sermon. It is a highly artificial piece of writing, set down in rhythmical prose; it uses a staccato style with short impressive phrases; and much of it is metrical. It employs forced and laboured antitheses. The Jews are frequently apostrophised in an artificial manner. So far from Melito's work being a homily, the key to its understanding, unless we are mistaken, lies almost certainly in the fact that what we have here is nothing else than a Christian Paschal Haggadah. As such it is unique in Christian literature.

Here it must be recognised that the primitive Christian Easter was simply a continuation of the Jewish Passover rite, which by the 1st century of our era was as firmly established among the Jews as the Christmas dinner is among ourselves. A Passover rite without the lamb had long been current in Judaism outside Jerusalem, even before A.D. 70, and the observance was as much domestic and social as specifically religious. When the early Christian converts from Judaism accepted Jesus as the Messiah and found a wholly new significance in the Exodus of God's people which was commemorated every spring, there is every reason to suppose that force of custom, apart from other reasons, would have encouraged the continuance of the annual Passover, which would now be given a vastly richer significance. The rite continued, with its ancient name; but it now became the annual feast of the Resurrection, which henceforward itself appropriated the title of the 'Pasch'. The mere fact that the Christian Easter everywhere bore the name of the 'Pasch' is a sufficient indication that it was only the continuation of the Jewish feast and not a new institution.

H

Now a prominent feature in the ritual of the Jewish Pasch was the discourse on the meaning of the feast pronounced by the presiding member of the gathering, usually the Pater familias, and known as the 'Haggadah'. The Mishnah laid down in some detail what the Haggadah was to include and it gradually took on a stereotyped form. Indeed the form still in regular use in Jewish families today appears to differ little from that ordered in the Mishnah tractate, *Pesachim*, at the beginning of the Christian era. Here[1] Rabbi Gamaliel insists that the presiding member shall always refer to three things. 'And these are they: Passover, unleavened bread, and bitter herbs: "Passover"—because God passed over the houses of our fathers in Egypt: "unleavened bread"— because our fathers were redeemed from Egypt; "bitter herbs"—because the Egyptians embittered the lives of our fathers in Egypt. In every generation a man must so regard himself as if he came forth himself out of Egypt, for it is written, *And thou shalt tell thy son in that day saying, It is because of that which the Lord did for me when I came out of Egypt.* Therefore are we bound to give thanks, to praise, to glorify, to honour, to exalt, to extol, and to bless him who wrought all these wonders for our fathers and for us. He brought us out from bondage to freedom, from sorrow to gladness, and from mourning to a Festival-day, and from darkness to great light, and from servitude to redemption; so let us say before him the *Hallelujah*.' These are precisely the themes of Melito's tract. The latter part of the quotation is closely paralleled by Melito c. 68: 'This is he who clothed Death with a garment of shame and bound the devil in anguish as Moses bound Pharaoh. This is he who smote iniquity, and made unrighteousness barren as Moses made Egypt. This is he who rescued us from slavery to freedom, from darkness to light, from death to life, from oppression to an eternal kingdom, and made us a new priesthood and a chosen people for ever. He is the Pasch of our salvation, he it is who in many men suffered many things'. Interdependence

[1] Pesachim X. 5.

seems certain. And the theme of the Bitter Herbs is developed in 92f.: 'Him whom the nations worshipped and whom the uncircumcised admired and the Gentiles glorified, for whom even Pilate washed his hands, him thou hast slain in the great feast. Therefore bitter to thee shall be the feast of unleavened bread, as it is written, "ye shall eat unleavened bread with bitter herbs". Bitter to thee the nails that thou hast sharpened; bitter to thee the tongue that thou hast incited against him; bitter to thee the false witnesses that thou hast set up against him; bitter to thee the scourges that thou didst plait; bitter to thee Judas whom thou didst hire; bitter to thee Herod whom thou didst follow, bitter to thee Caiaphas whom thou didst obey; bitter to thee the gall which thou preparedst; bitter to thee the thorn that thou didst gather; bitter to thee the hands that thou didst stain with blood. Thou hast slain thy Lord in the midst of Jerusalem.'

If we have correctly discovered the *Sitz im Leben* of Melito's tract, then it is a primary document for the history of the primitive Easter. We see how by the later 2nd century the functions of the president of the Passover gathering had passed to the Bishop. We can also observe the Exodus theme firmly established in the imagery of Easter whence it has never since been dislodged. We can see further the origins of the long drawn out Easter Vigil though there are no clear associations of the Pasch with Baptism in Melito. Whatever may have been matters of local custom in earlier times,[1] Christian Paschal practice only became systematised after the organisation of the catechumenate in the great cities towards the end of the 2nd century.

IRENAEUS

[Early edd. of *Adv. Haer.* by D. Erasmus (Basle, 1526), F. Feuardent (Cologne, 1596), J. E. Grabe (Oxford, 1702) and the Maurist, R. Massuet, O.S.B. (Paris, 1710). Later edd. by A. Stieren (Leipzig, 1848-53) and

[1] On this subject, perhaps I may be allowed to refer to my *I Peter. A Paschal Liturgy* (1954).

W. W. Harvey (Cambridge, 1857). Crit. ed. for G.C.S. in preparation; crit. text of Book iii, with notes by F. M. M. Sagnard, O.P., in S.C. xxxiv, 1952. Eng. tr. in A.N.C.L. Eng. tr. of *Demonstration of Apostolic Preaching* (see below) by J. A. Robinson (London, 1920); Fr. tr. of ditto by L. M. Froidevaux in S.C. lxii, 1959. Modern studies in English by F. R. M. Hitchcock (Cambridge, 1914) and J. Lawson (London, 1948). Further discussion with bibl. in B. Altaner, *Patrologie* (ed. 1958), pp. 118-25.]

Irenaeus, the most considerable Christian theologian of the 2nd century, was a native of Smyrna. The date of his birth can hardly be later than 140 as he asserts that as a young man he sat at the feet of his Bishop, Polycarp;[1] it may have been as early as 120 (T. Zahn, 115). He was by nature a man of tradition, and as such proud of his personal links with the Apostolic Age. At an unrecorded date he left Asia Minor for Gaul, where he became a leading personality in the Church. Quite possibly he spent some time in Rome on the way.[2] While a presbyter he was commissioned by his superiors at Lyons to take letters to Pope Eleutherus (*c.* 174-189) to seek toleration for the Montanists of Asia Minor.[3] The fierce persecution of 177 in Gaul[4] probably took place while Irenaeus was absent at Rome on this mission and Pothinus, the Bishop of Lyons, was martyred at the age of ninety.

As soon as peace was restored, Irenaeus succeeded as Bishop. He had a very successful episcopate, during which Christianity made great advances in Gaul, even if we discount Gregory of Tours' statement[5] that within a short space he had made the whole of Gaul Christian. Coming from Asia Minor Irenaeus naturally had sympathies with the Quarto-decimans; and when *c.* 190 the Paschal Controversy flared up again, he interceded with Pope Victor on their behalf and

[1] Martyred in 155 or 156; cf. p. 19.

[2] Cf. F. Sagnard, O.P., *La Gnose Valentinienne et le Témoignage de St. Irénée* (1947), pp. 57-62.

[3] There is nothing to suggest that Irenaeus was himself sympathetic towards the sect.

[4] For details of this we have the letter of the Churches of Vienne and Lyons, preserved in Eusebius, *Hist. Eccl.* v. 1ff.

[5] *Hist. Eccl.* V. xxiv. 18.

thereby, as Eusebius observed, by his 'irenical' (εἰρηνοποιός) activities fittingly bore testimony to his name.[1] Tradition accounts him a martyr, but without authority.[2]

Irenaeus wrote a long list of works. Of these only two survive, and in neither case in the language in which it was written.

To the earlier and longer of them, his treatise *Against Heresies*, he gave the cumbrous title 'Five Books of Unmasking and Overthrow of the falsely named Gnosis'. Considerable extracts of the original Greek made by later writers survive and the whole of it in a Latin translation. The date of this translation, which is of extreme literalness, has long been a matter of dispute. Whereas older scholars (among them W. Sanday) for the most part held that it was known to Tertullian and hence must have been almost contemporary, many scholars now hold that the dependence was the other way (H. Jordan, 350-400; A. Souter, 370-420). It was almost certainly used by Augustine in his *De Doctrina Christiana* ii. 40 (A.D. 396).[3] The translation is so literal and so bald that it is often possible to reconstruct the Greek with considerable certainty. Whatever its date the work is a primary text for students of ecclesiastical Latin.[4] Besides this Latin version, Books IV and V also exist in an Armenian translation, probably made direct from the Greek. A considerable number of Syriac fragments also survive, perhaps translated as the passages were needed rather than from a continuous rendering of the whole work.

The work *Against Heresies* strikes the reader as untidy, chiefly because Irenaeus did not write it on any prearranged plan. His original idea seems to have been to describe

---

[1] *Hist. Eccl.* V. xxiv. 18.

[2] Irenaeus' martyrdom was unknown to Eusebius. Nor does Jerome mention it in his *De Viris Illustribus* 35. In his *Comm. in Is.* ad. 64. 4f., however, he terms him a 'martyr' (P.L. xxiv. 623 A).

[3] B. Altaner 'Augustinus und Irenäus' in *Theologische Quartalschrift* cxxix (1949), pp. 162-72.

[4] Cf. S. Lundström, *Übersetzungstechnische Untersuchungen auf dem Gebiete der christlichen Latinität* (Lund, 1955).

('unmask') and refute ('overthrow') the Gnostic errors in two Books. And at the outset his intention apparently was to confine his attention to the doctrines of Ptolemy, the Valentinian Gnostic. But as he progressed he was led on to describe the systems of Valentinus himself, then of some of his pupils, particularly the charlatan Mark, and then several of the older Gnostics from Simon Magus onwards.[1] This task he carried through to the end of Book I, triumphantly concluding, with no exaggeration, 'Merely to describe such doctrines is to refute them.[2] Yet he will go on and add another Book directed to their explicit refutation. In the event, when he had reached the end of Book II, he found, happily for posterity, that there was still much more to be said. It may be added that from references in the text it is clear that the various Books were put into circulation as they were completed.

In the last three Books, which in form approach a series of *excursus* on specific points, Irenaeus deals with many broader topics. He elaborates the foundation principles of Christian theology. What was the Church's answer to all the fantastic and absurd doctrines of the Gnostics? It was to be found in the continuity of Christian belief to which there were two principal witnesses, the Gospels and tradition.

This system of orthodox faith was attested first of all by the Gospels. In these Gospels there is manifestly a record of historical events over against the esoteric and fantastic speculations of the Gnostic books. The Gospel is fourfold, and there could not be more or less than four Gospels. Its fourfold form corresponds to the four quarters of heaven, the four principal winds, the four-visaged ($\tau \epsilon \tau \rho a \pi \rho \acute{o} \sigma \omega \pi a$) cherubims, and the four universal (catholic) covenants,—of Noah, Abraham, Moses and Christ. Moreover Irenaeus recounted several highly interesting details about the Evangelists and his statements are still among the primary *data* for the criticism of the Gospels. 'Matthew edited a writing of the

---

[1] Cf. p. 38 (for Mark), p. 35 (for Simon Magus).
[2] 'Adversos eos victoria est sententiae eorum manifestatio'. I. xxxi. 4.

Gospel among the Hebrews in their own language, while Peter and Paul were preaching the Gospel in Rome and founding the Church. After their departure ("death"?) Mark, the pupil and interpreter of Peter, handed down to us in writing the things which were preached by Peter. And Luke, the attendant of Paul, recorded in a book the Gospel that was proclaimed by him. Afterwards John, the disciple of the Lord, who also leaned upon his breast, published the Gospel during his residence in Ephesus'.[1]

Irenaeus' other surviving work, his *Proof of the Apostolic Preaching*, is much shorter. Still known to Eusebius,[2] it had been lost to later scholars until it was recovered, early in this century, in a 13th-century Armenian MS., by K. Ter-Mekerttschian.[3] The treatise expressly refers to, and hence must have been later than, the *Adversus Haereses*. The Armenian translation, which was apparently made direct from the Greek and not *via* the Syriac, is of extreme literalness. Indeed, it has been suggested that it was made for Armenian students of Irenaeus, who needed a 'crib' to help them make out the Greek original.

After a short prologue (1-3), in which stress is laid on the need for orthodoxy both in faith and morals, the body of the treatise falls into two main divisions,—an exposition of the fundamental doctrines of the Apostolic Preaching (3-42) and the proof of these doctrines from the Old Testament (43-97). The work concludes with three chapters upholding the unity of revelation (98-100).

In general the theological standpoint and mode of argumentation have much in common with those of the *Adversus Haereses*. The work contains a defence of the Trinity and of the fact of Creation, an account of the Fall, the mode of preparation for Christ in the Old Testament and the culmination of the pre-Christian history in the Incarnation. One of the chief purposes of the Incarnation was to convey the gift of

---

[1] *Adversus Haereses* III. i. 1.   [2] *Hist. Eccl.* V. xxvi.
[3] It was first edited by him in conjunction with E. Ter-Minassiantz in T.U. 31. 1, 1907.

incorruption to fallen man, and among its consequences were the abolition of the Law of Moses, the calling of the Gentiles and the rapid spread of the Church.

These two treatises are but a small fraction of Irenaeus' literary work, though of the rest very little survives. Eusebius preserves an extract of some length from a letter 'On the Monarchy [of God]'. This was directed against a Roman presbyter who had once sat with his correspondent at the feet of Polycarp of Smyrna and later fallen away to Gnosticism.[1] Eusebius also mentions that Irenaeus wrote a 'most concise and exceedingly cogent work' 'On Knowledge', directed against the Greeks.[2] Among his other writings were works on the Easter Controversy. In *Adv. Haer.* I. xxvii. 5 and III. xii. 12 Irenaeus states his intention of refuting Marcion in a separate treatise, but if he ever did so, no trace of the book exists.

Before we conclude our account of Irenaeus, reference must be made to the famous four 'Pfaff fragments' on the Eucharist. The fragments first appeared early in the 18th century when C. M. Pfaff, Professor of Theology at Giessen, put them into the hands of the eminent Italian scholar, Scipio Maffei. Pfaff asserted that he had found them in the Library at Turin. They were first published by Maffei in 1713 in his *Giornale de' Letterati d'Italia*, and two years later Pfaff issued them himself in an annotated edition at The Hague (1715). As they dealt with the theology of the Eucharist and bore on contemporary controversies they at once attracted attention. Maffei expressed his doubts from the first as to whether they were Irenaean, and other scholars shared his suspicions. But Pfaff by his persistence went far towards silencing objectors, though he was evidently embarrassed by those who challenged him to produce fuller details. From then on the texts appeared regularly in editions of Irenaeus.

The *dénouement* came in 1900 when A. Harnack subjected the fragments to a thorough analysis. He demonstrated conclusively that they were an 18th-century fabrication; that all

[1] *Hist. Eccl.* V. xx.   [2] *Hist. Eccl.* V. xxvi.

four were closely related and must have come from a single source; and that it was morally certain that all were Pfaff's own composition. He pointed out that where they seemed to follow New Testament scriptures, the text used was none other than the *textus receptus* current in the modern printed editions of the Greek text. He also shewed that though Pfaff had taken care that the passages should have close points of contact with Irenaeus' *Adversus Haereses* these contacts were invariably with the relatively small parts of the Greek text known in 1713. Specially striking was the occurrence of the form ἐκκαλοῦμεν in the fragments, doubtless based on the word ἔκκλησις, which happened to be a misprint for ἐπίκλησις (at *Adv. Haer.* IV. xviii. 5) in the current text of Irenaeus. Most remarkable of all, the successive fragments reflect Pfaff's own theological interests,—his pietism, his Lutheran doctrine of the Eucharist, his ideals for reunion and his belief in a final Apocatastasis. The hoax had a quality of the dramatic and the inexplicable not without its parallels with Charles Dawson's forgery of the 'Piltdown Man'.[1]

---

[1] An entertaining instance of the practical use made of the Pfaff fragments, assumed genuine ('the originals have mysteriously disappeared'), will be found in F. W. Farrar, *Lives of the Fathers* i (1889), p. 105.

VIII.—THE ALEXANDRIANS

[C. Bigg, *The Christian Platonists of Alexandria* (Bampton Lectures for 1886; new ed. F. E. Brightman, 1913); R. B. Tollinton, *Alexandrine Teaching on the Universe* (1932); E. Molland, *The Conception of the Gospel in the Alexandrian Theology* (Oslo, 1938).]

BEFORE many decades had passed the Church became conscious of a call to interpret the revelation made in Jesus Christ in rational terms. In earlier chapters we have, indeed, already met with two attempts to give a rational account of Christianity, but neither had been at all satisfactory. The Gnostics with their bizarre systems had played havoc with the faith; and it soon became clear that there could be no place in Christianity for their undisciplined and fantastic speculations. Nor had the Apologists (except Melito and Tertullian who, in this as in other respects, stand apart) achieved a satisfying Christian metaphysic. They had adopted the Logos doctrine for apologetic purposes, but they had not come to terms with the fundamental themes of the Gospel nor constructed a genuine Christian theology. The one real exception we have so far met is Irenaeus. He was conscious at once of the achievements and the limitations of the Apologists and had a firm grasp of the redemptive theology inherent in the Gospel. But Irenaeus, however clear his theological perception, had limited powers of formulation. The real task was left to the Alexandrians to whom we now turn.

Christianity in Alexandria was at first of slow growth and our knowledge of its development down to the latter part of the 2nd century is very scanty. This is at first sight a little surprising when we recall that Alexandria was such a strong centre of Judaism and the traditional contacts between the

Jews of Palestine and those of Alexandria since the days of
the Ptolemies. We might have expected that Alexandria
would have become an early centre of Christianity. But this
is certainly not suggested by the author of the Acts of the
Apostles, whose whole interest was in the growth and
missionary work of the early Church northwards from
Jerusalem. We have very little on record of the early history
of Christianity in Egypt. And perhaps there is a reason for
our ignorance, for it is hard to believe that Christian ideas
did not reach this vigorous centre of Jewish culture at an
early date. There is much to suggest that it is connected with
the hold which Gnosticism had on early Christianity in Egypt.
Alexandria was the home of such influential Gnostics as
Valentinus and Basilides, and if the early Church of Alexandria were mainly under Gnostic influence, we might thus
explain the veil which orthodoxy has cast over its early
beginnings. There is much to be said for the view, symbolically expressed in the belief of Eusebius that the Alexandrian
Church was founded by St. Mark, the disciple of St. Peter,
that when orthodoxy developed in Alexandria in the later
2nd century it was mainly under the influence of Rome.
This would explain the respect traditionally shown at
Alexandria later for the Roman Church.[1]

PANTAENUS

Pantaenus is the earliest known representative of orthodox
Christianity in Alexandria. Since the days of Eusebius he has
also been accounted the first head of the Catechetical School;
but this was perhaps only a conjecture of Eusebius.[2] Clement
records that Pantaenus, 'the true, the Sicilian bee, gathering
the spoil of the flowers of the prophetic and apostolic
meadow, engendered in the souls of his hearers a deathless
element of knowledge';[3] and it is a safe deduction from this

[1] This thesis is defended by Walter Bauer in his *Rechtglaübigkeit
und Ketzerei im ältesten Christentum* (1935).

[2] So G. Bardy; cf. p. 119, note 1.

[3] Clement Alex., *Strom.* I. i. 11. Sicilian honey was generally held to
be of special excellence.

passage that Pantaenus was a native of Sicily and not, as Philip of Side conjectured, doubtless from Pantaenus' philosophical interests, of Athens.[1] According to Eusebius, Pantaenus evangelised among the peoples of the East, travelling as far as 'India' (perhaps Southern Arabia); and Clement and Eusebius agree that he was a highly successful teacher. Pantaenus, however, wrote nothing himself. In later times several works were ascribed to him by Jerome[2] and others; but in view of the testimony of Clement that the 'elders' (οἱ πρεσβύτεροι) did not write'[3] and that among the elders he certainly included Pantaenus, these attributions must be rejected. The real founder of the Alexandrian theology was Clement.

CLEMENT OF ALEXANDRIA

[Early edd. by P. Victorius (Florence, 1550) and F. Sylburg (Heidelberg, 1592). Good ed. by J. Potter [later Abp. of Canterbury], 2 vols., Oxford, 1715. J. P. Migne, *P.G.*, viii and ix. Crit. ed. by O. Stählin in G.C.S. (text, 3 vols., 1905-9; index vol., excellent, 1934-6). Crit. ed. of *Stromateis* Bk. VII (only), with notes by F. J. A. Hort and J. B. Mayor, London, 1903. Eng. tr. in A.N.C.L. Modern studies by R. B. Tollinton (2 vols., London, 1914); G. Bardy (Paris, 1926); J. Munck (Stuttgart, 1933); C. Mondésert, S.J. (Paris, 1944). E. Molland, *The Conception of the Gospel in the Alexandrian Theology* (Oslo, 1938), pp. 5-84. Further bibl. in *O.D.C.C.*, p. 300, and B. Altaner, *Patrologie* (ed. 1958), pp. 172f., 174f.]

Titus Flavius Clemens, probably a native of Athens, was born of pagan parents *c*. 150. Possessed from early years of an ardent desire to find the truth, he travelled far and wide until he found light at last in the teachings of Pantaenus at Alexandria. Here he was ordained presbyter and from *c*. 190 gave regular instruction in the Christian faith, probably mainly to those studying at the university. The current view that a regular Christian academy (the 'Catechetical School') was established by Demetrius (Bishop of Alexandria, 189-231) and that this had a continuous history down to the 4th century is improbable. This misconception doubtless arose

---

[1] Frag. apud H. Dodwell, *Dissertationes in Irenaeum* (1689), p. 488.
[2] *De Viris Illustribus* 36.   [3] *Eclogae* 27.

from Eusebius' partiality to ideas of succession and the list of heads of the 'School' drawn up by Philip of Side.[1] More probably there existed a much less formal centre of instruction entirely under Clement's direction and responsibility. When the persecution broke out under Septimius Severus in 202, Clement withdrew from Alexandria, and this is almost the last we hear of him. Perhaps Demetrius did not try to persuade such an unconventional teacher to come back when the persecution ended. It appears that Clement spent his later years in Cappadocia.

Clement is the first known Christian scholar. Possessing a vast erudition, he was familiar alike with the Scriptures and an immense number of pagan authors (though he knew these last often through *florilegia* and handbooks rather than from their actual works). He wrote fluently, but his works were discursive. The principal writings which have come down to us are the *Paidagogos*, the *Protrepticos* and the *Stromateis*. On the basis of a passage at the outset of the *Paidagogos*, where Clement is expounding the triple method by which the Logos achieves our salvation, these three writings have been held to constitute a trilogy. The Logos, he says, first of all 'converts' us ($\pi\rho o\tau\rho\acute{\epsilon}\pi\omega\nu$), then He 'disciplines' us ($\pi\alpha\iota\delta\alpha\gamma\omega\gamma\hat{\omega}\nu$) and finally He 'instructs' us ($\acute{\epsilon}\pi\iota\ \pi\hat{\alpha}\sigma\iota\nu\ \acute{\epsilon}\kappa\delta\iota\delta\acute{\alpha}\sigma\kappa\omega\nu$).[2] But while this analysis suggests that Clement's plan was to embody his teaching in a trilogy and that of this trilogy the first two items were the *Protrepticos*, ($\pi\rho o\tau\rho\epsilon\kappa\tau\iota\kappa\acute{o}\varsigma$) and the *Paidagogos* ($\pi\alpha\iota\delta\alpha\gamma\omega\gamma\acute{o}\varsigma$), it is less certain that the *Stromateis* ($\sigma\tau\rho\omega\mu\alpha\tau\epsilon\hat{\iota}\varsigma$) was the third. Let us examine briefly these three writings in turn.

(1) The *Protrepticos*, or 'Hortatory Discourse to the Greeks' (not 'to the *Gentiles*', as Jerome renders it) is an earnest appeal to his readers to give ear to the Logos, whose music can win over the hardest of hearts. After a powerful

---

[1] G. Bardy, 'Aux Origines de l'École d'Alexandrie' in *Rech. S.R.* xxvii (1937), pp. 65-90; id., *Vivre et Penser* [wartime *R. Bibl.*] ii (1942), pp. 80-109.

[2] *Paidagogos* I. 1.

critique of paganism and its horrors and of the false gods and doctrines which its philosophers and poets defend, Clement bids us exchange these outmoded forms for the far more sublime teachings of the Gospel. The treatise was probably written c. 190.

(2) The *Paidagogos*, which is in three Books, is a continuation of the *Protrepticos*. It depicts Christ as the ideal Guide for the human soul. At Baptism, indeed, we become babes (νήπιοι) in Christ and are thus brought back to the beginning, but there is also implanted in us the potentialities of true knowledge (γνῶσις), that is, of perfection; and we should strive to advance towards it. In his account of our moral growth, he is evidently largely dependent on the moral conditions and temptations of Alexandria in his day. He gives many details as to how the Christian should regulate his daily life in such matters as eating and drinking, rest and refreshment, clothing, relations with his fellow-men, sex, and so on. The ideal is one of ordered simplicity in which the good things of life are to be enjoyed, but with due restraint. The work concludes with the splendid hymn to Christ ('The Bridle of Colts Untamed').

(3) The third and much the longest of Clement's works was the *Stromateis*. 'Stromateis', a word which literally meant 'Carpet Bags' and was in regular use for a collection of undigested literary material, can be rendered into English as 'Miscellanies'. Clement's unsystematic mind doubtless found this form of composition congenial. The work followed no predetermined plan but the argument developed as he wrote. The work as we have it is in eight Books. But it is unfinished, and Clement does not seem to have put it into shape beyond the end of Book VII, as Book VIII would appear to be a collection of notes. Appended to Book VIII are the *Excerpta ex Theodoto* and the *Eclogae Propheticae*; both items are extracts from Gnostic writings. On some of these extracts Clement had apparently made his own running comments, but their highly compressed form makes it very difficult to identify which words are Clement's own.

In the *Stromateis*, Clement reverts again and again to the themes of his earlier treaties. Book I treats of the importance and uses of Greek philosophy for the Christian; Book II shews how the Christian revelation far surpasses the highest achievements of human reason and how faith is the foundation of all true knowledge. Books III and IV deal especially with the ethical aspects of Christian belief and elaborate its great superiority to the moral teaching of the Gnostics. Emphasis is laid on the high moral standards required of the Christian both in the married and the celibate state and his readiness for martyrdom in their defence. In the three remaining books he develops the character and beliefs of the 'True Gnostic', as contrasted with the ideals of Judaism and Greek philosophy.

Clement's other surviving writings include:

(1) The *Hypotyposes* or 'Sketches' (ὑποτυπώσεις). The title is misleading, perhaps purposely so; for the work was a commentary on the Jewish and Christian Scriptures in eight books which was designed as a supplement to the works we have just considered. A small part of the work has survived in fragments of a Latin version made by an unknown hand at the instigation of Cassiodorus (*c.* 540). These fragments, generally known from the title of the original edition of M. de la Bigne,[1] as the *Adumbrationes*, all come from four of the Catholic Epistles (1 Pet., Jude, 1, 2 John).

(2) *Who is the Rich Man that is being saved*? This is an attractive homily on Mk. x. 17-31, especially the words 'It is easier for a camel to go through the eye of a needle than for a rich man to enter the Kingdom of God'. Its theme is the stewardship of wealth, that worldly riches, though not evil in themselves, should be used with detachment. The concluding section of the homily recounts the well-known story of the aged John the Apostle rescuing the young man who had lapsed and become a robber.

(3) Clement also wrote several other treatises of which next to nothing has survived, among them *On the Pasch*, *The*

[1] Issued at Paris, 1575.

Ecclesiastical Canon, or against the Judaisers, Disquisitions on Fasting and Scandal, An Exhortation to Patience, or to the Newly Baptised, On the Prophet Amos, and *On Providence.* Two sentences have also been preserved from Clement's *Twenty-first Letter.* The list of titles is a striking testimony to the range of Clement's interests.

ORIGEN

[Best collected ed. by the Maurist, C. de la Rue, O.S.B. (4 vols., Paris, 1733-59; vol. iv completed by his nephew, C. Vincent de la Rue, O.S.B.), repr. with additions in J. P. Migne, P.G. xi-xvii. This is gradually being replaced by mod. crit. texts in G.C.S., incl. *Contra Celsum* (ed. P. Koetschau, 1899), *Comm. in Jn.* (ed. E. Preuschen, 1903), *De Principiis* (ed. P. Koetschau, 1913). Text of 'Discourse with Heracleides' ed. J. Scherer, Cairo, 1949. *Philocalia,* ed. J. A. Robinson, Cambridge, 1893. Translations in A.N.C.L. More recent translations of *Contra Celsum* by H. Chadwick (important; Cambridge, 1953), of *De Principiis* by G. W. Butterworth (London, 1936), of *De Oratione* and *Exhortatio ad Martyrium* by J. J. O'Meara (A.C.W., 1954). Studies of Origen's life and work by P. D. Huet (in ed. of Origen's works, 2 vols., Rouen, 1688), E. R. Redepenning (2 vols., Bonn, 1841-6), J. Daniélou, S.J. (Paris, 1948; Eng. tr., London, 1955). For further bibl. see *O.D.C.C.,* p. 993.]

None of the early fathers merits closer study than Origen.[1] Apart from his other claims on our attention, he is the most outstanding theologian of pre-Nicene times, if not of the whole Patristic period; and his literary productivity was enormous. His remains include a long series of formal compositions, as well as regular expositions of Scripture in the church services which in his later years were taken down by short-hand copyists. It is true that owing to the distrust of his teaching, especially from the 6th century onwards, many of his writings have disappeared. Others have reached us through the medium of translators, and of translators whose renderings, as we shall see, cannot always be trusted.

---

[1] The principal source for Origen's life is Book VI of Eusebius' *Ecclesiastical History.* Eusebius, a native of Caesarea in Palestine where Origen had spent his later years, was a warm admirer of Origen. He tells us that besides Origen's writings, he drew on the six Books of Pamphilus' *Apology for Origen* (unfortunately only the first Book, in Rufinus' Latin version, survives). Gregory Thaumaturgus' *Address to Origen* (cf. below, p. 175) also contains valuable biographical material.

But even so, we still possess a considerably greater extent of Origen's writings than of any other pre-Nicene writer.

Origen was born in Egypt *c.* 185, probably at Alexandria, of parents who brought him up in a Christian home and won him from his earliest years to an ardent Christian faith. According to Eusebius, he was educated in the 'Catechetical School' under Clement,[1] but whether Origen really came under the influence of Clement, as has been commonly supposed, is doubtful, as Origen nowhere mentions Clement in his writings, not even where a reference to him would seem almost inevitable.[2] During the persecution under Septimius Severus (202), his father Leonides suffered martyrdom, and tradition records that Origen, desirous of the same glorious end, was only restrained from his purpose by his mother's hiding his clothes to keep him indoors. When peace was restored to the Church, Demetrius, the Bishop, put Origen in charge of the instruction of the catechumens. This probably marked the institution of a regular catechumenate at Alexandria to prepare candidates for Baptism at the ensuing Easter.[3] Origen gave himself to the task with great zest. 'His manner of life was as his doctrine, and his doctrine as his life.'[4] He began to practise many austerities, entered on a life of prayer, fasting and voluntary poverty, and in an excess of zeal and an over rigid interpretation of Matt. xix. 12 mutilated himself. Eager to equip himself as fully as he could for his task, he not only sat at the feet of Ammonius Saccas and studied the pagan philosophers, but also travelled widely. It is recorded that in 212 he paid a short visit to Rome where he heard Hippolytus preach.[5] In 215 he visited Arabia and, three years later (218), Antioch, where he was

[1] Eusebius, *Hist. Eccl.* VI. vi. On the 'Catechetical School', cf. above, p. 118.
[2] J. Munck, *Untersuchungen über Klemens von Alexandrien* (1933), p. 224f.
[3] Cf. G. Bardy in *Vivre et Penser* [wartime *R.Bibl.*] ii (1942), p. 85.
[4] Eusebius, *Hist. Eccl.* VI. v. 7.
[5] This has been the usual deduction from Eusebius, *Hist. Eccl.* VI. xiv. 10, taken in conjunction with Jerome, *De Vir. Illustr.* 61. But it is possible Origen heard Hippolytus at Alexandria.

received by Julia Mammaea, the mother of Alexander
Severus. Meanwhile, when conditions at Alexandria were
disordered by the troubles connected with the visit of Caracalla (215), Origen had made his way to Palestine. While he
was here, though he was only a layman, he accepted invita-
tions to preach from the Bishops of Caesarea and Jerusalem.
Such activity on the part of a layman was contrary to
Egyptian practice and Demetrius, regarding it as a breach of
discipline, recalled Origen to Egypt. He now ceased to have
charge of the catechumens and became free to devote himself
for the next years entirely to his theological and Biblical
studies and to spread the faith among the educated. In this
work he had the generous help of his friend, Ambrose, a
wealthy convert from Valentinianism, who put several stenographers at his disposal. This was the period to which his
De Principiis and earlier Commentaries belong.

In 230 Origen paid another visit to Palestine. The Bishops
who had invited him to preach in Palestine fifteen years
earlier now ordained him presbyter. This precipitated a
crisis on his return to Alexandria, so that in 231 Origen was
deprived of any official position in the Alexandrian Church.
He accordingly left Egypt for Caesarea in Palestine where he
settled and continued to teach and preach for the rest of his
life. He continued to travel extensively. On a journey to
Arabia, he engaged in a theological disputation with Beryllus,
Bishop of Bostra, and persuaded him to renounce his
Monarchianism. During the Decian persecution (249-250)
he was imprisoned and subjected to torture in an unsuccessful
attempt to secure his defection. His physical strength, however, was broken by his sufferings and he died shortly
afterwards at Tyre (*c.* 253-4). His tomb at Tyre was shown
to travellers until modern times.[1]

Origen's principal writings may be divided into four
groups: (1) Biblical writings; (2) The theological treatise 'On
First Principles'; (3) The Apology against Celsus; and
(4) Practical writings. To these must be added (5) His

[1] Cf. B. F. Westcott in *D.C.B.* iv, p. 103.

Disputations, including the *Discourse with Heracleides*; (6) His Correspondence; and (7) the 'Philocalia'. The last named is a collection of extracts from his writings, put together more than a hundred years after his death by St. Gregory Nazianzen and St. Basil for the use of their monks in Cappadocia on the banks of the Iris. It contains many passages not known to exist elsewhere and is an important witness to the Greek text of certain of his writings, notably the *Contra Celsum*.[1]

(1) Among Origen's Biblical writings, the *Hexapla* occupies a place apart. This monumental work, begun while Origen was still at Alexandria, was not completed until well into his Caesarean period (*c*. 245). It was an edition of the Old Testament text which contained in six parallel columns the Hebrew text, the Hebrew text in Greek characters[2] and then the four Greek versions of Aquila, Symmachus, the Septuagint and Theodotion. In places these six columns were extended to as many as nine, by the addition of other versions.

The complete work must have been of vast bulk and was probably never copied in its entirety. St. Jerome expressly states that he used the copy preserved at Caesarea.[3] Early in the 7th century its Septuagintal column was rendered very literally into Syriac by Paul, the Monophysite Bishop of Tella, and this text is of great importance for textual critical purposes (as a witness to the LXX).[4]

[1] Critical edition by J. A. Robinson, Cambridge, 1893.

[2] The purpose of the second column was apparently liturgical, to enable Jews ignorant of Hebrew to read the Hebrew text in public worship. This was shewn by H. Halévy, 'L'Origine de la Transcription du Texte Hébreu en charactères grecs dans l'Hexaple d'Origène' in *Journal Asiatique*, sér. ix, xvii (1901), pp. 335-41. Cf. P. E. Kahle, *The Cairo Geniza* (1947), pp. 86-8. It appears from Melito of Sardis that this practice was also followed by the Christian Church. Cf. T. W. Manson in *Dominican Studies* ii (1949), p. 191f.

[3] 'Commentarioli in Psalmas' apud G. Morin, O.S.B., *Anecdota Maredsolana* iii. 1 (Maredsous, 1895), p. 12.

[4] The surviving Greek fragments of the Hexapla have been collected by F. Field in *Origenis Hexaplorum quae supersunt* (2 vols., Oxford, 1867-75).

Origen's exegetical treatises fall into three groups,—Commentaries, Homilies and Scholia. The aim of the Commentaries was scholarly, namely to expound the text scientifically (though this did not preclude their author from allegorising); the Homilies were primarily edificatory; while the Scholia were detached notes on particular passages.

The *Commentaries* (or 'Tomes'), begun at Alexandria, occupied Origen through most of his life. They are the finest part of his exegetical work and won the warm admiration of Jerome (who had little interest in the Homilies). There is no set which survives *in toto* in the original Greek, but large sections of the Commentaries on Matthew and John have reached us. The Commentary on John, the longest of all, extended to 32 Books, of which the first five came from his Alexandrian period. Origen's devotion to the Fourth Gospel largely explains its great length. A considerable part of it is also taken up with the refutation of the Gnostic Heracleon.[1] Origen also commented on Luke, and the majority of the Pauline Epistles. Much of the Greek text of his Commentary on Romans has recently been recovered on a Toura papyrus.[2] As regards the Old Testament, Origen commented on Genesis, on several of the Psalms, on nearly all the Prophets and on the Song of Songs (twice); but very much has been lost. The second of Origen's Commentaries on the Canticles was praised by Jerome in the highest terms[3] and it is in Jerome's Latin version that it survives.

The *Homilies*, which contain Origen's pulpit expositions of Scripture, all come from his Caesarean period. The earliest series of homilies derives from notes made by Origen himself before delivery, but from *c*. 245 onwards he allowed steno-

[1] Cf. above, p. 38.

[2] On this see pp. 132f. Cf. also H. Chadwick, 'Rufinus and the Tura Papyrus of Origen's Commentary on Romans' in *J.T.S.* x (1959), pp. 10-42. Dr. Chadwick shews (against Scherer) that though Rufinus *more suo* had taken considerable liberties with the text, he had faithfully reproduced the substance of Origen.

[3] 'Origenes, cum in ceteris libris omnes vicerit, in Cantico canticorum ipse se vicit'. *Prol. in Hom. in Cant. Cant.*, init.

graphers to take his Homilies down. Of the 500 homilies of
Origen which came into circulation some 240, together with
some fragments, survive in Latin versions. Forty of them are
on the Gospel of Luke; these, the earliest, date from c. 234.
The rest are on various portions of the Old Testament,
especially the first four Books of the Pentateuch. It would
appear that at least on occasion they were delivered at
Jerusalem. The Homily on the Witch of Endor (I Sam.
xxviii), which has come down in Greek, is noteworthy for the
attention it attracted among later writers. Origen contended
that the witch really conjured up Samuel from the dead, a
view rejected both by Eustathius of Antioch and Gregory of
Nyssa.

The *Scholia* (σχόλια or σημειώσεις), philological and
historical notes on particular passages or verses, date mainly
from Origen's earlier years. He is known to have composed
such for the first four Books of the Pentateuch, Isaiah,
Ecclesiastes, the Psalms, the Gospels of Matthew and John,
Galatians and Revelation. Only brief extracts survive.

(2) Origen's *De Principiis*, the purpose of which is to
expound a coherent system the Christian teaching about God
and the Universe, is the most ambitious work on speculative
theology of pre-Nicene times. Though it is one of Origen's
earliest writings, it is highly characteristic of him, both in
method and content. 'His voluminous later writings are little
more than an expansion of the ideas there set down'.[1]

Unfortunately, the greater part of the original Greek text
has been lost,[2] and it survives complete only in a Latin
version made by Rufinus of Aquileia in 398. Rufinus, however,
took great liberties with the text. His purpose in translating
it was to commend its theology to the Western world at a
time when Origen's orthodoxy was widely challenged,
notably by St. Jerome, and Rufinus tells us that when he
came to passages which he found doctrinally objectionable,

[1] C. Bigg, *The Christian Platonists of Alexandria* (ed. 1913), p. 193.
[2] The longest Greek fragments (from Books III and IV) are preserved
in the *Philocalia* (cf. above, p. 125).

he presumed that they were the insertions of heretics and accordingly suppressed or modified them, or put in their place unobjectionable passages on the same subject from Origen's other writings. That Rufinus in fact handled the text very freely is borne out by comparison of his version with various passages from the original Greek which have come down to us. At almost the same date (398) Jerome made a literal version with the contrary purpose of proving Origen unorthodox. Apart from a few brief fragments, this version has been lost.

The *De Principiis* is in four Books which treat successively of God, the World, Freedom and Scripture. They are introduced by a Preface in which Origen insists that the source of all true doctrine is Christ, who illuminated the Prophets before His Incarnation no less than the inspired writers of the New Covenant. This doctrine has been transmitted through an ordered succession of teachers down to the present day.[1] But some of this teaching has reached us in a fragmentary or uncertain state. When is the soul united with the body? What is the nature of the devil? What is an incorporeal being? (For he notes that the word 'incorporeal' is not found in Scripture.) And are God and Christ incorporeal? These are the kind of problems to which the Christian theologian must address himself and which will form the subject of the ensuing books.

Book I deals with God and the spiritual world generally, i.e., besides the Father, Son and Holy Ghost, with the realm of created spirits, i.e. both angels and demonic beings. God is beyond all definition, pure intelligence and absolute unity. The Son, who is the Divine wisdom, is the Image of the Invisible God; He is the Word, the Truth, the Life, the Resurrection and the Way. Already we have evidence of Origen's subordinationism. The dominion of the Father extends over the whole created universe; that of the Son or Logos to all rational creatures; while that of the Spirit, with

---

[1] Illa sola credenda est veritas quae in nullo ab ecclesiastica et apostolica discordat traditione. *De Principiis*, praef. 2.

His mission of sanctification, is confined to the Church, both in this world and in the next. The angels and spirits, he goes on to explain, form a hierarchy. The chief characteristic of a reasonable being is the capacity to choose between good and evil. Hence the angels, in exercising this gift, fell. The evil angels are those who with Satan are called in Scripture the 'princes of this world'. But in the end evil will be conquered and all beings, including Satan, will return to their primitive state (the 'apocatastasis'). In ch. vii Origen elaborated another of his doctrines, which caused so much offence in later times, the view that the stars have souls.

In Book II Origen proceeds to treat of the material world and of man. Despite the external diversity of creatures the world has a unity which belongs to it as a kind of organism. The universe will end as it began. Yet he held to the doctrine of a plurality of worlds which eternally succeed one another. With ch. vi he opens his treatment of the Incarnation. The soul of Christ, like the souls of other men, was endowed with free will; but He alone possessed the plenitude of the Divine word. In a long discussion of the human soul, he closely aligns it with the pure spirits, fancifully suggesting that its name ($\psi\nu\chi\eta$, 'soul') shews it to be a 'cooling' ($\psi\tilde{\nu}\chi\sigma s$, 'cold') of the Divine love into a more solid form. The latter pages of the Book treat of eschatological matters.

Book III is mainly taken up with the problems of free will and of the Divine Providence in its relation to human action. While our present life is one of continual struggle with the Devil and the flesh, in the next life there will be a final victory of good over evil, when even the Devil will be saved. We shall then attain complete conformity with God ($\delta\mu\sigma\iota\omega\sigma\iota s$ $\tau\tilde{\omega}$ $\theta\epsilon\tilde{\omega}$) and reach the state when God will be all in all (1 Cor. xv. 28).

Most of Book IV is concerned with the principles of Scriptural exegesis. Here are set out the methods that Origen adopted in his Commentaries and other exegetical writings. The threefold sense of Scripture is again described. Much in the Bible, and especially in the Old Testament, cannot be understood literally. Who can suppose that for the first three days after the creation there was no sun or moon or stars? Or that God planted the Garden of Eden like a gardener, or that He walked in the garden while Adam hid his nakedness? Or that Moses forbade the eating of the griffin, a fabulous animal? Or that in the Temptation Story, Jesus literally went to the pinnacle of the Temple? No doubt the Bible contains much history. But whereas the whole lends itself to a spiritual interpretation from beginning to end, there is much in Scripture which has no literal message to convey.

The final chapter (ch. iv) contains an epitome of the whole work.

(3) In the field of apologetics, Origen's most important writing was his work against Celsus. The treatise, which is in eight Books, dates from c. 245. It was written at the insistence of his friend and patron, Ambrose, who had met with Celsus' work and felt it would do much harm if it were not answered. Origen himself, indeed, was convinced that the work needed no reply. The best answer was to follow Christ before His calumniators and be silent. But a request from Ambrose could not be disregarded, so Origen set about refuting Celsus' argument step by step. Hence arose the *Contra Celsum*.

The case for Christianity finally rests on its moral excellence. This is the principal answer to the arguments which Celsus derives from the pagan philosophers and his trivial criticisms of the Christian Scriptures. Moreover, Celsus' claim to be fully acquainted with the Christian case is just bragging. 'If he had read the Prophets which are admitted to be enigmatical and obscure; if he had gone through the evangelical parables, the law, the history of the Jews and the writings of the Apostles and, having read them without prejudice, had tried to penetrate their meaning, he would not say with such assurance, "I know all" ($\pi\acute{a}\nu\tau a$ $\gamma\grave{a}\rho$ $o\tilde{\iota}\delta a$). We ourselves, who have studied all these things closely, would not dare to say "I know all", for we love the truth' (I. xii). And the objections which Celsus makes to particular incidents and passages in the Scriptures will not stand. These last can be shewn to accord with what we should expect of God. The miracles of the Bible, so far from being an offence, are wholly defensible. Origen constantly appeals to the strength of Christ's power in the lives of Christians who shine as stars ($\phi\omega\sigma\tau\hat{\eta}\rho\epsilon\varsigma$) in the world of his own day as a testimony of Christian faith.

For the student of Origen the work is valuable not only for its testimony to Origen's range of knowledge, but for its indication of the particular philosophical sources which Origen studied.

(4) Two of Origen's practical writings call for notice. His treatise on Prayer is deservedly held in high esteem.[1] 'No writing of Origen is more free from his characteristic faults, or more full of beautiful thoughts.[2] The work, which was written in answer to a number of questions raised by his patron, Ambrose, probably dates from 233-234, i.e. shortly after Origen's removal to Caesarea. Origen upheld the view that prayer in its fullest sense may be addressed only to the Father. He defended this thesis on the Scriptural basis that Christ is Himself our High Priest and Intercessor, and though He far transcends the heavenly host of Cherubim, He has a place in the Divine hierarchy lower than the Father. The work incorporates a long section in which Origen expounds the Lord's Prayer. This is of much interest for the history of its exegesis. Thus in a long and careful discussion of the word 'supersubstantial', Origen concludes that this has reference to the supernatural Bread, which nourishes our souls as the Word of God. There is no reference here either on the one hand to our need of purely earthly food nor on the other to the sacramental Bread of the Eucharist.

Slightly later in date is the 'Exhortation to Martyrdom' written to encourage two of his friends, Ambrose, and the

[1] This is illustrated by the three recent English translations, by Dr. E. G. Jay, by Dr. H. Chadwick in L.C.C. and by Prof. J. J. O'Meara in A.C.W.

[2] B. F. Westcott in D.C.B. iv, p. 124.

presbyter, Protoctetus, both of whom had been thrown into prison during the persecution under Maximinus Thrax (235). After a general exhortation to martyrdom (1-5), Origen warns his readers against idolatry and apostasy (6-10), exhorts them to persevere unflinchingly in bearing the cross (11-12), commends the examples of the martyrs in II Maccabees (22-27), delineates the various kinds of martyrdom (28-44), and attacks idolatry in general (45f.). He ends by renewed exhortations to perseverance (47-50). The treatise has much in common with the writings of Tertullian and Cyprian on the same subject as well as the Pseudo-Cyprianic *De laude Martyrii*.

(5) Our knowledge of Origen has recently been still further extended by the discovery in 1941 of a number of 6th century papyri in a quarry at Toura, a few miles from Cairo, which was used as a munitions dump during the late war. The most considerable, which bears the title: 'Discussions (διάλεκτοι) of Origen with Heracleides and the Bishops who are with him',[1] is the verbal record of unrehearsed dialogues which took place in a church in Arabia in or about 245. Origen had been invited by the bishops to disentangle certain theological perplexities which were disturbing the community. There is no suggestion of a trial for heresy and the discussion seems to have been quite informal. We owe the record of this life-like debate to stenographers, who have transmitted it to posterity just as it took place.[2]

The problems discussed in the first part of the *Discussions* are the Divinity of the Son, the nature of prayer, the character

[1] The fullest account of the whole find to date is still O. Guérard, 'Note préliminaire sur les papyrus d'Origène découverts à Toura' in the *Revue de l'Histoire des Religions* cxxxi (1946), pp. 85-108. Some of these texts have since been published by M. Jean Scherer. They include, besides (1) the *Discussions*, (2) extracts from Books I and II of *Contra Celsum* and (3) large portions of Origen's Commentary on Romans (cf. above, p. 126).

[2] As A. D. Nock observes, the preservation of this record of an informal discussion is unique in ancient literature and unparalleled outside Augustine. See *American Journal of Archaeology* lv (1951), p. 283.

of the Lord's Body and the mechanism of the resurrection. Heracleides having objected that Origen's formula of 'two Gods' for the Father and the Son was polytheistic, Origen defended it on the ground that in many places of Scripture, 'two' were 'one'. Adam and Eve, though two, had only one flesh (Gen. ii. 24); St. Paul asserted that 'he that is joined unto the Lord is one spirit' with him (1 Cor. vi. 17); above all, Christ Himself had said: 'I and My Father are one' (Jn.x.30). The disputants finally agree that the formula 'two Gods' is admissible, and that what the two Persons have in common is a single power (δύναμις μιά ἐστιν).

Next follows an extended discussion with a certain Dionysius, probably also a Bishop, on whether the soul in man is to be identified with his blood. Origen argues that besides physical blood there is the blood of the interior man and that it is this which is to be equated with the soul and survives physical death. In the concluding section of the *Discussions* Origen discusses the question of the soul's immortality.

Among other MSS. of Origen found at Toura were a fragmentary treatise *On the Passion*,[1] an early text of the *Contra Celsum* I and II, and exegetical fragments on Rom., I Cor. and I Reg. xxviii.[2]

(6) Of Origen's large correspondence only two items survive, viz. (i) a Letter to Gregory Thaumaturgus,[3] commending the study of Scripture; and (ii) a Letter to Julius Africanus, defending the canonicity of the three fragments of the Greek Daniel not found in the Hebrew, viz. the Prayer of the Three Children in the Fiery Furnace (iii.24-90), the

[1] Fragments of this have been published by P. Nautin in *Homélies Pascales II: Trois Homélies dans la Tradition d'Origène* (Sources Chrétiennes 36, 1953).

[2] The Toura MSS. also contained hitherto unknown texts of the commentaries of Didymus the Blind on Genesis, Job, the Psalms, and Zechariah. This Commentary of Didymus on the Psalms has been the subject of an important recent study by Dr. A. Gesché of Louvain.

[3] On Gregory Thaumaturgus, cf. pp. 174-6.

Appendix on Susanna, and the Story of Bel and the Dragon.[1] Origen's attitude to the Greek Daniel here is indefensible; but it was in line with that generally held in the early Church until Jerome showed the true nature of the Deutero-canonical books.

From this brief survey of Origen's writings, we must be struck by the immense range and variety of his interests. He was active as an exegete, as a philosopher, as a theologian and as a spiritual writer; and in all these capacities his competence was outstanding. The chief criticism which the modern student is apt to make of Origen's outlook is his want of historical sense. This profoundly affected his understanding of the Bible and indeed his whole theology of the Incarnation. As a philosopher he has traditionally been ranked with the 'Platonists' or, in more recent times, with the 'Neo-Platonists'. But Dr. Henry Chadwick has recently shewn how extensively he was also affected by Stoic influences. It seems likely that his debt to Platonism has been exaggerated and that it is wrong to regard him as the exponent of any one philosophical system. Indeed, the popular belief that he was directly influenced by the system of Plotinus is ruled out by chronology. His doctrine of the Godhead could not commend itself permanently to Christian thought on account of its subordinationism. The unfettered speculations of his fertile mind, which were only meant as hypotheses, though they later came to be understood as if they were matters of personal belief, led to his too ready condemnation. In recent times, students of the Fathers have been ready to take a less prejudiced view of Origen and to recognise his supreme place among the pre-Nicenes.

[1] The three items are found in the 'Apocrypha' of the English version.

IX.—THE AFRICAN WRITERS

THE early Christian writers who belonged to the Roman province of Africa, i.e. Carthage and its hinterland, stand in striking contrast to the Alexandrians whom we have just been considering. The transition from Clement and Origen to Tertullian has been compared with that of a traveller 'hurried from a fair and smiling prospect to a rugged country under scowling skies'.[1] While the Church in Alexandria was in danger of being enmeshed by the charms of philosophy, early Christianity in Africa was wholly out of sympathy with the Greek spirit. It was in Africa that Latin gained its first secure hold on the Church. We begin with Tertullian.

TERTULLIAN

[The best of the older edd. is that of F. Oehler, 3 vols., Leipzig, 1851-4. Crit. edd. of separate works in course of publication in C.S.E.L. and Corpus Christianorum. Many good annotated edd. and translations of separate works also exist. For further bibl. see *O.D.C.C.*, p. 1334.]

Tertullian was born at Carthage of pagan parents not later than the year 160. He received a good education in law and rhetoric, and also gained a mastery of Greek. He made the law his profession and went to Rome, where he gained a reputation as a jurist.[2] Having been converted to Christianity *c.* 196, he returned to Carthage where he at once threw himself with ardour into propagating his newly found faith. To bear public testimony to his Christian profession, he exchanged the Roman toga for the philosopher's *pallium*. He also began writing with zest, and many of his writings date

[1] H. B. Swete, *Patristic Study*, p. 61.
[2] He is probably to be identified with the jurist Tertullian of the *Pandects*.

from the first years after his conversion. Whether or not, as Jerome[1] asserts, he ever became a presbyter is uncertain. But his dour outlook could not find enduring satisfaction in the Church. He needed a system which made of asceticism not a counsel but a precept. So some ten years after his conversion he was drawn towards the rigorist system of morals propagated by the Montanists and *c.* 207 became a member of the African branch of the sect. He died at Carthage at some date after 220.

Tertullian was the most prolific of the Latin Fathers in pre-Nicene times. Of a fiery and rugged temperament, he was by nature a rebel and would hardly have fitted happily into any *milieu*. He first abandoned the pagan society in which he had filled an important position in civil life and then the orthodox Christianity to which he had been converted, to become in his later life a member of an extremist schismatic sect. But he was destined to exercise a remarkable influence on Western Christendom. He adapted the Latin language, over which his sway was in many respects without parallel, for theological purposes with remarkable success. Besides being the first considerable Christian Latin writer, he was also the first great Latin thinker. His theological perception was so sharp and his range so wide that he created at one stroke the theological vocabulary of the Western Church. He is also a primary witness to the pre-Nicene Biblical text. For the most part he used the Greek Bible and translated it into Latin as was required.

Tertullian's crisp and terse style makes a heavy demand on the reader's attention. It was well described by Vincent of Lerins when he wrote that almost every word is a sentence.[2] Almost all his writing is controversial; and with his complete command of language, he became a master of invective. He suffers more than any other of the Fathers from translation.

---

[1] *De Vir. Ill.* 53. The absence of Biblical commentaries or works of exegesis among Tertullian's writings favours the view that he was never ordained.

[2] *Commonitorium*, c. 18: 'Quot paene verba, tot sententiae'.

But the success of his dialectic varies. Despite his acute powers of observation, he does not always carry his reader with him. His argumentation too often resembles a display of fireworks. Yet Tertullian can on occasion convince. His *Apology* was a devastating and unanswerable attack on contemporary paganism.

Tertullian's writings, which treat a large range of themes, all bear the marked individuality of their author.[1] A few of them can be identified as belonging to his Montanist period; but otherwise, apart from occasional cross-references, they cannot be dated or arranged in any chronological order. They survive in very few copies, and many of his works have perished altogether. Certain MSS. known to the earlier editors of Tertullian have since been lost, and for two of his writings included in the editions (*De Pudicitia, De Jejunio*) there is now no known MS. source. This was also true for *De Baptismo* until 1916 when Dom Wilmart succeeded in finding a MS. at Troyes (cod. 523). For several of Tertullian's works the sole source is the important 'Codex Agobardinus' (Paris cod. 1622), formerly in the possession of Agobard, Bishop of Lyons (d. 840).

I. *Apologetic Writings*

(1) *Ad Nationes* (197). Tertullian wrote this defence of Christianity very soon after his conversion, drawing largely on Varro's *Antiquitates* for his description of paganism. The treatise, which is in two Books, was written at a white heat of passion. It abounds in brilliant thrusts, but it is ill argued. It was preparatory to the *Apology*, technically far superior and written a few months later.

(2) The *Apology* (end of 197), the greatest of Tertullian's works. Though formally addressed to the governors of the

[1] Owing to the uncertainty in the dating of Tertullian's writings, any arrangement of them is somewhat arbitrary. The order followed here is that in B. Altaner's *Patrology*, where they are disposed in three groups according to their subject-matter and then in each group a conjectured chronological order. For convenience of reference they are here numbered as in Altaner.

Roman Provinces (*praesides provinciarum*) it was really designed for the general public. It sought to counter the rapidly growing feeling against Christianity which led up to the persecuting edict of Septimius Severus in 202. Christians, he says, are often charged with secret crimes (*occulta facinora*, 6), with infanticide, Thyestean banquets, incest. But charges of this kind can be easily answered, since they rest on 'rumour alone'. All the more attention, then, is due to the public crimes laid at their feet,—contempt for the accredited religion and a corresponding want of patriotism (*intentatio laesae divinitatis*, 27) and, even worse, high treason (*titulus laesae augustioris majestatis*, 28). 'Every individual province, every city has its own gods. . . . We, we alone, are forbidden a religion of our own.' None the less it is with the Christians that the future lies. 'We are of yesterday, but we have filled your whole world, your cities and their quarters (*insulae*), your country towns and your settlements, even your camps, your tribes, the decuries of your judges, the palace, the senate, the bar. We have left you only your temples. We can count your armies; the Christians of a single province exceed them in number' (38).

The *Apology* has far better MS. attestation than any of Tertullian's other writings, owing, no doubt, to its popularity from the first; and it was known in an ancient Greek version to Eusebius. The text exists in two forms and it has sometimes been suggested that both recensions go back to Tertullian himself. The problem is still unsolved, but it seems likely that the 'Fuldensis' MS. preserves the original text, while the other form, found in the majority of the MSS., is a revision of a scribe of the Carolingian school.

(3) *De Testimonio Animae* (after 197). An extended discussion of the phrase in the *Apology* (ch. 17): 'O testimonium animae naturaliter christianae'. The heathen testify to their belief in such fundamental Christian truths as the unity of God, the permanence of the soul and the existence of evil spirits by their daily exclamations: 'Which may God grant',

'If God will', 'God shall judge between us', and so on.

(4) *Ad Scapulam* (212). An open letter to Scapula, the Proconsul of Africa, who outstripped others of proconsular rank in throwing Christians to the wild beasts and even having them burnt. There appears to be a reference in it to the solar eclipse of 14 August 212.

(5) *Adversus Judaeos* (200-206). Tertullian argues that the law of justice has now given way to the law of love and that the promises made to Israel have passed to the Gentiles. Only the first part is genuine (1-8); the remainder (9-14) is the work of an inferior writer, who took as his basis *Adversus Marcionem* iii.

II. *Doctrinal and Polemical Writings*

(6) *De Praescriptione Haereticorum* (c. 200). In this masterly treatise Tertullian sets forth certain fundamental principles by which all heresies can be shewn to be in error.[1] *Praescriptio* is the technical legal term for the statement which the defendant in a law suit inserted in his speech containing the grounds on which he urged further proceedings in the case should be stopped. Tertullian holds that the *praescriptio* whereby orthodoxy can stop the pretensions of heretics is the circumstance that truth has been entrusted to Catholic Christianity. It is the Church alone which possesses ancient Catholic tradition, the Holy Scriptures and the right to interpret them. Heretics think that the truth can be reached by an intellectual quest and justify themselves by the text in the Gospel: 'Seek and ye shall find'. But they overlook the context of these words, which were given at the outset of the Lord's ministry when He had not yet committed the great truths to the Apostles. But now all has been revealed and there is no place for philosophy. 'What has Athens to do with Jerusalem? What has the Academy to do with the Church?

[1] In the modern editions the work consists of 56 chapters, but it properly ends at ch. 45a. On the remaining chapters (46b-end), see 6(a) below.

What have heretics in common with Christians?' Our Porch is the Porch of Solomon.[1] 'Away with those who bring forward a Stoic or Platonic or dialectic Christianity. We have no need of speculative inquiry after we have known Christ Jesus; nor of search for the truth after we have received the Gospel' (ch. 7). The Apostles and their successors played a fundamental part in enabling the Gospel to reach us. With the Scriptures as their basis they formulated the 'rule of faith' and this faith was handed down especially in the Apostolic sees. It is this tradition of the truth, manifest and patent to all, which stands over against the secret doctrines of the Gnostics. 'The one faith of countless Christians derives not from error, but from tradition'.[2] Over against this traditional and ancient faith all heresies are but the creations of yesterday.

(6a) *Libellus adversus Omnes Haereses*. Appended to the *De Praescriptione*, i.e. chs. 46b-56 in the editions, is a short treatise listing thirty-two heresies. It is clear from its style that it cannot be by Tertullian. It has been widely supposed to rest on the (lost) 'Syntagma Against Heresies' of Hippolytus.[3] According to E. Schwartz[4] it is an anti-Origenist compilation by Pope Zephyrinus or one of his clerics which was translated into Latin by Victorinus of Pettau.

(7) *Adversus Marcionem* (in five Books). This was Tertullian's most ambitious and longest work, and is our most extensive authority for Marcion's teaching. Incidentally, as Tertullian's method of attack required him to make extensive quotations from the Old and New Testaments, the treatise is also one of the principal witnesses for the Old Latin Biblical text.

Tertullian took great pains over the treatise. An original draft, dating from *c*. 200, he suppressed altogether as inadequate. A second draft, he tells us, was stolen from him

[1] Cf. Jn. x. 23; Acts iii. 2, v. 12. With allusion to the 'Stoics', the philosophers of the 'Stoa' (=Porch).

[2] Quod apud multos unum invenitur, non est erratum sed traditum (28).

[3] Cf. below, p. 163.		[4] *Sb* (Bayr.), 1936, No. 3.

and circulated against his will in an incorrect form. The text which survives is a third recension; of this the first four Books date from *c*. 208, while the fifth and last dates from *c*. 211. The work opens with a hideous picture of Pontus with its grim climate and savage inhabitants; but all these horrors are nothing compared with the barbarities and treachery of its native, Marcion. The passage, which is a piece of invective unmatched in Patristic literature, prepares the reader for the ruthless treatment of Marcion in the body of the work. In Books I-III Tertullian seeks to establish the unity of God against Marcion's distinction between the Good God of the Christian revelation and the merely Just God of the Old Testament. Books IV and V attack Marcion's Biblical text and dispose of Marcion's imagined contradictions between the Old and New Testaments.

(8) *Adversus Hermogenem* (*c*. 200). Hermogenes, a painter by profession, was an otherwise unknown 2nd-century Gnostic. He taught an extreme form of dualism and had already been attacked in a lost treatise of Theophilus of Antioch.[1] Tertullian's work contains a vigorous defence of the doctrine of creation.

(9) *Adversus Valentinianos* (*c*. 207). This treatise has many points of contact with the previous one. Tertullian here draws extensively on the attack on the Valentinians in Irenaeus, *Adv. Haer*. I.

(10) *Scorpiace* (213), i.e. a 'Remedy against the Sting of the Scorpion'. It is directed against certain Gnostics who depreciated martyrdom. It probably dates from the summer of 213, when the persecution under the Proconsul, Scapula, was raging.

(11) *De Carne Christi* (210-213). The treatise is a vigorous defence of the reality of the flesh of Christ against the docetism of the Gnostics, Marcion and other heretics. So insistent was Tertullian on His full assumption of our flesh

---

[1] Eusebius, *Hist. Eccl*. IV. xxiv.

that he denied Our Lady's virginity *in partu*.[1] He also expressed the opinion, found in other pre-Nicene writers (cf. Is. liii. 14), that Christ in the days of His flesh had an ugly countenance.[2]

(12) *De Carnis Resurrectione* (210-212). A complement to the preceding. It defends the resurrection of the body against the Gnostics.

(13) *Adversus Praxean* (after 213). Though it comes from Tertullian's Montanist years, the treatise contains the clearest statement of the Catholic doctrine of the Trinity from pre-Nicene times. The work is directed against a certain 'Praxeas', who defended at Rome a Monarchianist (Patripassianist) view of the Godhead and attacked Montanism. The absence of all reference to 'Praxeas' in Hippolytus is surprising in view of his first hand acquaintance with Rome and his special interest in combating Monarchianist teaching. So it has been asked whether 'Praxeas' may not be a nickname ('busybody') and conceal Pope Callistus or perhaps Epigonus, the disciple of Noetus. Tertullian tells us that Praxeas 'managed two pieces of the devil's business: he drove out prophecy and introduced heresy. He put to flight the Paraclete and crucified the Father' (ch. 1). The main purpose of the work was to defend the orthodox doctrine of the Godhead. The author clearly insists on the unity of God and the trinity of persons. It contains the earliest occurrence of the Latin word *trinitas* in Christian literature (ch. 3).

(14) *De Baptismo* (*c*. 200-206). This is the only pre-Nicene treatise dealing expressly with Sacramental theology. It is also an important liturgical source, for in defending the traditional teaching on Baptism, Tertullian notes many details of the practice of the rite, including the completion of Baptism by chrismation and the laying on of hands. He is unusual in deprecating the baptism of infants. He also denied the validity of heretical baptism, here anticipating Cyprian.

[1] Virgo quantum a viro, non virgo quantum a partu, ch. 23.
[2] Nec humanae honestatis corpus fuit, ch. 9.

The treatise is based on an earlier Greek work of his which has been lost.

(15) *De Anima* (*c.* 210). Apart from the treatise *Against Marcion*, this is the longest of Tertullian's works. It contains the first extended discussion of the soul in Christian literature, which is developed in relation to the errors of contemporary Gnosticism; and much use is made of the early 2nd-century medical writer, Soranus of Ephesus. The work is in three sections: (1) chs. 4-22. On the nature of the soul. Tertullian defends the view, ultimately Stoic, that the soul has a corporeal element and is not purely spirit; (2) chs. 23-41. On the origin of the soul. Against all doctrines of pre-existence and creationism Tertullian upholds a crude Traducianism. On this basis he explains the transmission of original sin (*vitium originis*) from parent to child; (3) chs. 42-58. On death, sleep, dreams and the resting place of the soul after death. The treatise is the subject of an elaborate commentary by Professor J. H. Waszink (Amsterdam, 1947).

III. *Moral and Practical Writings*

(16) *Ad Martyras* (*c.* 197). This short treatise is designed to comfort a group of Christians who had been thrown into prison and were expecting martyrdom.

(17) *De Spectaculis* (*c.* 197). In this treatise, addressed to catechumens, Tertullian denounces all forms of the pagan theatre.

(18) *De Oratione* (198-204). This is the earliest Christian treatise on prayer and also contains the oldest surviving exposition of the Lord's Prayer. It wants the finished style of most of Tertullian's writings and is perhaps a collection of sermon notes.[1] The *Paternoster* is termed 'an epitome of the whole Gospel'.[2] A long section (13-27) deals with various practices relating to public prayer (washing the hands, lifting them up and spreading them out, taking off the overcoat,

---

[1] E. Evans, *Tertullian's Tract on The Prayer* (1953), p. xi.
[2] Breviarius totius Evangelii, ch. 1.

sitting down as soon as the prayers are over, moderation of the voice, refusing the kiss of peace, women's dress and covering of the head, and not kneeling on Saturdays); it has been suggested that these all come from a section added to an original homily when it was published.[1] The treatise ends with an *encomium* on Christian prayer.

(19) *De Patientia* (200-203). Here Tertullian commends the virtue of patience to catechumens, conscious of not possessing it himself, but acting like a sick man praising health.

(20) *De Paenitentia* (203). This tract throws important light on the administration of penance in the early Church. It describes a form of penance exacted of adult catechumens before baptism (4-6) and the 'canonical penance' demanded from the baptized who had been guilty of the serious sins (murder, idolatry, adultery; 7-12). No one could receive this latter penance more than once.

(21) *De Cultu Feminarum* (c. 200). In two (independent) books, he urged modesty in apparel. Ornaments and cosmetics come from the devil. Love of dress (*cultus*) arises from ambition, love of make-up (*ornatus*) from prostitution.

(22) *Ad Uxorem* (c. 203). In these two books, addressed to his wife ('my best-beloved fellow-servant in the Lord'), he dealt with the issue of second marriages. Though in this, his Catholic period, he was prepared to tolerate second marriages, provided the new husband was a Christian, he recommended against them; and urged his wife, should he die first, to remain a widow.

(23) *De Exhortatione Castitatis* (c. 206). Here [contrast (22)], he strongly opposed second marriages as 'a form of adultery'.

(24) *De Monogamia* (c. 217). He reasserts this view of remarriage, finding its theological basis in Monotheism.[2]

[1] E. Evans, op. cit., p. xiif.
[2] Unum matrimonium novimus sicut unum Deum, c. 1.

(25) *De Virginibus Velandis* (before his lapse to Montanism, i.e. before 207). All virgins must always be veiled in public and not only when in church.

(26) *De Corona* (211). Tertullian here commends a soldier for refusing to wear the soldier's crown on the ground that the emblem was essentially pagan. He went on to maintain that service in the army as such was incompatible with profession of the Christian faith. The treatise belongs to his early Montanist period and contains his first attack on the Catholic clergy.[1]

(27) *De Idolalatria* (date uncertain; perhaps *c.* 212). A fierce attack on idolatry and all secular avocations which might be held to countenance it.

(28) *De Fuga in Persecutione* (*c.* 212). Persecution is Divinely ordained; therefore to take flight when it comes is directly to resist the will of God.

(29) *De Ieiunio adversus Psychicos* (date uncertain). A defence against the 'Psychics' (i.e. the Catholics) of Montanist practice in the matter of fasting.

(30) *De Pudicitia* (217-222). Over against his earlier view in *De Paenitentia* [20, above] Tertullian here denies that the 'Church of the Bishops' has the power to forgive sinners. He refers ironically to a peremptory decree to the contrary (*edictum . . . et quidem peremptorium*) of the Chief Pontiff who is the Bishop of Bishops (*Pontifex . . . Maximus, quod est episcopus episcoporum*). It is generally held that the Pontiff described in these terms can only be the Bishop of Rome and, if so, Pope Callistus (217-222). Tertullian now distinguishes between *peccata remissibilia* and *peccata irremissibilia*; for serious sins such as adultery and fornication there can now be no forgiveness.

(31) *De Pallio* (*c.* 210). He defends the practice of wearing the philosopher's pallium in place of the *toga*, the cloak of the Roman citizen.

[1] Novi et pastores eorum in pace leones, in proelio cervos, ch. 1.

MINUCIUS FELIX

[Crit. edd. of text by C. Halm (C.S.E.L., 1867) and J. P. Waltzing (Louvain, 1903; ed. Teubn. Liepzig, 1926); other edd., also trr., listed O.D.C.C., p. 905. P. Monceaux, *Histoire littéraire de l'Afrique Chrétienne* i (1901), pp. 463-508.]

The attractive little treatise of Minucius Felix known as the *Octavius*, which survives in a single 9th-century MS. in the Bibliothèque Nationale,[1] takes the form of a dialogue between Caecilius, a pagan, and Octavius, a Christian. Minucius Felix, the author, appears in the capacity of judge as a third speaker, but he fills only a subordinate part. The main speakers, lawyers by profession, defend their positions with ease and grace. The reader's interest is sustained through the fact that the speakers, who are fully conversant with Roman mythology, introduce an abundance of allusions to pagan (esp. Roman) classical mythology and history. If there is an absence of specifically Christian material, this may be explained by the conventions of the Dialogue and need not imply an inadequate grasp of the faith by the writer.

Little is known about the author. It used to be generally thought that he was a native of Rome, but there is good reason to suppose, with a number of recent scholars, that he belonged to Africa. Many points of affinity between the *Octavius* and Tertullian's *Apology* and Cyprian's *Quod Idola Dii non sunt* would support this view. Indeed its affinities and literary connexions with Tertullian's *Apology*, however they are to be explained, would seem to require some definite inter-dependence. But on which side does the dependence lie? Here it is not possible to be sure. Already within a few generations of Minucius' death opinion seems to have been divided. Lactantius apparently regarded Minucius as the elder, whereas Jerome definitely regarded him as the borrower from Tertullian. In 1868 A. Ebert argued for the priority

[1] Formerly in the Vatican, it was presented by Leo X to Francis I, whence it found its way into the Bibliothèque Royale. It now bears the shelfmark Bibl. Nat. lat. 1661. It is at the end of the codex containing the text of Arnobius. There is a 16th-century copy of the MS. at Brussels.

of Minucius and he was followed by a long series of critics. But scholars are now tending to revert to a later date. In its support are the facts (1) that Jerome is a far more reliable authority than Lactantius on literary questions; (2) that Christians seem free from persecution, which would fit well the period 202-249; and (3) various literary allusions which occur in both writings.[1] If, indeed, the Caecilius of the *Octavius* is to be identified with the Marcus Caecilius who erected a triumphal arch at Cirta (Constantine) to the honour of Caracalla (211-217) as proposed by H. Dessau,[2] the question would be settled. But this identification is very precarious. In any case the citation of the *Octavius* by Lactantius proves that it cannot be later than the 3rd century.

The *Octavius* is in the form of a dialectical contest which takes place at Ostia between Cecilius Natalis, a pagan, and Octavius, a Christian, with Minucius Felix, also a Christian, as the umpire. On neither side are the arguments of any profundity. Cecilius, who opens the dispute, upholds the religious and philosophical scepticism prevalent in the cultured world of his time. He reproaches the Christians for their dogmatism on such subjects as the nature of God, Creation, Providence, the resurrection of the body and the next life, matters (he urges) on which the proper attitude is one of ignorance. He also upbraids their nonconformity in matters of worship. No man can do better than follow the traditional cult to which the Roman Empire owes its greatness. A religious sect which is recruited from the lowest orders of society and teaches errors deserve only scorn. As everything is uncertain, it is best to keep the ancient beliefs.

Octavius then deals with these objections. After defending the propriety of subjecting such matters to intellectual examination, he upholds the unity of God and the Divine providence. He next criticises pagan idolatry. It is quite mistaken to attribute to it the power of the Roman Empire.

[1] This evidence, however, is strangely at conflict in different passages.
[2] H. Dessau, 'Minucius Felix und Cäcilius Natalis' in *Hermes* xl (1905), pp. 373-86.

If the oracles from time to time forecast correctly, this is accidental and proves nothing. Divination is full of error. The worship of the Christians on the other hand is pure and their doctrine sublime. Moreover, pagans have no right to scoff at Christian teachings about the last things. The germ of the doctrine of the resurrection of the body is to be found in their own philosophers, Pythagoras and Plato, and the idea of future retribution exists in the classical poets. The Christian ideal of life is incomparably superior to that of the pagans. It is we 'who do not show wisdom in our dress but in our hearts, who do not proclaim great things but live them, who are proud of having obtained what philosophers have sought in their utmost efforts but failed to find' (xxxviii. 6).

At all this Cecilius admits his certain defeat without waiting for the umpire to give his verdict. 'After this we retired, all three joyful and happy: Cecilius because he believed, Octavius because he was victorious, and I because of the conversion of the one and the victory of the other' (xl. 6).

CYPRIAN

[Text ed. by J. Fell-J. Pearson (1682) and S. Baluze-P. Maran (1726). Crit. ed. by W. Hartel (C.S.E.L., 1868-9). Life by E. W. Benson (1897). Further bibl. in *O.D.C.C.* p. 364.]

Cyprian, like Tertullian, was converted to Christianity when he was already in middle life and filled an important public position. Born *c.* 200-210, probably at Carthage, where he became a teacher of rhetoric, he was won to the Christian faith by a presbyter Caecilian in 246. Two years later he was ordained presbyter and soon afterwards (248), at the insistence of the laity but not without some resistance on the part of the clergy, who doubtless resented the rapid promotion of such a recent convert, became Bishop of Carthage.

Early in 250 the life of the Church throughout the Empire was suddenly thrown into turmoil. Decius, who was eager for a return to the ancient religion of Rome and saw in Christianity the chief hindrance to its restoration, instituted a persecution of the Church on a scale hitherto undreamt of.

He sought to deprive the Church of its leaders and by making apostates by bribery and deceit, to destroy its *morale*. Fabian, Bishop of Rome, was put to death in January 250, and Decius achieved a wide measure of success. Innumerable Christians lapsed, either by complying with the demand for sacrifice or, more often, without actually sacrificing, by procuring a false certificate of compliance and thus compromising their position. The result was chaos. With the principles of ecclesiastical discipline still in the making, complete confusion reigned as long as the persecution raged. What treatment was to be meted out to those who lapsed from the faith? And who was to administer discipline? Though authority was commonly held to reside in the clergy, and above all in the Bishops, there were others who believed that those who had suffered persecution thereby secured a unique status and special prerogatives in the Church.

On the outbreak of the persecution early in 250, Cyprian withdrew from Carthage and administered the affairs of the Church from a hide-out. When the persecution ceased in the spring of 251 he returned to his see to find himself faced with a host of problems. In the matter of the lapsed there were advocates of rigorism and of laxity, and Cyprian found himself confronted with much opposition. Malcontents among the clergy, doubtless especially those who had never wanted him to be Bishop, charged him with over-leniency and over-severity in turn and a schismatic party formed under Novatian.[1] In this situation, Cyprian's administrative abilities were of great service to the Church. He favoured the settlement of the points in dispute by synodical action and thus won for synods the status which led them to play such an important part in the later history of the Church in Africa.

In the next years Cyprian was faced by many practical problems arising out of the serious plague which ravaged the Empire (252-254). His later years were troubled by controversy over the question of how far heretical Baptism was valid. In this matter Cyprian upheld the traditional

[1] On Novatian and his schism, cf. below, pp. 181-3.

African position requiring rebaptism against Pope Stephen.

When in 257 persecution broke out again under Valerian, Cyprian was sent into exile to Curubis. In the next year he was brought back to Carthage and put to death on 14 September 258 in the gardens of the proconsular Villa Sexti, outside the city. He was the first Bishop in Africa to gain the crown of martyrdom. The vivid account of his trial and death in the 'Acta Proconsularia' is almost certainly genuine.[1]

Cyprian was a born administrator, always ready to take a broad practical view of affairs. Once he had made up his mind, he was never hampered by intellectual hesitations. He generally favoured moderation. In dealing with the lapsed, he sought to steer a middle course between the rigorism of Novatian and the over-leniency of Felicissimus. As we shall see, he often applied his mind to the same moral problems as Tertullian had done. But he was as far in advance of Tertullian in his judgement as he fell behind him in brilliance.

Cyprian's natural bent towards administration rather than theology is reflected in the large place which his correspondence occupies in his remains. All his writings enjoyed great popularity. Over a century later Augustine found it necessary to insist that despite the unique regard which he had for the great African bishop, his works were not to be regarded as Scripture.[2] What is virtually a contemporary list of them is to be found in Cyprian's *Life*, written by his deacon, Pontius, in the year after his death.[3] Another very early list is the so-called Cheltenham List, first published by T. Mommsen, where they are appended to a list of the Scriptural books.[4]

Cyprian's individual writings were:

(1) *Ad Donatum* (246). The earliest of his writings, it is written in a cumbersome style. It is an apology for Christianity

---

[1] Cf. below, p. 197.

[2] Contra Cresconium, 2. 31. 39; cf. Ep. 93 ad Vincentium, 10. 35.

[3] On this life, cf. A. Harnack, *Das Leben Cyprians von Pontius. Die erste christliche Biographie* (T.U. 39.3, 1913).

[4] On this, cf. W. Sanday, 'The Cheltenham List of the Canonical Books of the New Testament and of the Writings of Cyprian' in *Studia Biblica et Ecclesiastica* iii (1891), pp. 217-325.

addressed to his friend Donatus. Cyprian elaborates the
benefits conferred by Christianity and stresses its superior
morals to those of the pagan world. He wrote it shortly after
his Baptism.

(2) *De Habitu Virginum* (*c.* 248), addressed in the first place
to consecrated virgins. It was before the time of religious
communities for women, when those who took vows continued to live in their own homes. Cyprian extols the virgin
state. He insists that those who pledged themselves to it
must dress plainly, avoid cosmetics, use their possessions for
the support of the poor, and avoid wedding parties and the
baths. The treatise was largely dependent on Tertullian's
De Cultu Feminarum.

(3) *De Lapsis* (early 251). This was a pastoral letter to the
Church of Carthage when the persecution was over. It states
the principles on which those who had lapsed should be
treated. Cyprian sought to avoid the opposing excesses of
laxity and severity. All who had fallen must submit to
penance of some kind. Cyprian distinguished between those
who had succumbed under torture and those who had
renounced their faith without resistance. He stressed the
caution needed in readmitting apostates to communion.
Apostasy was a very grave offence and those who had fallen
should remember that nothing is hidden from the eyes of
God. The treatise was read at the Council which met at
Carthage in the spring of 251 and set out in substance the
principles followed by Cyprian in the ensuing controversy.

(4) *De Catholica Ecclesiae Unitate* (251). This, the most
celebrated of Cyprian's treatises, has generally been supposed
to have been composed shortly before the Council held about
Easter 251 in view of the threat of schism in the Church; but
recently Fr. M. Bévenot, S.J., and others have put it slightly
later, after the Novatianist schism had actually begun.
Cyprian insists that the Church of Christ must be one, and
that schisms and heresies are the work of the devil. The unity

of the Church follows from the unity of its foundation, namely St. Peter, and this has been in no way impaired by the gradual extension of the Church over the world. From one sun there come many rays, from one spring many brooks, from one trunk many branches. 'No doubt the other Apostles were all that Peter was, endowed with equal dignity and power, but the start comes from him alone, in order to show that the Church of Christ is one' (ch. 4). To be in this one Church is the only hope of salvation. 'He cannot have God for his Father who has not the Church for his Mother' (ch. 6). The unity of the Church is symbolised by the seamless robe of Christ and that no salvation is possible outside it by the house of Rahab the harlot. In the latter part of the treatise Cyprian pleads that the faithful will preserve charity and remain in the unity of Christ.

Special interest attaches to the fourth chapter of this treatise which exists in two recensions. In one of these (the so-called 'Primacy' text, because it contains the words *primatus Petro datur*) Peter occupies a more prominent position than in the other. Until recently it was widely held that the 'Primacy recension' was the work of a later scribe who interpolated Cyprian in the interests of the Papal position. But in recent years, largely through the researches of Dom John Chapman and Fr. Maurice Bévenot,[1] there has come a growing consensus of opinion that both forms of the text go back to Cyprian. According to Fr. Bévenot, who has made a thorough study of the manuscript tradition, the 'Primacy text' is original, being the form in which the treatise was sent to Rome, in which form it was aimed especially at Novatian, the intruded Bishop of Rome, while the other text was modified for circulation in Africa where Cyprian was confronted with the excessive claims for Stephen in the matter of heretical Baptism.

(5) *De Dominica Oratione* (251-252). This treatise is an

[1] *St. Cyprian: The Lapsed, the Unity of the Catholic Church* (A.C.W., xxv, 1957).

exposition of the Lord's Prayer, again largely dependent on
Tertullian. After extolling its great merits Cyprian comments
on its individual clauses. The 'daily bread' (*panis cottidianus*)
is Christ in the Eucharist, 'the bread of those who are in
union with His Body'. He concludes with some general re-
flexions on the Lord's Prayer as a whole, and on prayer in
general. He characteristically emphasises the need of uniting
prayer with fasting and almsgiving.

(6) *Ad Demetrianum* (252). A strong attack on Demetrianus,
an unknown pagan, who had ascribed the misfortunes of the
times to the Christian abandonment of the pagan gods.
Cyprian replied that on the contrary they were God's punishment for the unbelief and the vices of the pagan world, and
especially the persecution of the Christians. The pagan gods
were no gods, but only demons.

(7) *De Mortalitate* (252-253). A pastoral letter to console
those suffering from the plague then raging in Africa. Many
believers were perplexed when they saw its relentless toll of
Christians and non-Christians alike. The Christian, Cyprian
insists, should regard death not as an object of fear, but as a
reward. He should look forward with joy to his true destiny
in Paradise.

(8) *De Opere et Eleemosynis* (252-253). Here Cyprian stresses
the meritorious character of good works and almsgiving.
They are a divinely appointed means of cancelling sins, and
hence a complement of Baptism. No almsgiver should fear
that he will be impoverished. Rather he performs deeds
which are highly agreeable in the eyes of God.

(9) *De Bono Patientiae* (256). This work dates from the
period of the Baptismal Controversy. Cyprian shows, with
arguments drawn from Tertullian, the difference between the
true patience of the Christians and that inculcated by the
philosophers. Our supreme example of patience is to be found
in God and Christ.

(10) *De Zelo et Livore* (256-257). This treatise was occasioned by the rancours that arose out of the Baptismal controversy. Cyprian here uses Biblical examples and texts to show the evils of jealousy and envy.

(11) *Ad Fortunatum de Exhortatione Martyrii* (257). A treatise written to encourage Fortunatus to stedfastness in the face of the Valerianic persecution. This Cyprian will do, he tells Fortunatus, not by writing a treatise of his own, but by bringing together Biblical texts and illustrations on the subject.

(12) *Ad Quirinum* (Testimoniorum libri III). This work contains collections of Biblical texts. Books I and II (248) are directed against the Jews. In Book I under twenty-four headings he shews the errors of the Jews; in Book II, under thirty headings, the Godhead and mission of Christ. In Book III, which was added later, he demonstrates under 120 headings the moral duties of the Christian. The work is of great value to the student of the Latin Bible. It shews that Cyprian used the Gospels in a text which was almost identical with that contained in the MS. k (formerly at Bobbio, now at Turin).

(13) *Quod Idola Dei non sunt* (*c.* 246). This work, which draws extensively on Minucius Felix and Tertullian, is of doubtful authenticity as it is not found in the catalogues of Pontius or Mommsen. It first refutes polytheism; then demonstrates the unity of God; and finally treats of Christ.

A large collection of Cyprian's letters has also survived. They deal with the same practical and theological matters as his treatises. With his administrative efficiency, he carefully preserved copies of his correspondence and these appear to have been the ultimate source of the letters which have come down to us. They are important for the history of his age, and they add many details not found in Cyprian's treatises though they do not modify, or substantially add to, what can be deduced about Cyprian and his theology from the study of his writings.

X.—HIPPOLYTUS AND THE CHURCH OF ROME

HIPPOLYTUS

[First collected ed. by J. A. Fabricius (2 vols., Hamburg, 1716-18; repr., with additions, in J. P. Migne, *P.G.* x 261-962). For works which have come to light more recently, see under individual items. Crit. texts ed. by H. Achelis, G. Bonwetsch, and others in G.C.S. (1897ff.). Many of Hippolytus' writings in Eng. tr. in *A.N.C.L.* (vols. vi and ix, p. 2); Eng. tr. of the *Philosophumena* by F. Legge (2 vols., London, 1921). The best critical study of his theology is A. D'Alès, S.J., *La Théologie de Saint Hippolyte* (1906). A. Hamel, *Kirche bei Hippolyt von Rom* (1951). There are also several notable items on Hippolytus in T.U., esp. in the period 1889-97. The recent work of J. M. Hanssens. S.J., *La Liturgie d'Hippolyte*, Ses Documents, Son Titulaire, Ses Origines et Son Caractère (Rome, 1959), is of the first importance on all questions relating to Hippolytus. For further bibl. see *O.D.C.C.*, p. 642.]

The first member of the Roman Church who can be said to stand out as a distinct personality (if we exclude such 'foreigners' as Justin and Marcion) is Hippolytus. Yet, by a strange irony, it is because we know so much more about Hippolytus than about any other of his Roman predecessors or contemporaries that we are made aware of our ignorance of him and the Church to which he belonged. There can be little doubt that Hippolytus was also an enigma to his own generation. Not the least remarkable and unexpected fact about him is that, though he was excommunicated from the orthodox Rome community and became the first of the Anti-Popes, only a generation or two later he was held in high veneration and reckoned as a saint.

After his death the facts of his life were quickly forgotten. In the next century neither Eusebius nor Jerome could name the see over which he presided. On a monument which Pope Damasus (d. 384) put up in Hippolytus' memory, he is represented as once a disciple of the schismatic Novatian in his earlier days, a view which receives no support from other

sources and is intrinsically improbable, as Novatian did not
appear on the scene until several years after Hippolytus'
death. Prudentius (d. *c.* 410) is so ignorant of Hippolytus that
in a poem in his praise he confounds him with the Hippolytus
of Greek mythology. Still later writers, wishing to provide
him with a see, asserted that he became Bishop of Porto.

Modern interest in Hippolytus dates from 1551 when a
headless statue of the Bishop was recovered just outside Rome
during excavations on the Via Tiburtina.[1] It represents the
Bishop seated on a chair,—that is, in the position of a
teacher,—with a calendar of the dates of Easter inscribed on
the two sides of the base of his chair and a list of his writings
on the left hand curved portion of the basis. The statue is
contemporary and perhaps was constructed in Hippolytus'
lifetime. It bears witness at any rate to the high repute in
which Hippolytus must have been held in Rome.

From then on interest in Hippolytus has progressively
increased. Portions of his literary remains gradually came to
light and in 1716-18 J. A. Fabricius issued a collected edition
of his known writings. But it was not until the middle of the
19th century that Hippolytus began to emerge as a definite
personality from the pages of the ninth book of his *Philosophumena*. In 1842 there was found on Mount Athos a
manuscript of what proved to be the most important chapters
of this work. The manuscript did not reveal the name of its
author, and when it was first printed at Oxford in 1851,
E. Miller, the editor, issued it under the name of Origen. But
it soon became clear that this attribution was mistaken.
Several scholars, of whom the most distinguished was J. J. I.
von Döllinger, recognised it as a lost work of Hippolytus and
before long this ascription was generally accepted. It threw

---

[1] As Professor J. M. Hanssens points out, the facts concerning the
recovery of the statue are less accurately known than is commonly
supposed. Until recently, the statue was preserved in the Lateran
Museum. In 1959 it was removed to the entrance hall of the Vatican
Library, where the imposing figure, who is circumspectly described (if
my memory can be trusted) as *vir ecclesiasticus doctissimus*, welcomes
all readers on arrival.

a quite unexpected light on the history of the Church at Rome in the early 3rd century.

A further stage was reached in 1897 when the Berlin Academy of Sciences began its edition of Hippolytus' writings. It now became possible to read the scattered and poorly transmitted works of Hippolytus in a critical text. In the present century a quite unexpected discovery was made. In 1916 R. H. Connolly[1] established to the satisfaction of most subsequent scholars that the liturgical and canonical document hitherto known as 'the Egyptian Church Order' and believed to be of the 5th century was the work of none other than Hippolytus of Rome. In this way Hippolytus suddenly came into prominence as the author of the most important liturgical monument of pre-Nicene times. Shortly after the conclusion of the Second World War a daring attempt was made by Dr. P. Nautin to dislodge Hippolytus from the high position he had come to hold by challenging his authorship of the *Philosophumena*. But this thesis, so brilliantly expounded in *Hippolyt et Josippe* (1947),[2] has made few converts. More recently still, the Alexandrian connexions of

---

[1] As already stated above. Cf. pp. 95f.

[2] Nautin's main thesis in *Hippolyt et Josippe* was that many of the writings currently ascribed to Hippolytus really belong to a slightly later writer, Josippus ('Joseph'). He argued that certain discrepancies between the *Philosophumena* and the fragment *Contra Noetum* precluded common authorship. The *Contra Noetum* is certainly the work of Hippolytus; hence the author of the *Philosophumena*, and also the subject of the Lateran statue, is Josippus. To Josippus we also owe the *De Universo* and the Chronicle. Nautin, however, has hardly established his case. Though his brilliant and provocative pages have elicited some valuable and miscellaneous researches into the whole question of Hippolytus' literary remains, the careful scrutiny to which they have recently been subjected has only established their traditional authorship on a firmer basis. Among the recent items bearing on the question is a series of articles by M. Richard in the *Mélanges de Science Religieuse* v (1948), pp. 294-308; vii (1950), pp. 237-68; viii (1951), pp. 19-50; x (1953), pp. 13-52, 145-80; G. Bardy, 'L'Énigme d'Hippolyte' in the same periodical v (1948), pp. 63-88; an important study of B. Capelle, O.S.B., 'Hippolyte de Rome' in *Recherches de Théologie Ancienne et Médiévale* xvii (1950), pp. 145-74, in which on linguistic and other grounds the unity of authorship between the two groups of Hippolytus' writings is shewn to demonstration; cf. also id. xix (1952), pp. 193-202; Dom B. Botte, in *idem*, xvi (1949), pp. 177-85 and xviii (1951), pp. 5-18;

Hippolytus have been upheld by Dr. J. M. Hanssens, S.J., in his *La Liturgie d'Hippolyte* (1959).

What, in the light of all these remarkable discoveries can we be said to know of Hippolytus? It has been conjectured that, if not himself born in the East, he belonged to one of the many groups of Oriental Christians then settled at Rome. A reference in the *Philosophumena* to Pope Victor (*c.* 189-198; he is the 'Blessed Victor') may indicate he had close relations with him; and if so we may perhaps conjecture from his chronological interests that as a young man he helped Victor to construct an Easter calendar which would make the Roman Church independent of the Jews. By 212, when Origen made his visit to Rome, he must have become a figure of considerable repute in the Roman Church, for Origen records that he sat at Hippolytus' feet. We learn from the *Philosophumena* that his middle years were taken up with a bitter dispute with Victor's successor, Zephyrinus (198-217), and Zephyrinus' right-hand man and (later) successor, Callistus (217-222). The conflict seems to have been a struggle between the conservatives and the moderns. The rapid expansion of the Church of Rome and the large flow of new converts was raising the question whether the traditional standards of discipline should be relaxed. The older practice had been to exclude those who had fallen into serious sin for ever[1] from ecclesiastical communion, however great their repentance. Zephyrinus and Callistus were eager to abandon the old rigidity and allowed those who had been guilty of adultery and other serious sins, after suitable penance, to receive the Church's absolution. Hippolytus, a strong conservative, was shocked at such laxity (as he thought it). Moreover, Hippolytus had other reasons for distrusting Zephyrinus. He could not accept the teaching on the Trinity propagated by Zephyrinus and his party. To Hippo-

and a review by J. Daniélou in *Recherches de Science Religieuse* xxxv (1948), pp. 596-8. The stylistic differences between the *Contra Noetum* and the *Philosophumena* are sufficiently explained by the long interval between them.

[1] At any rate after a single reconciliation.

lytus their moderate sympathy with Noetus, who laid great stress on the unity of the Godhead, seemed only veiled Sabellianism. These animosities, resting on moral and theological grounds, gave Hippolytus his opportunity. He proceeded to attack Zephyrinus and Callistus in unmeasured terms. He brought to light incidents in Callistus' murky past which shewed him to be a complete scoundrel and a thief who on account of some discreditable financial dealings had been sentenced in the criminal court and exiled to Sardinia. When Zephyrinus died in 217, Hippolytus and his community refused to recognise Callistus, and a schism resulted with Hippolytus as a rival Bishop of Rome.

In this, the first recorded schism in the Roman Church, Hippolytus continued to govern his community under the pontificates of Urban (222-230) and Pontian (230-235). A new situation arose in 235 when persecution broke out under Maximinus Thrax. Hippolytus and Pontian were both exiled to Sardinia, where they both died shortly afterwards from the rigours of convict life. The bodies of the two exiled Bishops were brought back in honour to Rome on 13 August 236 or 237, that of Pontian being laid to rest in the Cemetery of Callistus and that of Hippolytus on the Tiburtine Way. Meanwhile, the two communities had united on a successor and honours were accordingly given to both. Hence the dispute was forgotten and both Pope and Anti-Pope were recognised as saints and have retained their place in the Roman Calendar.[1]

Hippolytus was the most prolific writer of the Church of Rome in pre-Nicene times. Indeed the extent of his surviving writings, though many of them are only fragments, is larger than that of all the other Roman writers of the first 300 years put together. His range of learning was comparable with that of Origen. He had a wide knowledge of the Bible, especially the Old Testament, on which his speculations were largely nourished. He was also keenly interested in the chronological

[1] In the *Depositio Martyrum* of 354, the oldest list of martyrs, we find the entry 'Idus Aug. Ypoliti in Tiburtina et Pontiani in Callisti'.

aspects of sacred history, and had considerable arithmetical competence; he was also curious about the speculations of the Greeks on the origin of the universe and matters of mythology. On the other hand he seldom mastered his subjects. His learning overburdened him and he fell far behind Origen in philosophical ability or spiritual understanding.

Hippolytus' writings may be grouped as follows: (1) Exegetical; (2) Theological; (3) Anti-Heretical; (4) Chronographical; (5) Philosophical; (6) Homiletical. To these must now be added (7) The *Apostolic Tradition* which is discussed elsewhere.[1] Few of them have come down to us entire in their original form.

(1) The longest of Hippolytus' Biblical writings is his *Commentary on Daniel*. Much of the Greek is recoverable from catena fragments, while the entire text is preserved in a Slavonic version. It dates from *c.* 204 and is the oldest Christian commentary on any Biblical book to survive.

Hippolytus rests his interpretation throughout on types.[2] The two elders who persecute the wife of Joachim foreshadow the Jews and the heathen, the two chief persecutors of the Church. Finding the four kingdoms in Dan. ii and vii symbolised in the Empires of Babylon, Persia, Greece and Rome, Hippolytus discovers the Antichrist in the little horn of the fourth animal. In places the text has suffered from interpolation, e.g. the passage where Christ's birthday is given as 25 December, a date for 'Christmas' which is almost certainly not earlier than the fourth century.[3]

Another of Hippolytus' Biblical writings to survive is his *Exposition on the Song of Songs*. It is a collection of homilies rather than a commentary. Until this century only fragments

---

[1] Among writings occasionally ascribed, probably incorrectly, to Hippolytus, are the *Muratorian Fragment on the Canon* and *Ad Diognetum* 11 and 12. On these, cf. above, pp. 68-70, 27f.

[2] The Biblical text used of Daniel (which includes the story of Susanna and the Hymn of the Three Children) is that of Theodotion.

[3] G. N. Bonwetsch, 'Die Datierung der Geburt Christi in den Danielkommentar Hippolyts' in N.G.W.G. Phil. hist. Kl. (1895), pp. 515-27.

were known, but in 1901 N. Marr published a continuous (Georgian) text. The point where the text breaks off, at Can. iii. 7, is probably where Hippolytus himself ended his commentary, as no fragment from any later point of the Biblical text is extant. Here for the first time the love *motif* of the Song of Songs is interpreted as the love between God and the Church, His mystical bride, or alternatively (and here Hippolytus is not entirely consistent) as the love between God and the individual soul. It was an interpretation destined to have an immense influence among later exegetes and spiritual writers from Origen onwards.

Otherwise little survives of Hippolytus' many writings on the Old and New Testaments. A work on the *Blessing of Jacob* (Gen. xlix) is extant in Greek and also in Armenian and Georgian. Another on the *Blessing of Moses* (Deut. xxxiii) is complete only in Armenian and Georgian. Fragments of a work *On the Psalms* have also come down to us.

(2) The only work on a theological theme by Hippolytus which survives is his treatise *On the Antichrist*. With the Scriptures as his basis, he expounds the manner of Antichrist's coming,—when he will be revealed, whence and from what tribe he will come, how his name is indicated in Scripture by the number 666 (Rev. xii. 18), his mode of working error and stirring up tribulation against the saints, how he will glorify himself as God and meet his end, the sudden revelation of the Lord from heaven, the conflagration of the world, the heavenly reign of the saints with Christ and the punishment of the wicked by fire (ch. 5). The treatise, which dates from *c*. 200, is probably Hippolytus' earliest writing. It was written to allay the fears by which many Christian hearts were filled at a time when the threatening persecution of Septimius Severus was widely held to prelude the end of the world. Hippolytus bade his readers take comfort from the Scriptures where they would learn that the Antichrist would not appear before the dissolution of the Roman Empire. The

work is the most extended discussion of the Antichrist to be found in early Christian literature.

(3) Of Hippolytus' writings on the history of doctrine, the most extensive is the *Philosophumena*, already mentioned. Its bitter and harsh attacks on his contemporary, Callistus, so uncalled for and out of place in a work of which the ostensible object was to be a universal handbook against heresies, almost forces us to conclude that the whole work was conceived with this piece of invective in view. There are several signs in the work that it comes from an ageing and embittered man, and in any case it is later than Callistus' death (222). It may perhaps be dated *c.* 230.

The *Philosophumena*, as it has survived in the Mount Athos MS., appears to be nearly complete.[1] Its plan is to prove that the heresies which have prevailed in Christendom from the outset are in substance only a number of rehashes of the teachings of the various Greek philosophies. So in Book I we have an outline history of Greek philosophy, based mainly on (often unreliable) Hellenistic sources. Books II to IV treat of astronomy, magic, and other ancient superstitions. In Book V Hippolytus reaches his main theme, the direct refutation of false forms of Christian teaching. Hippolytus' limitations as a writer become very apparent. His treatment is desultory, his style cumbrous and devoid of literary merit, while his attempts to connect each of the Christian heresies with a particular Greek philosopher are superficial and forced. Moreover, he lacks historical sense and his descriptions of the heresies do not inspire confidence. He can be relied on only in so far as he reproduces the earlier heresiologists correctly. Perhaps he had most of his own to contribute in the case of the Valentinians. Though he took Irenaeus as his main source, he says that, in view of

---

[1] This was argued by A. d'Alès, S.J., *La Théologie de St. Hippolyte* (1906), pp. 80ff., against earlier writers. D'Alès held that what Miller printed as Book IV was in fact Books II to IV and thus linked on to Book I, which had long been known, and had been regularly printed, under the name of Origen.

the allegations of Mark, the Gnostic, that Irenaeus had
misrepresented Valentinus, he had himself made an independent investigation of the subject and established the accuracy
of Irenaeus' statement.[1] But in general he is less successful. His
account of Basilides diverges widely from that found in other
authorities; and it seems more probable that these differences
are due to Hippolytus' use of poor sources or mishandling of
reliable ones rather than to any trustworthy information.

We learn from the preface to the *Philosophumena*, as well
as from the list of Hippolytus' writings in Eusebius and
Jerome, that he also wrote another, but shorter, anti-
heretical work known as the *Syntagma*. Photius, to whom the
work was still available, describes it as a small book directed
against thirty-two heresies, beginning with the Dositheans.
R. A. Lipsius, who has been followed by most subsequent
scholars, held that though the *Syntagma* is now lost it formed
the basis of three later anti-heretical works, viz. the Pseudo-
Tertullianic *Libellus adversus Omnes Haereses*,[2] Epiphanius'
Panarion and Filaster of Brescia's *Liber de Haeresibus*. If
this contention is correct, it was through this writing, and
not his *Philosophumena*, that Hippolytus was to exert such
a very great influence on the later heresiologists.[3] From these
later derivatives the substance of the *Syntagma* can be reconstructed. It is probably to be dated in the earlier part of
Zephyrinus' pontificate, say *c.* 205.

A fragment of another anti-heretical writing from the pen
of Hippolytus goes under the name of the *Contra Noetum*.
It is preserved in Cod. Vat. gr. 1431. It is described in its
title as a Homily, but this view, though defended by E.
Schwartz,[4] has been generally rejected. As the work makes

[1] *Philosophumena* VI, 40-56, esp. 43.

[2] Cf. above p. 140.

[3] E. Schwartz (*Zwei Predigten Hippolyts*, p. 37) describes Lipsius'
contention as a 'shadow without substance' (*ein Schatten ohne Inhalt*).
He thinks that the *Syntagma* was written in Greek by Zephyrinus or
one of his clerics and translated into Latin by Victorinus of Pettau
(cf. p. 187). But his arguments do not convince.

[4] *Zwei Predigten Hippolyts*, in Sb (Bayr,), 1936, Heft 3. This view
was held earlier by C. C. J. Bunsen, *Hippolytus*, Germ. tr. i, p. 182.

use of the *Philosophumena*[1] with which it appears to be closely connected, it must belong to the later years of Hippolytus' life. There are some grounds for thinking that it is a fragment of a work which also attacked other forms of Monarchianism, notably Artemas (or Artemon), and is to be identified with the work named by Theodoret 'The Little Labyrinth'[2] and attributed, probably correctly, to Hippolytus.[3]

(4) Hippolytus was keenly interested in chronological problems. His early attraction to the subject is reflected in his choice of *Daniel* as the subject of his commentary. Two of his later incursions into this field survive:

(i) Hippolytus' 'Chronicle' (χρονικῶν βιβλὸς) or 'Synagoge' (συναγωγὴ χρόνων) was a chronicle of world history extending from the Creation to the date of writing (234-235). Its purpose was to reassure those who were fearing a speedy end of the world that the end was not yet. He endeavours to prove by three different routes that at the time of writing only 5,738 years had elapsed since the Creation, whereas the Day of Judgement and the millennium were not to be expected until the year 6000. The Chronicle made use of that of Julius Africanus (221) and the chronological section of Clement of Alexandria's *Stromateis* (1. 109-36) but it had few chronographical merits and its calculations were subordinated to its apologetic purpose. A portion of the Greek survives in a Madrid MS. (No. 4701; 10th-11th century), and the whole in three independent Latin versions (the 'Excerpta Latina Barberi'; and the two 'Libri Generationis') and also in an Armenian translation.[4] T. Mommsen established that it was

[1] Nautin also admits this, despite his belief in difference of authorship. Cf. pp. 157f.

[2] *Haer. Fab. Comp.* ii. 5. This is in contrast to the title 'Labyrinth' *sans phrase* for the *Philosophumena*. cf. τὸν λαβύρινθον τῶν αἱρέσεων (*Philos.* x. 1 [5]).

[3] So R. H. Connolly, *J.T.S.*, xlix (1948), pp. 73-9.

[4] P. Nautin's contention that the chronological system of the 'Chronicle' differs from that of Hippolytus' Commentary on Daniel has been disposed of by M. Richard in his articles on 'Comput et Chronographie chez Saint Hippolyte' in *Mélanges de Science Religieuse* vii (1950), pp. 237-68, and viii (1951), pp. 19-50.

used in the form of the 'Liber Generationis II' by the famous 'Chronographer of 354'.

(ii) The 'Apodeixis Ton Chronon', mentioned on his statue. This work contained not only the Easter tables which were engraven on the sides of the statue, but also, it would seem, an account of the principles on which the tables were drawn up. The latter is now lost. The tables are based on a sixteen-year cycle, and record the dates of Easter from 222 to 233. Here we have the first known attempt to provide the Christian Church with a chronological system for determining the date of the Christian Pasch. It would have the gratifying result of making the Church independent of the Jews, and it was presumably hoped that it would be generally accepted through Roman influence. This table, and probably also the rest of the Apodeixis, would have been compiled at the first date, i.e. in 222 as in the comparable case of calendars at the beginning of the Book of Common Prayer. The table, in fact, must very soon have revealed its weaknesses. For it had oversimplified the astronomical conditions of the problem and in a few years its calculated date for Easter bore no relation to the 'Paschal moon'.

(5) It is probable that Hippolytus' work 'Against the Greeks', which is listed on the statue as $Πρὸς$ "$Ελληνας$ $καὶ$ $πρὸς$ $Πλάτωνα$ $ἤ$ $καὶ$ $περὶ$ $τοῦ$ $παντός$ and also mentioned at the end of the *Philosophumena* (x. 32) is to be identified with the work ascribed by Photius (Cod. 48) to 'Josephus', or on the basis of a marginal note in Photius MS. to 'Caius'. We learn from Photius that the work was in two books and that the author charged Plato with contradictions, attacked the false doctrines of the Platonist Alkinous (prob. Albinus) on the soul and the resurrection, and proved that the Jewish people were more ancient than the Greeks. An interesting passage from the work is preserved by John of Damascus in his *Sacra Parallela*, where the conditions of the souls of the righteous and of sinners in Hades as they await the final resurrection are described. But the work itself has been lost.

(6) What appears to be the substance, at least, of one of Hippolytus' sermons has recently been recovered.

From the 'Paschal Chronicle' (early 7th cent.) we learn that Hippolytus was the author of a treatise on the Pasch. This work was generally supposed to have been lost (apart from fragments) until Pére C. Martin[1] claimed in 1926 to have identified it among the spurious homilies ascribed to St. Chrysostom. He pointed to a number of parallels to Hippolytus' language and thought in the sermon; and his contention seemed to receive remarkable confirmation when ten years later he found a text of the homily expressly attributed to 'Hippolytus, the Bishop of Rome and martyr' in a Grottaferrata MS. (B.a.LV; 8th-9th cent.).[2] Subsequent study,[3] however, has shewn that the claim as originally stated will not stand. In its present form the sermon cannot be earlier than the 4th century, for it presupposes the Arian controversies. Moreover, its insistence on Christ's full humanity, combined with His 'angelic nature', is foreign to the thought of Hippolytus.

None the less the affinities of much of the sermon to Hippolytus are indisputable and there is every reason to believe, with Dr. P. Nautin, that it has a Hippolytean basis.[4]

The sermon describes the parallelism between the Passover of the Jews (the 'Pasch') and our Redemption in Christ. It draws out, stage by stage, the foreshadowing of the Passion of Christ in the events narrated in Exodus 12. The whole Exodus story was fulfilled in Christ, who is Himself

[1] C. Martin, S.J., 'Un περὶ τοῦ πάσχα de S. Hippolyte retrouvé?' in *Rech. S.R.* xvi (1926), pp. 148-65. It is the last of the six sermons among the spuria in P.G. 59. 735-46.

[2] C. Martin, S.J., 'Fragments palimpsestes d'un discours sur la Pâque attribué à saint Hippolyte de Rome (Crypt. B. a LV)' in *Annuaire de l'Institut de Philologie et d'Histoire orientales et slaves* vi (=*Melanges Franz Cumont*) (Brussels, 1936), pp. 324-30.

[3] R. H. Connolly in *J.T.S.* xlv (1944), pp. 192-200.

[4] According to Nautin, other writers who made use of the (genuine) Hippolytus on the Pasch are Gaudentius of Brescia (Hom. on the Exodus) and the author of the *Tractatus Origenis* (prob. Gregory of Elvira), Tract. ix.

the true Pasch. There are good reasons for thinking that it ultimately goes back to an early Christian Paschal Haggadah such as we find in Melito of Sardis.[1]

Hippolytus' remains show him to have been a polymath, possessed of encyclopaedic interests. He had an ardent and devoted following, but probably it was small. He doubtless appeared to the rapidly expanding and progressive Roman Church of the early 3rd century as a reactionary, so it is not surprising that his writings, over-burdened with ill-digested learning, compilatory rather than constructive, and the work of one who had mastery neither of his subject matter nor of his style, were allowed to drop into oblivion. The modern student, unless he has an uncommon tenacity of purpose, is not likely to succeed in reading Hippolytus in long stretches at a sitting. His writings are mainly useful for the purposes of reference. Nevertheless, posterity has reason to be grateful to Hippolytus for the considerable light which his writings, often fragmentary and scattered, throw on the obscure history of the pre-Nicene Church.

[1] Cf. above, pp. 104-9.

XI.—LATER GREEK WRITERS

In this chapter we return to the East and deal with a number of Greek writers of the 3rd century who do not easily lend themselves to classification by schools.

SEXTUS JULIUS AFRICANUS

[Collection of fragments by M. J. Routh, *Reliquiae Sacrae* (ed. 2, 1844), ii, pp. 238-309; repr. in J. P. Migne, *P.G.* x, 63-94. New ed. of Epp. by W. Reichardt in T.U., xxxiv. 3 (1909). H. Gelzer, *Sextus Julius Africanus und die byzantinische Chronographie* (2 vols., 1880-98). Further bibl. in *O.D.C.C.*, p. 755.]

Sextus Julius Africanus, despite his name, had no connexion with Africa. He was a native of Jerusalem who became a military officer under Septimius Severus. During a campaign in Osrhoene in 195 he made the acquaintance of the king of Edessa. Later he held an important administrative position at Emmaus in Palestine. While he was here a successful embassy to Heliogabalus (218-222) bore fruit in the rebuilding of the township and its renaming as Nicopolis. From Nicopolis he corresponded *c.* 240 with Origen, then resident at the neighbouring town of Caesarea, on the Scriptural authority of the additions to the Book of Daniel.[1] In another letter to a certain Aristides he dealt with the genealogies of Christ in the Gospels. He died probably not later than 250. Despite a later tradition (Dionysius bar-Salibi) to the contrary, it is unlikely that he was ever ordained priest.

Of his writings, the chief is his *Chronicle.* This work, the first known Christian 'History of the World', became the primary source of later Byzantine chronography, including

---

[1] Cf. above, pp. 133f.

the celebrated 'Chronicle' of Eusebius-Jerome. Only fragments survive. Its purpose was largely apologetic, viz. to shew the greater antiquity, and hence the superiority, of the Biblical history over that of the pagan world. The work, which began with the Creation, puts the birth of Christ 5,500 years later; Africanus reckoned that the world would end after a total period of 6,000 years, i.e. in A.D. 500. The date of composition is indicated by its latest date, i.e. the year from the Creation 5721 (A.D. 221).

Julius' other work, the 'Embroidered Girdles' (*Κεστοί*), which also survives only in fragments, is an encyclopaedic work on the sciences and the arts (war, medicine, agriculture, etc.) dedicated to Alexander Severus. Though Julius was a Christian when he wrote it, there is apparently nothing Christian about it.

DIONYSIUS OF ALEXANDRIA

[Fragments orig. collected by S. de Magistris (Rome, 1796). Crit. ed. by C. L. Feltoe (Cambr. Patr. Texts, 1904); Eng. tr. by id., London, 1918. Further bibl. in *O.D.C.C.*, p. 402, and in B. Altaner, *Patrologie* (1958), p. 187.]

After Origen's departure from Alexandria in 231, the most outstanding theologian in the city until Athanasius was Dionysius 'the Great'.[1] He was born probably of pagan parents, in the last years of the 2nd century. When Heraclas succeeded to the see of Alexandria on the death of Demetrius (231), Dionysius, already a presbyter, was appointed to the headship of the 'Catechetical School'. In 247, sixteen years later, Dionysius succeeded Heraclas to a troubled episcopate. In 248 serious persecution broke out against the Christians at Alexandria. In 249 when the Decian persecution raged, Alexandria suffered severely and Dionysius, whose life was in peril, fled and spent a considerable time in the Libyan desert. After his return, he took part in several important doctrinal and ecclesiastical controversies. He sought to

[1] He is already 'the Great' to Peter of Alexandria and Eusebius. Cf. C. L. Feltoe, op. cit., p. xi.

mediate in the heated dispute over heretical baptism between
Cyprian and Pope Stephen, advocating that each Church
should preserve its own customs and observe tolerance. In
the persecution under Valerian (257-258) he was brought
before the Prefect, Aemilianus, and again banished. On the
issue of the Rescript of Gallienus in 260 he returned to his see.
His last years were largely taken up with the troubles arising
out of Sabellianism. Ill health and advanced years made him
unable to take part in the Council which met at Antioch in
264-265 to deal with the question of Paul of Samosata.
Shortly afterwards, probably in 265, he died.

Though Dionysius wrote on a great variety of subjects, his
writings survive only in fragments, some of them, however,
of considerable length.

To his years at the 'Catechetical School' we must probably
assign a treatise 'On Nature' (περὶ φύσεως), several fragments
of which are preserved by Eusebius in his *Praeparatio
Evangelica*. It was a defence of the unity of the cosmos and
Divine providence against the doctrine of atoms, taught by
Democritus and Epicurus. Other writings which probably
belong to this period are his Book on Trials (ὁ περὶ πειρασμῶν)
and various exegetical works. None of these survives; but it
seems probable that passages from his Commentary on
Ecclesiastes were excerpted by later writers.

His letters, fragments of which are preserved by Eusebius,
are on a variety of subjects, among them the Novatianist
Schism and the lapsed, the rebaptism of heretics, and his
exile during the persecution. Special interest attaches to his
Easter Letters, as the earliest surviving Paschal Letters
(ἐπιστολαὶ ἑορταστικαί). In later times these Letters
became an important institution in Egyptian Church life.
The custom grew up of the Bishop issuing an encyclical every
year at the Epiphany season for circulation among his
suffragans, giving precise information as to the date of Easter
and commenting on practical matters. The fragments which
derive from Dionysius show that they had not yet become as
stereotyped as they became later. It is not certain that they

were as yet issued regularly every year nor that in a given year the Bishop sent the same letter to all his suffragans as was the later practice. But they are interesting testimony to the early history of the custom.

Of his theological writings the most important is his letter to Pope Dionysius of Rome (259-268) on the doctrine of the Godhead. The correspondence arose out of the discussions on the nature of the Godhead prompted by Sabellius. Dionysius of Alexandria was charged before his namesake at Rome with teaching subordinationist doctrines and a council which met at Rome in 262 issued a synodical letter rejecting the opposed views of both the Bishop of Alexandria and Sabellianism. Dionysius wrote to the Pope defending his position and then followed this letter on with a full justification in a work in four books which he entitled *Refutation and Defence* (βιβλία ἐλέγχου καὶ ἀπολογίας). The correspondence shews that the Bishop of Alexandria, in his fear of Sabellianism, had in fact used analogies and forms of expression about the Son which anticipated those of Arius. But on being pressed Dionysius explained them to the satisfaction of the Bishop of Rome, and his reply to the Pope appears to have been fully approved by Athanasius in the next century. It is an interesting fact that neither here, nor elsewhere, does Dionysius ever make mention of Origen.

THEOGNOSTUS AND PIERIUS

[Fragments in J. P. Migne, *P.G.* x, 235-42 (Theognostus) and 241-6 (Pierius). L. B. Radford, *Three Teachers of Alexandria*. Theognostus, Pierius, Peter (1908).]

After Dionysius there are three further pre-Nicene Alexandrian writers of note. The first two may be regarded as followers of Origen; the third was an avowed opponent.

THEOGNOSTUS (d. *c.* 282) held the headship of the Catechetical School, probably in succession to Dionysius.[1] He was

---

[1] Philip of Side (cf. H. Dodwell, *Dissertationes in Irenaeum*, Oxford, 1689, p. 488) seems mistaken when he puts Theognostus' headship of the School after that of Pierius.

M

the author of a work on systematic theology which he entitled *Hypotyposeis*. According to Photius, who has a full account of the work,[1] it expounded the principles of theology on an ordered plane in seven books. Theognostus had evidently take Origen as his model. He betrays his influence, e.g. in the long disquisition on the angels and evil spirits which fills the whole of the fourth book. Only a few fragments of the work survive.[2] Despite the subordinationism of his theology, Athanasius appeals to him (with Origen) for support against the Arians.[3]

PIERIUS, whom Jerome termed 'the Younger Origen',[4] was a leading Alexandrian presbyter under Bishop Theonas (282-300), and noted also as an ascetic and a preacher. According to Philip Sidetes[5] he was, like Theognostus, Head of the Catechetical School.[6] There is a tradition that he and his brother Isidore were 'martyred' ($\dot{\epsilon}\mu\alpha\rho\tau\dot{\upsilon}\rho\eta\sigma\alpha\nu$);[7] this may not mean more than that he suffered. According to another tradition Pierius was at Rome in his later years. Possibly the two are combined by supposing that he was at Rome through exile.

The few scattered references in early writers to Pierius, when taken together, indicate that his writings took the form of homilies. Only a few fragments survive.[8] Their character is described by Photius (Cod. 118); but he is more concerned with their orthodoxy than describing their contents. The subject of two of them, however, appears to have been 'the Gospel of Luke' and 'the Pasch and Hosea'.

---

[1] Cod. 106

[2] Fullest collection of fragments in M. J. Routh, *Reliquiae Sacrae* (ed. 2), iii, pp. 405-22; cf. also F. Diekamp, 'Ein neues Fragment aus den Hypotyposen des Alexandriners Theognostus' in *Theol. Quartalschrift* lxxxiv (1902), pp. 481-94.

[3] *Ep. ad Serap.* iv. 9-11; *De Decr.* xxv.

[4] *De Vir. Ill.* 76: ut Origenes iunior vocaretur.

[5] Cf. above p. 119.

[6] Eusebius *H. E.* VII. xxxii. 26-7 or 30 asserts that Achillas was head of the school under Theonas; but we have pointed out the insecurity of this evidence.

[7] Cf. de Boor, T.U. v. 2 (1888), p. 170f.

[8] Collected in M. J. Routh, *Reliquiae Sacrae* (ed. 2), iii, pp. 423-35.

PETER OF ALEXANDRIA

[Fragments in M. J. Routh (ed.) *Reliquiae Sacrae* (ed. 2, Oxford, 1846), iv, pp. 19-82; repr. in J. P. Migne, *P.G.*, xviii. 449-552. Eng. tr. in A.N.C.L. xiv (1896). L. B. Radford, *Three Teachers of Alexandria*. Theognostus, Pierius and Peter (1908), pp. 58-86. Further bibl. in *O.D.C.C.*, p. 1052.]

Tradition holds that Peter taught in the Catechetical School at Alexandria; but, as we have seen,[1] the existence of such a School down to this late date is very improbable. At the beginning of the 4th century he succeeded Theonas (*c.* 282-300) in the Bishopric of Alexandria. Eusebius praises him in high terms,[2] testimony the more remarkable in that Peter was a strong opponent of the Origenistic theology. When the Diocletianic Persecution broke out in 303, Peter retired from Alexandria and administered his diocese from his retreat. In his absence Melitius, Bishop of Lycopolis, made a bid to displace Peter and exercise the primacy over Egypt. After the persecution had ended, Peter repudiated the intruder at a Synod at Alexandria (late 305 or early 306) and the result was a definite schism which persisted as 'Melitianism' in Egypt for centuries. It has been the traditional view that Peter also excommunicated Arius.[3] When the persecution was renewed under Maximin, Peter suffered a martyr's death (November 311). There are several recensions of his 'Acta' (Latin, Greek, Syriac, Coptic), but all are so heavily overladen by legend that any kernel of historic truth they may contain cannot be isolated.

Of Peter's extensive writing, very little survives. It includes:

(1) A short Letter to his flock, doubtless written from his hiding place, warning the Alexandrian clergy and faithful against dealing with Melitius. It was discovered by S. Maffei in the 'Theodosian Collection' in the Verona Chapter Library.[4]

[1] Pp. 118f.   [2] *Eccl. Hist.* VII. xxxii. 31.

[3] That there is more evidence for the traditional view than has been customarily supposed in modern times has been shewn by Dr. W. Telfer, 'St. Peter of Alexandria and Arius' in *Anal. Boll.* lxvii (1949), pp. 117-30.

[4] It was first published in his *Osservazioni Letterarie*, iii (1738), pp. 11-18. It is reprinted in *P.G.* xviii. 11-18.

(2) A set of fourteen canons on 'Penance', dating from 306, which were later taken up into the Eastern canonical collections. They deal mainly with the treatment of those who had lapsed in the Persecution, the chief matter in which he found himself in disagreement with Melitius. Peter's attitude was marked by reasonableness and good sense. These canons seem originally to have formed part of Peter's Paschal Letter for the same year.

Of Peter's other writings little is known beyond their titles. Three short passages from a treatise 'On the Godhead' are quoted in the *Acta* of the Council of Ephesus (431); they strongly repudiate Origen's subordinationism. Another fragment is quoted by Leontius of Byzantium[1] from Peter's work 'On the Coming to us of our Redeemer', perhaps another title for the same work. Leontius elsewhere preserves two passages from Peter's treatise 'That the Soul does not pre-exist and that it has not been cast into a Body in consequence of sinning', clearly from its title a very anti-Origenistic work. There also survive several Syriac fragments of what appears to be a genuine work 'On the Resurrection'. There are a few other fragments which have little claim to authenticity.

GREGORY THAUMATURGUS

[Works in J. P. Migne, *P.G.* x. 963-1232. Crit. ed. of Gregory's Address to Origen by P. Koetschau, Tübingen, 1894. Life by Gregory of Nyssa in J. P. Migne, *P.G.* xlvi, 893-958. There also exist Syr., Armen., and Lat. lives, none of any value. Further bibl. in *O.D.C.C.*, p. 589f.]

Gregory Thaumaturgus (*c.* 213-*c.* 270), a member of a distinguished family of Neo-Caesarea in Pontus, was educated for the law. In or about 233 he paid a visit to his sister at Caesarea in Palestine, where his brother-in-law was Imperial governor. Here he and his brother-in-law met Origen, where both came under his spell, and were converted to the Christian faith. After remaining for five years in Origen's company, Gregory returned to his native city. Shortly afterwards he was appointed Bishop and from then on exercised

---

[1] *Contra Nestorianos et Eutychianus* I. i.

a remarkable influence. Indeed, if report can be trusted, before long he had converted almost the whole country to Christianity so that hardly any pagans were left in the land. He numbered among his pupils St. Macrina the Elder, the grandmother of St. Basil and St. Gregory of Nyssa, and was thus by an historic link a forerunner of the Cappadocian theology. In 264-265 he took part in the Synod of Antioch on Paul of Samosata. According to 'Suidas', he died in the reign of Aurelian (270-275). Later he became the object of a considerable cultus.[1]

To judge by his remains, Gregory's interests were chiefly practical. His writings are:

(1) The 'Prosphoneticus', or 'Address to Origen'. This is panegyric which he delivered at the Palestinian Caesarea the on taking leave of Origen. Besides information about Origen and his teaching methods, it tells us much about Gregory himself. It suffers somewhat from an artificial use of rhetoric, a reflection of Gregory's youth, but it wins our sympathy by the ardent esteem in which Gregory held his master.

(2) His Creed. This is a longer document than the ordinary creeds, and contains a clear and precise positive exposition of the doctrine of the Trinity.[2] According to a tradition recorded by St. Gregory of Nyssa, it was communicated to Gregory Thaumaturgus supernaturally on the eve of his consecration to the episcopate by St. John the Evangelist. Its genuineness seems adequately guaranteed.

(3) A 'Metaphrase of Ecclesiastes'. This is hardly more than a paraphrase of the Septuagintal text. Though the work is generally attributed in the MSS. to St. Gregory of Nazianzen (among whose works it has been commonly printed), it really belongs to Gregory Thaumaturgus, as Jerome and Rufinus both recognised.

[1] See W. Telfer, 'The Cultus of St. Gregory Thaumaturgus' in *H.T.R.* xxix (1936), pp. 225-344.

[2] The autograph still existed at Neo-Caesarea in Gregory of Nyssa's days.

(4) A Canonical Epistle. This was in origin a letter sent by Gregory to some unknown Bishop who sought his guidance on a number of practical matters, largely arising out of the devastation of Pontus and Bithynia by the Goths in 253-254. It was incorporated by canonists of later times into their collections. The Letter contains valuable information on the penitential discipline of the early Church.

(5) A Letter addressed to Theopompus, which survives only in a Syriac version. It is a philosophical colloquy on the impassibility of God.

FIRMILIAN OF CAESAREA

[Firmilian's letter to Cyprian is preserved in Cyprian's *Opera*, Ep. 75 (ed. W. Hartel, C.S.E.L., iii (2), pp. 810-27).]

Firmilian, Bishop of Caesarea in Cappadocia and a leading personality in the Church of his time, was, like Gregory Thaumaturgus, a warm admirer of Origen. He took a prominent part in the matter of the *lapsi* and the affair of Paul of Samosata. The only one of his many writings to survive is a letter to Cyprian of Carthage in which he supported him in the Rebaptism controversy against Stephen, Bishop of Rome. The letter was written in Greek but it survives in a Latin translation, probably the work of Cyprian himself.[1] He defended the view that all Baptisms by heretics are null and void.

PAUL OF SAMOSATA

[G. Bardy, *Paul de Samosate* (S.S.L. iv, 1923; new ed. 1929), F. Loofs, *Paulus von Samosata* (T.U. xl. 5; 1924). H. de Riedmatten, O.P., *Les Actes du Procès de Paul de Samosate* (Paradosis vi; 1952), with the best collection of fragments, pp. 135-58. Further bibl. in *O.D.C.C.*, p. 1034.]

Paul, a native of Samosata, was one of the first Christian leaders to combine ecclesiastical office with high civil rank and a life of considerable splendour. He was the protégé of

---

[1] The letter is in Cyprian's correspondence, Ep. 75. It has been argued that this version has been interpolated; but without sufficient reason.

Zenobia, the celebrated Queen of Palmyra, and after Antioch had passed over to the Kingdom of Palmyra following Valerian's defeat by the Persians in 260, Paul became Zenobia's procurator (*ducenarius*) and at the same time Bishop of Antioch. Here he met with much opposition from his flock both from his mode of life and from his theology. He was charged with teaching an extreme form of 'adoptionist' doctrine. His case was brought before a series of Councils at Antioch, and at the last and most influential of these he was finally condemned in 268. But as long as he enjoyed the protection of Zenobia Paul could not be dislodged from his bishopric and he retained his see until the fall of Palmyra (272) deprived him of her protection. The Emperor Aurelian then ordered that Paul's cathedral should be surrendered to the person nominated Bishop by the Bishops of Rome and Italy. It was the first known intervention of the secular power in defence of orthodoxy.

The documents from which Paul's doctrines have to be reconstructed are:

(1) The Synodal letter of the Council of Antioch of 268, of which considerable extracts are preserved in Eusebius, *H. E.* VII. 30. Eusebius, however, was more interested in Paul's moral obloquies than his teaching about which he tells us little. Several modern scholars have claimed that the dogmatic parts of the letter can be recovered from later writers who were directly dependent on it.

(2) The stenographic minutes (*acta*) of a public disputation between Paul and a presbyter, Malchion, who came forward as a supporter of the orthodox Christology. These minutes appear to have been put into circulation by the Synod of 268 with its encyclical letter; but the authenticity of the fragments which have been ascribed to these *acta* is doubtful. Their earliest certain appearance is in 429 when Eusebius, who later became Bishop of Dorylaeum, put them into circulation with passages of Nestorius' teaching. As Malchion's doctrines had affinities with the later doctrines of

Apollinarius, R. Devreesse, M. Richard, G. Bardy[1] and others
have held that the Antiochene *acta* were really Apollinarian
forgeries such as abounded in the early 5th century. Dr.
H. de Riedmatten, however, has recently defended their
authenticity.

(3) A set of five fragments of 'Discourses addressed to
Sabinus' ascribed to Paul. These are preserved in a 6th-
century catena known as the *Doctina Patrum de Incarnatione
Verbi* (ed. F. Diekamp), but they can hardly be genuine in
their present form.

(4) The Letter which Hymenaeus, Bishop of Jerusalem, and
five other Bishops who took part in the Council of Antioch
are supposed to have sent to Paul before the synod deposed
him. It contains a long creed which the Bishops put to Paul
for his acceptance. It is doubtful, however, if the Letter is
genuine. It has no early attestation and its theology appears
at one point to reflect the teaching of Nestorius.

It thus seems that though Paul became the focus of a
small *corpus* of literature, no writing in which he himself
set out his views has survived unadulterated, if, indeed, at all.
The most reliable source for his doctrines is to be sought in
the few traces which have survived of the disputation at
Antioch in 268.

METHODIUS OF OLYMPUS

[Works in J. P. Migne, *P.G.*, xviii. 9-408. Crit. ed. by G. N. Bonwetsch
in G.C.S. xxvii (1917). Eng. tr. in A.N.C.L. G. N. Bonwetsch, *Die
Theologie des Methodius von Olympus* (1903). Further bibl. in *O.D.C.C.*,
p. 895.]

Methodius occupies a notable place among the Fathers as
one of the first opponents of Origen's theology. Perhaps it
was his hostility to Origen which explains the silence of
Eusebius and hence our lack of information about him. The
earliest references, in Jerome[2] and Socrates[3], are untrustworthy and conflicting,—but it seems probable that Metho-

---

[1] Cf. *Rev. S.R.* xxvi (1952), pp. 294-6, abandoning his earlier view.
[2] *De Vir. Ill.* 83.   [3] *H. E.* VI. 13.

dius was Bishop of Olympus in Lycia and suffered a martyr's death in Chalcis in 311.

Methodius was the author of several works, mostly in the form of dialogues. Jerome pays tribute to his abilities[1] and the virtues of his style.[2] He strove after literary effect—wrote poetry, and endeavoured to imitate Plato. But he hardly reached his high ambitions.

His *Symposium* or *Banquet*, the only writing which has come down to us complete in its original Greek, is a dialogue modelled on Plato's treatise with the same title. But whereas Plato commended Love (Eros), Methodius here expounds the excellence of virginity. Ten virgins in turn sing the merits of chasity. Their praises lead up to a final hymn in twenty-four strophes sung by Thecla, one of the ten virgins, which addressed to Christ the Bridegroom and the Church His Bride.

Considerable portions of the Greek of two other works survive:

(1) *Aglaophon: or On the Resurrection*, a work directed against Origen. It attacks the pre-existence of the soul and maintains the identity of the resurrection body with that which has lived on earth. It is so named from Aglaophon, a physician of Patara, in whose house the dialogue took place;

(2) A treatise *On Free Will*, which attacks the dualism and determinism of the Valentinian Gnostics. Evil is not a self-existing principle, but an energy (ἐνέργεια) from an evil spirit, the devil, who does not exist in his own right, but is a creature of God who fell through disobedience. Apart from occasional gaps, the whole work survives in a Slavonic translation.

Other works of Methodius survive only in Slavonic. They include writings on the food laws of the Old Testament, on the mystical interpretation of the references to leprosy in Lev. xiii and on the leech in Prov. xxx. 15. Among his lost writings are commentaries on Genesis and Canticles; a work on the Pythonissa directed against Origen, and an extensive

---

[1] Disertissimus vir, *Comm. in Dan. ad* xii. 13.
[2] Nitidi compositique sermonis, *De Vir. Ill.* 38.

work against Porphyry. The disappearance of this last is particularly regrettable as it was the first reply to Porphyry's celebrated attack on Christianity.

THE DIALOGUE OF ADAMANTIUS

[Ed. princeps by J. R. Wetstein, Basle, 1674, repr. in J. P. Migne, *P.G.* xi. 1711-1884, among the works of Origen. Crit. ed. by W. H. van de Sande Bakhuiyzen in *G.C.S.* (1901). See also *O.D.C.C.*, p. 16.]

A Dialogue by an unknown author, 'On the Correct Faith in God' (*De Recta in Deum Fide*), has come down to us in variant Greek and Latin forms. Its author and place of origin are alike unknown. In the Greek version the writer's name is given as 'Adamantius who is also Origen'; but the Adamantius who is the mouthpiece of orthodoxy in the Dialogue cannot be the great Alexandrian, since he draws freely on Methodius of Olympus who, as we have just seen, was one of Origen's chief critics. This last fact also requires us to date the Dialogue not earlier than the last years of the 3rd century. On the other hand, the fact that it was written before the end of the Great Persecution makes it impossible to put it after 313. The Latin translation is the work of Rufinus. The first two sections are directed mainly against Marcion, the other three against Bardesanes. It may be that the author, knowing of Origen's reputation as a theologian and not aware of his particular 'heresies', intended the historic Origen (who was also known as 'Adamantius') to be his mouthpiece. If so, there is no need to suppose that the author wished to mislead his readers, as the dialogue form was a recognised literary device. On the other hand Basil the Great and Gregory of Nazianzen both ascribed the work erroneously to Origen.

XII.—LATER LATIN WRITERS

WE pass now to give some account of a miscellaneous group
of Latin writers and begin with Novatian, the first Latin
theologian of Rome.

NOVATIAN

[The best of the earlier edd. is that of J. Jackson (London, 1728). Crit.
ed. of 'De Trinitate' by W. Yorke Fausset (Cambr. Patr. Texts, 1909).
Eng. tr. by H. Moore (London, 1919). The best study of his theology
is A. d'Alès, S.J., *Novatien* (1924). Further bibl. in *O.D.C.C.*, p. 968,
s. v. 'Novatianism'.]

Novatian, probably a native if not of Rome at any rate of
Italy,[1] first came into prominence as a presbyter during the
Decian persecution when the Roman see was vacant for over
a year after Fabian's martyrdom on 20 January 250. From
his correspondence with Cyprian,[2] we learn that in the early
stages of the persecution Novatian took a leading part in
handling the pressing question of the lapsed at Rome and
that at first he acted in close collaboration with the Bishop
of Carthage. It appears that Novatian had set his hopes on
succeeding to the Roman see. When after fourteen months
Cornelius was elected Pope (March 251), Novatian in his dis-
appointment set himself up as the leader of a rival group at
Rome which stood for a rigorist position in regard to the
lapsed. He was encouraged in his stand by a certain Novatus,
a malcontent from Carthage, who with strange inconsistency
had upheld at Carthage a laxist view on the same question.
Novatian duly secured consecration from three Italian
Bishops,—they were described by Cornelius as simple and

[1] No weight can be attached to Philostorgius' assertion (*Hist. Eccl.*
VIII. xv) that Novatian came from Phrygia.
[2] Letters 30 and 36 in the Cyprianic corpus are by *Novatian*.

honest men, but as half intoxicated during the ceremony,—
and claimed to be the rightful holder of the Roman see.
Novatian secured a considerable following in many parts of
the Church and the Novatianist schism (in the East under the
name of καθαροί) continued for a long time. The treatment
to be meted out to Novatianists who abjured their schism
was the subject of the eighth Nicene Canon.

The longest and most important of Novatian's writings is
his *De Trinitate*, one of the very few Latin discussions of
the Trinity in pre-Nicene times. It is written in rhythmical
prose and probably dates from the years before he fell into
schism. It treats successively of God the Father and His
attributes (1-8); of the Divinity of Christ and the nature of
the Incarnation (9-28); of the Holy Spirit (29); and of the
Divinity of the Son in its relation to the unity of God (30-1);
and one of its principal objects was to combat the teaching
of the Monarchians, in both its dynamic and modalist forms,
which flourished at Rome in the earlier half of the 3rd century.
Jerome described the treatise as 'so to speak an epitome of
Tertullian';[1] but the only known work of Tertullian's to
which this would apply would be his *Adversus Praxean*,—
Tertullian never wrote a treatise *De Trinitate*,—and the
resemblance is not very close. Jerome's assertion, indeed, in
conjunction with the facts that Novatian wrote in Latin and
that the treatise survived among the works of Tertullian (in
MSS. now lost), seems to have misled modern historians of
doctrine; for in some ways Novatian is closer to Irenaeus and
in others to Hippolytus than he is to Tertullian, with whom
the resemblances are not very striking. There is a strong
subordinationist element in his teaching which he shares
with Irenaeus and Hippolytus.

The only other writing which has come down under
Novatian's name is his work 'On Jewish Foods' (*De Cibis
Judaicis*). Its thesis is that the Jewish food-laws are no longer
applicable to Christians, to whom all foods except meats
offered to idols are lawful. The purpose of the Jewish laws was

---

[1] quasi ἐπιτομήν operis Tertulliani, *De Vir. Illustr.* 70.

temporary, viz. to teach the Jews by visible signs the nature of moral distinctions. In his original state of innocence, man found his food by looking upwards and picking the produce of the trees. It was only after man had fallen that he had to bend down and till the soil, and then, owing to the need for a more robust food to sustain him for the toil imposed, required flesh-meat. But all these foods, being the creation of God, are good. The Jewish law discriminating meats cannot therefore be understood literally. It must be taken symbolically. The only food forbidden to Christians is that offered to demons. For though everything is clean as long as it belongs to God's creation, it ceases to be so when it is offered to idols. A passage in which Novatian advises for reasons of health against drinking early in the morning (6), resembles, and is perhaps dependent on, Seneca, *Ep.* 122. 6.

Two other writings which have come down in the Cyprianic *corpus*, the *De Spectaculis* and the *De Bono Pudicitiae*, probably also belong to Novatian. The former is an attack on the theatre to which (he says) no true Christian will go. How debased are the spectacles of the stage especially when contrasted with God's work as revealed in the glory and beauty of the natural order! In the latter, Novatian described the different stages of moral purity. At the top stands virginity, then abstention from cohabitation in the married state, and then the faithfulness of man and wife. The treatise has affinities with Tertullian's *De Virginibus Velandis*, *De Cultu Feminarum* and *De Pudicitia* and with Cyprian's *De Habitu Virginum*.

ARNOBIUS OF SICCA

[Text in J. P. Migne, *P.L.*, v. 349-1374; crit. edd. by A. Reifferscheid in C.E.S.L. iv (1875), also by G. Marchesi, Turin, 1935. Eng. tr. by G. E. McCracken in A.C.W., vols. viif. Further bibl. in *O.D.C.C.*, p. 90.]

Arnobius was a pagan rhetorician of Sicca Veneria in Africa Proconsularis who towards the end of his life sought admission to the Church. When the Bishop was hesitant to admit to the fold a convert hitherto known only as a determined adversary, Arnobius decided that he could best establish his sincerity and serve the Church by writing an apology for his newly won faith. To this end he wrote *c.* 300 his *Adversus Nationes*.

The work, which is preserved in the single Paris MS., Cod. lat. 1661,[1] is in seven books. Books I and II seek to establish that the calamities of the times, which pagans persisted in ascribing to the gods' displeasure at their neglected worship, really come from the operation of natural laws. There is nothing in Christian doctrine to justify the hostility of the gods. Nor did these calamities begin with the Christian era. After disposing of such charges, Arnobius makes in Books III to VII a direct attack on the pagan religions.

The treatise has few merits. From the literary point of view it is badly constructed and verbose, has much tedious rhetoric, and is full of contradictions. Arnobius in general prefers irony to argument. Nor in the matter of theological content is the work satisfactory; for Arnobius seems to have had little understanding of the Christian faith. He never quotes, and almost never even refers to, Scripture and he speaks disparagingly of all kinds of exterior worship. He also seems ignorant of the filiation of Christianity to Judaism.

LACTANTIUS

[Works in J. P. Migne, *P.L.* vi and vii. Crit. ed. by S. Brandt and G. Laubmann in C.S.E.L. xix (1890) and xvii (1897). Eng. tr. in A.N.C.L. R. Pichou, *Lactance* (1901). Further bibl. in *O.D.C.C.*, p. 778.]

From Arnobius it is natural to pass to his much more able pupil, Lactantius, also an African by birth. Lactantius deservedly acquired a high reputation as a rhetorician both in his own day and again at the revival of learning, so much so that he came to be dubbed the 'Christian Cicero'. Diocletian summoned him from Africa to teach rhetoric at his new capital of Nicomedia. When the persecution broke out in 303 he was obliged to hand in his resignation; but he continued to

[1] It is the MS. which also preserves the text of Minucius Felix (cf. above p. 146).

live on at Nicomedia, where for several years he had only precarious means of support. Much later Constantine persuaded him to go to Trier as the tutor of his son Crispus. This is the last we hear of him.

Lactantius' works were for the most part apologetic. The longest and most ambitious was his treatise on the *Divine Institutes*. This apology, a defence of Christianity in seven books, was designed as a reply to the ever more formidable pagan attacks which were appearing with the rapid growth of Christianity in the later 3rd century. Among the more notable contemporary critics of the faith was a certain Hierocles, Procurator of Bithynia, who was then resident in Nicomedia, and it is probable that Lactantius had Hierocles prominently in view.

In his first two Books, 'De falsa religione' and 'De origine erroris', Lactantius is concerned to refute the superstitions of the pagan world and to demonstrate the truth of monotheism. The pagan gods are in reality only demons under the control of the devil. The third Book, 'De falsa sapientia', is directed against the pagan philosophies. Over against their mutually destructive systems is the system of truth revealed in Christ. This brings the author to the subject of Book IV, 'De vera sapientia et religione', where the knowledge and worship of God brought to man from heaven are described. In Book V, 'De justitia', Lactantius, after describing the disappearance of righteousness from the earth, argues that men are brought back to it through Christ. Its basis is the common sonship of all believers to God, with its corollary of their equality (*aequitas*). In Book VI ('De vero cultu'), the true worship of God is shown to consist in the exercise of this righteousness. The concluding Book, VII ('De vita beata'), describes the Last Things and the worship of heaven. Some MSS. of the work contain considerable additions, among them addresses to Constantine and passages with dualistic doctrines. Indeed the longer text may be original and the other a revised text made by Lactantius when the addresses to Constantine seemed no longer appropriate.

Lactantius issued later an *Epitome* of the work (*c.* 315). In some measure it can be considered an independent work as it has a number of improvements.

Lactantius also wrote two further works with an apologetic purpose, viz. *De Opificio Dei* (*c.* 303-304) and *De Ira Dei* (not before 314). In the former he maintained against the Epicureans that the beauty and adaptation to purpose in the human organism and its powers of reasoning shew it to be a work of God. In the *De Ira Dei* he argued against the Epicurean and Stoic teaching on the impassibility of the Godhead and defended the existence and necessity of the Divine wrath.

Of particular interest is Lactantius' *De Mortibus Persecutorum*. He shews the fate of all who persecute the Church. After an introductory section in which the author describes the deaths of Nero, Domitian, Decius, Valerius and Aurelian, he turns to his own times and gives vivid accounts of the crimes and deaths of Diocletian, Maximian, Galerius, Severus and Maximin. It carries the story down to the agreement of Constantine and Licinius after the Battle of the Milvian Bridge in 312 (the so-called 'Edict of Milan'). As Lactantius here regards Licinius as a supporter of the Christian cause, the book must be earlier than 320-1, when Licinius publicly abandoned his patronage of the Church. The fullness with which it describes some of the secular events of the time makes it one of the primary authorities for the history of the early 4th century. Lactantius' view that the moving spirit in the Great Persecution was not Diocletian, but Galerius, is now very widely accepted. The attribution of the treatise to Lactantius has often been contested, partly because he is not so named in the title in the MSS., partly because its impassioned and bitter language against the pagan state and its rulers is in contrast with the more urbane attitude of the *Divine Institutes* and Lactantius' other apologetic works. But the majority of scholars now rightly (it would seem) believe it to be authentic.

VICTORINUS OF PETTAU

[Crit. text in C.S.E.L. xlix (1916). For further bibl. see *O.D.C.C.*, p. 1419f.; E. Peterson in *E.C.* xii (1954), col. 154f., s. v. 'Vittoriono di Pettau'.]

Victorinus, Bishop of Poetovio (now Pettau in Styria), was the first Biblical exegete to use Latin. Very little is known of him beyond the fact that he was put to death in 304 in the Diocletianic Persecution. But though he was an extensive writer, his works are nearly all lost; they were probably distrusted on account of their author's Millenarianism.[1] His *Commentary on the Apocalypse* has come down to us in a 15th-century Ottobonian MS. (lat. 3288A), now in the Vatican, and reflects its author's chiliastic doctrines. Victorinus also wrote a work on the Creation, *De Fabrica Mundi*. This last survives in a Lambeth Codex (414; 9th century) whence it was edited by W. Cave in 1688.

COMMODIAN

[Ed. princeps by N. Rigaltius, Toul, 1649, repr. in J. P. Migne, *P.L.*, v. 201-62. Crit. edd. by E. Ludwig (Bibl. Teubn., 1877-8) and B. Dombart (C.S.E.L., 1887). Further bibl. in *O.D.C.C.*, p. 317.]

As we have no information about Commodian except what can be deduced from his writings[2] and these tell us very little about their author, widely divergent views have been, and still are, held about his date and person. The view which had become traditional, that he was a native of Gaza who settled in the West and belonged to and wrote in the 3rd century, was challenged by H. Brewer, S.J., in 1906. Since then many dates between the 3rd and 5th centuries have been given to him. Brewer himself dated his poems at about 460 and their place of origin the South of Gaul (Arles). More recently, Professor Courcelle has argued his dependence on both Orosius (early 5th century) and Salvian (*c.* 400-*c.* 480). Quite

---

[1] According to Jerome (*De Vir. Ill.* 74), Victorinus wrote Commentaries on Gen., Ex., Lev., Is., Ezek., Hab., Eccl., Cant., Matt., Rev.

[2] The section on Commodian in Gennadius, *De Vir. Ill.* 15 is also wholly dependent on his poems.

N

recently (1957) Dr. Josef Martin has defended the traditional
date, contending that Commodian was a fellow countryman
of Cyprian and that he was dependent on Cyprian's *Testi-
monia* for his Biblical quotations.

The longer of Commodian's works, his *Instructiones*, is a
collection of eighty acrostic poems of varying length. These
are in two books, the former addressed to pagans and Jews,
and the latter to catechumens and believers. The text as it
has come down is very corrupt. His other poem, the *Carmen
Apologeticum*, is an apology in 1,060 hexameters addressed to
pagans and Jews. Commodian's language is strongly influenced by popular forms and is often obscure; and his verifi-
cation is based more on word accent than on quantity.
Commodian's theology shews marked Sabellian and Millen-
arian affinities. It is probably for this reason that his poems
were included among the apocrypha in the Gelasian Decree.

XIII.—HYMNODY; ACTS OF THE MARTYRS; INSCRIPTIONS

In this, the final chapter, we shall examine some forms of early Christian literature which stand apart from the mainstream of Patristic documentation. They fall readily into certain well defined groups. We begin with hymnody.

EARLY CHRISTIAN PSALMODY

There can be no doubt that from the first the Christian Church used in her worship the Psalms which she inherited from Judaism. She had every reason to be aware of their Messianic content as Christians have been ever since. But to these the Church soon spontaneously added compositions of her own. In the New Testament, apart from the superb canticles of Lk. i and ii (Magnificat, Benedictus, Nunc Dimittis) there are clearly traces of hymns in the Pauline Epistles (e.g. the opening verses of Eph. and I Tim. iii. 16), while the place of the hymn in Christian worship is reflected in 'the new song' of Rev. v. 9f. and elsewhere. These early hymns are not metrical compositions, but, like the Psalms, were written in a rhythmical prose. No doubt many of them had a short life and were soon replaced by others so that the earliest have mostly disappeared.

In the next stage, it would seem, if our extant sources are representative, that the hymn developed especially in Gnostic milieus. These include the 'Pearl Song' or the 'Hymn of the Soul' in the *Acts of Thomas* (6f.), the hymn which Christ says with His Apostles in the *Acts of John*, and the Naassene hymn preserved in Hippolytus' *Philosophumena* 5. 10. 2. All these are more of the nature of religious poetry than hymns for use in public worship and flowed naturally from the 'intellectualism' of the Gnostics.

THE ODES OF SOLOMON

Akin to these compositions are the interesting early collection of hymns, known as the 'Odes of Solomon', which were first published from a Syriac MS. by J. Rendel Harris in 1909. Their poetic form is modelled on that of the Old Testament Psalms, and this fact, combined with their occurrence in the MS. next to the *Psalms of Solomon*, has lent some countenance to the view that the Odes were of Jewish *provenance* and had later undergone Christian interpolation. But it is more probable that they were Christian from the first. They perhaps date from the late 1st century and may have emanated from Gnostic circles. In 1912 F. C. Burkitt[1] drew attention to the existence of a second (imperfect) Syriac text of the Odes in the British Museum MS. Add 14538. This supplied the text of several further Odes. It is likely that they were composed in Greek, though recently Professor A. Vööbus has maintained that their original language was Syriac.[2]

The Odes are written in an allusive language and deal with a variety of subjects. Ode 12 is a hymn addressed to the Logos; Ode 17 deals with the Lord's Descent into Hell; Ode 19 with the Conception of the Blessed Virgin from the Father through the power of the Holy Spirit. Many of them appear to have references to Baptism, and there is much to be said for the view that they were written for a Baptismal setting.

ORTHODOX HYMNODY

Two early compositions free from any taint of unorthodoxy, which from their wide diffusion by the 4th century are probably to be assigned to a pre-Nicene date, are the

[1] *J.T.S.* xiii (1912), pp. 372-85.
[2] A. Vööbus, *Celibacy a Requirement for Admission to Baptism in the Early Syriac Church* (Stockholm, 1951).

celebrated Greek morning and evening hymns known as the
'Gloria in Excelsis' and the 'Phos Hilaron'. They are not in
any real sense a pair, for they have reached us by independent
traditions.

The former is familiar through its place in the Western
liturgy. It is found, in a somewhat modified form, in the
(probably genuine) Athanasian *De Virginitate* and in the
(late 4th-century) *Apostolic Constitutions*.[1] It is also included
in the collection of fifteen 'Odes' after the Psalter in the
Codex Alexandrinus of the Bible. It is in substance a hymn
of praise in rhythmical prose which was originally not
specially designed for the Eucharistic liturgy. The *Liber
Pontificalis* asserts that it was introduced into Mass by Pope
Telesphorus (*c.* 128-139), but this statement is historically
worthless. Elsewhere the *Liber Pontificalis* states that Pope
Symmachus (498-516) ordered it to be said every Sunday and
on the feasts of martyrs. Its first occurrence in the Roman
Mass books is in the MSS of the Gregorian Sacramentary.

The 'Phos Hilaron', familiar from its inclusion in English
hymnals as 'Hail! Gladdening Light', is a vesper hymn, also
of very early date. Its origin is equally obscure. It is still
regularly sung at the *Hesperinon* in the Byzantine daily office.
Its earliest datable occurrence is in Basil's *De Spiritu Sancto*
xxix (73), where the writer says its authorship was unknown
to him.

THE CHRISTIAN SIBYLLINE ORACLES

[Crit. ed. by J. Geffcken (G.C.S., 1902); more recent ed. by E. A.
Kurfess [Munich, 1951]. Eng. tr. into blank verse by M. S. Terry
New York, 1890. For further bibl. see *O.D.C.C.*, p. 1253.]

The authority ascribed by the pagans to the 'Sibylline
Books' provoked imitation from Jewish and Christian
writers. Early in the Christian era a collection of fifteen

---

[1] VII. 47. That the form of the text in the *Apostolic Constitutions* is
not original has been conclusively proved by Dom Bernard Capelle,
O.S.B., in *R.H.E.* xliv (1949), pp. 439-57.

books of 'Sibylline Oracles' in Greek hexameters was compiled, prefaced by a prose prologue describing the supposed origin of the items. Books IX, X and XV are missing altogether. Of the other twelve Books, VI, VII and VIII—and perhaps also XI—appear to be of purely Christian origin, while the rest are Jewish. Books I and II give an account of world history, in the form of prophecy, from its beginnings to the fall of Rome. Book III contains an apology for Jewish monotheism, with another history of the world. Books IV and V describe the history of Rome in the time of Nero, written from the Jewish standpoint, while Book VI consists of a hymn to Christ. Book VII is a conglomeration of eschatological prophecies and moral and ritual prescriptions. Book VIII treats of the nature of Christ and His miraculous Birth. This Book (lines 217-50) contains the celebrated acrostic poem, based on the words $X\rho\epsilon\iota\sigma\tau\grave{o}s$ $\theta\epsilon o\tilde{v}$ $v\iota\grave{o}s$ $\sigma\omega\tau\grave{\eta}\rho$ $\sigma\tau\alpha\upsilon\rho\acute{o}s$.[1] Books XI to XIV, of less religious interest, contain another account of world history, more or less imaginative in character.

The books, which are of various dates, were quoted by many of the Christian fathers, and were widely held to be authentic. The Jewish items in the collection vary in date from the time of the Maccabean revolt (168-165 B.C.) down to the reign of Hadrian (117-138). The Christian portions seem for the most part to be not earlier than the 3rd century. It has sometimes been held, however, that the hymn to Christ in Book VI is of Gnostic origin and may date from the 2nd century.

ACTS OF THE MARTYRS

[There is a useful collection of texts translated into English by E. C. E. Owen, *Some Authentic Acts of the Early Martyrs* (1927). Much fuller material is assembled by the Bollandists in their monumental *Acta Sanctorum*, arranged in the order of the feasts of the saints in the ecclesiastical calendar (publication began in 1643 and has now reached

---

[1] This acrostic was embodied by Constantine in his *Oratio ad coetum sanctorum*, 18, and by Augustine in a Latin rendering in *De Civitate Dei*, xviii. 23.

'November'); also by T. Ruinart, O.S.B., *Acta Primorum Martyrum Sincera et Selecta* (1689). Critical studies by H. Delehaye, S.J., *Les Origines du Culte des martyrs* (Subsidia Hagiographica, xx, 1912), and id., *Les Passions des Martyrs et les genres littéraires* (1921). Further texts and studies in *Analecta Bollandiana*, the quarterly review issued by the Bollandists (1882ff.).]

A particularly attractive and moving body of documents from primitive Christianity are the accounts of the deaths of the early martyrs. Many of them owe their preservation to the common practice of commemorating the death of the martyrs, at first locally and then more widely, on the anniversary of their death. This day, being the day on which they gained their crown and entered heaven, was known as their birthday (*natalitia*). On these anniversary festivities the records would be publicly read, sometimes at the actual site of the martyrdom, sometimes in the local basilica, and thus in many cases, though not always, the origin of the texts was liturgical.

The form of these documents varied. At its simplest it was a stenographic record of what was said in the courts at the martyrs' trial, to which would be added a brief account of his death; and occasionally some member of the Christian community found it possible to obtain this record from the official minutes,—sometimes at a price,—from the civil authorities. In other cases the 'Acta' are the record of the court scene by eye-witnesses, perhaps in the form of a letter written to tell some neighbouring community what had taken place. Or the narrative might have been drawn up by the local community expressly for liturgical use. In this case the text would go back to the first (or possibly subsequent) anniversary of the martyr's death and thus not be contemporary to quite the same extent. Or there were other cases, when the age of the persecutions was over and many of the early martyrs were little more than names, that the texts needed for liturgical purposes had to be constructed on a very limited body of historic evidence. Here we cannot do more than refer to some of the genuine Acts which survive from the age of persecution.

(1) *Martyrdom of St. Polycarp.* The martyrdom of St. Polycarp, which took place at Smyrna in 155 or 156,[1] is recorded in a contemporary letter from the local Church to the neighbouring Church of Philomelium and 'to all the Christian congregations of the world belonging to the Catholic Church'.[2] This, the oldest of the Acts of the Martyrs to survive, is clearly an eye-witness account of Polycarp's last days and its genuineness has never been seriously questioned.[3] Some passages in it have become deservedly famous, among them the altercation between the Proconsul and Polycarp at his trial. The Proconsul bade the Bishop 'swear by the Fortune of Caesar, repent, say "Away with the Atheists". Polycarp, gazing with a steadfast countenance on the crowd of lawless heathens in the stadium, waved his hand to them, sighed, and looking up to heaven said "Away with the Atheists". And when the Proconsul pressed him further and said "Swear and I set you free; Curse Christ", Polycarp replied, "Eighty and six years I served him and He did me no wrong. How can I blaspheme my King that saved me?" ' (ix. 2f.). There follows a vivid description of Polycarp's death. As the flames from his pyre were having no effect on his body, the people ordered a slaughterer to kill him with a dagger thrust. The exact day and hour of the martyrdom is recorded at the end of the Epistle.

(2) *The Acts of St. Justin and his Companions.* As mentioned above,[4] St. Justin was martyred at Rome under the City Prefect, Rusticus, who held the office from 163 to 167. A short time before, Justin had defeated the Cynic philosopher Crescens, in a public disputation. But, as L. Duchesne remarks, Crescens 'had other weapons at his command'[5] and successfully encompassed Justin's death. The Acts show that Justin was martyred with six others, a woman, Charito, and

---

[1] On St. Polycarp and the date of his death cf. above p. 19.

[2] So the address is given in the title of the MSS.

[3] Eusebius incorporated a considerable portion of the text in his *Ecclesiastical History* (IV. xv. 3-45).

[4] P. 49.   [5] *Histoire ancienne de l'Église* i (1906), p. 208.

five men. In their simplicity and directness, the Acts are manifestly based on a stenographic report of the trial. E. C. E. Owen[1] thinks he can detect a certain 'donnishness' in some of Justin's replies to his accusers, such as we might expect from the philosopher Justin. The Acts were unknown to Eusebius, though their genuineness cannot be doubted. Not the least impressive element in them is their brevity and simple sincerity.

(3) *The Martyrs of Vienne and Lyons*. As in the martyrdom of St. Polycarp, the record here is in an epistolary form, being the letter sent by the Churches of the two Gallic towns of Vienne and Lugdunum to the Churches of Asia and Phrygia. Eusebius was understandably so moved by the account that he included it not only in his (lost) collection of Acts of the Martyrs, but also in his *Ecclesiastical History*, V. i. Fortunately by its inclusion in the latter place the text has been preserved. It narrates the martyrdom of St. Pothinus, the immediate predecessor of St. Irenaeus and now over ninety years old,[2] and of several others with the attendant circumstances. The actual court scene is not as closely described as in the case of the martyrdom of Polycarp, but there is a touching and graphic account of the courageous stand of the martyrs and their Christian supporters. The account was the work of a writer with considerable descriptive powers. It has often been conjectured that the author was Irenaeus, but this cannot be proved and is perhaps not very likely.

(4) *The Acts of the Scillitan Martyrs*. The Acta, which are among the earliest documentary evidences of Christianity in North Africa,[3] record the martyrdoms of seven men and five women from Scilli (site unknown), who were put to death at Carthage on 17 July 180. The text exists in various Latin forms as well as in an early Greek version. The Latin text, in

---

[1] *Some Authentic Acts of the Early Martyrs* (1927), p. 48.

[2] Irenaeus apparently was away from Lyons at the time, cf. p. 110.

[3] The evidence for the so-called Madauran Martyrs is very insecure. See *O.D.C.C.*, s.v., p. 841.

its original unadorned and impressive simplicity, was first
published by the Bollandists in 1889.[1] The document
records how Speratus, in the name of himself and others, made
profession of his Christian faith before the proconsul
Saturninus and refused to swear by the genius of the Emperor
and to renounce his creed. All twelve were put to death.

(5) *The Passion of St. Perpetua and her Companions.* This
document records the martyrdom which took place in the
amphitheatre at Carthage under Septimius Severus on
7 March 203. It incorporates pieces written in the dungeon by
two of the martyrs themselves. Ch. i is a prologue due to the
compiler, ch. ii briefly makes the reader *au fait* of the historical
situation; chs. iii-x and xi-xiii are due respectively to the
martyrs Perpetua and Saturus themselves (the compiler
provides the link in ch. xi); in xiv-end, the compiler gives a
picture of the martyrs' combat and death and ends with a
peroration.

The Passion is a very moving document with its simple
record of the brutalities inflicted on the martyrs and their
courage and Christian sentiment. We learn how a group of
five Carthaginian Christians,—Vibia Perpetua, a woman of
twenty-two years, of good family, with two other young
people, Saturninus and Secundulus, and two slaves, Revo-
catus and Felicitas,—all catechumens, were arrested. Soon
afterwards a sixth, Saturus, gave himself up of his own
accord. Shortly before Perpetua's own record breaks off
(ch. x), she notes that she must soon enter the amphitheatre
and another must continue her report. There is a vivid
picture of the martyr's combat and death in the later
chapters.

The style and language of the narrative portions of the
'Passion' have affinities with those of Tertullian and he has

[1] *Analecta Bollandiana*, viii (1889), pp. 5-8. Cf. also J. A. Robinson
in Texts and Studies I, ii (1891), pp. 112-16. The closely similar Greek
text had been issued some years earlier by H. Usener in the scarce
Index scholarum Bonnensium per menses aest. a. 1881. It was also
printed by J. A. Robinson, op. cit., pp. 113-17 (facing the Latin text).

sometimes been considered the compiler of the work; and it has even been argued that the document shows traces of Montanist theology. But this is very uncertain.

(6) The *Acta Proconsularia Cypriani*. This account of the martyrdom of St. Cyprian[1] appears to be based on three separate documents: (a) The Report of Cyprian's interrogation before the Proconsul, Aspasius Paternus, on 30 August 257, leading to his exile to Curubis; (b) The Report of his interrogation before the Proconsul, Galerius Maximus, leading to his sentence to death on 14 September 258; (c) An eye-witness description of his execution at Villa Sexti near Carthage on the same day. These documents have been made into a continuous text by the editor, who has added a few connecting sentences.

(7) *Martyrdom of St. Marinus*. We learn details of the martyrdom of Marinus from Eusebius, *Ecclesiastical History* VII. xv, who doubtless bases his account on local Caesarean sources and tradition. Marinus was a soldier who was beheaded at Caesarea in Palestine under Gallienus in 262. He had been offered the post of centurion, but his capacity to fill it was challenged by another candidate, who urged that being a Christian he would be unable to offer the requisite sacrifices. On professing his creed Marinus was given three hours to decide. His bishop met him outside the court, took him to the altar, and persuaded him to choose between his sword and the Book of the Gospels. He chose the latter and was executed. This account is not known to have ever circulated as a separate document.

(8) *Martyrdom of St. Marcellus the Centurion*. These Latin 'acta', which record the trial and death of a centurion at Tingis in North Africa, exist in two related texts.[2] Disgusted at the heathen banquets which marked the Emperor's birthday, Marcellus cast his soldier's belt away; testified in a loud

---

[1] On Cyprian, cf. above, pp. 148-54.
[2] Texts, with discussion, in [H. Delehaye, S.J.] 'Les Actes de S. Marcel le Centurion' in *Analecta Bollandiana* xli (1923), pp. 257-87.

voice: 'I serve Jesus Christ the Eternal King'; added that he would no longer serve the Emperors; and publicly renounced service in the army. On 30 October 298 he was formally charged with violating military discipline and beheaded. This was one of the occasional martyrdoms which took place under Diocletian before the outbreak of the Great Persecution in 303. Obviously the circumstances were such as would have entailed death at any date.

CHRISTIAN INSCRIPTIONS

[The most convenient collection of early Latin Christian inscriptions is E. Diehl (ed.), *Inscriptiones Latinae Christianae* (3 vols., 1925-31). C. M. Kaufmann, *Handbuch der altchristlichen Epigraphik* (1917). Further bibl. in *O.D.C.C.*, p. 695.]

The literary remains of the Patristic period receive a notable addition in the early Christian inscriptions but owing to the relative poverty of the Church in pre-Nicene times they cannot compare in extent or quality with the better known contemporary examples from the pagan world. Among the most widespread are the simple epitaphs, for at least the name of the person buried was recorded on the grave stones in the cemeteries. Well-known examples of these come from the catacombs; but in most cases these are too brief to be reckoned as 'literary'. Only two can receive particular notice here.

ABERCIUS

[The Greek text with English trans. is in J. B. Lightfoot, *The Apostolic Fathers* II. i (1889), pp. 492-501. Further bibl. in *O.D.C.C.*, p. 5.]

The most interesting inscription of pre-Nicene times is the Greek epitaph of Abercius, Bishop of Hieropolis in Phrygia Salutaris. This text, brought to light by W. M. Ramsay in 1883, was composed by the Bishop himself for his tomb in his seventy-second year. It had an interesting history in that when, apparently in the late 4th century, a writer at Hieropolis wrote a 'Life of Abercius' (which has come down to us in various forms) he drew extensively on the inscription, and this was the only form in which its contents were known until the inscription itself was recovered.[1] The epitaph is a remarkable piece of writing. It relates how Abercius had been led by the 'Chaste Shepherd' (Christ) on his travels to distant Rome and Nisibis in the Far East and everywhere had found the same faith and been welcomed with the same hospitality. He describes in allusive language the Christian Eucharist in symbolic terms (which is described as the Fish ($IX\ThetaY\Sigma$) and with a mention of the mixed chalice) and notes its universal currency. The inscription, which was presented to Leo XIII by the Sultan Abdul Hamid, is now in the Museum of Christian Inscriptions in the Lateran.

PECTORIUS

Another Latin inscription which, though of less interest, has considerable affinities with that of Abercius is that of Pectorius, found in 1830 in an early Christian cemetery not far from Autun. Both J. B. Pitra, who first published it, and G. B. de Rossi attributed it to the early part of the 2nd century, but epigraphical and other evidence has convinced subsequent scholars that its chiselling is much later (350-400). The wording of the inscription, however, seems to belong to a much earlier period; and this may be due either to conscious archaising or the use of a much earlier text. It has some notable resemblances to that of Abercius. The Fish symbolism is again used; and both Baptism ('the immortal fountain of Divine waters') and the Eucharist ('the honey-sweet food of the Redeemer of the Saints') are mentioned. At the last lines of the epitaph, Pectorius begs his parents and brothers to remember him 'in the peace of the Fish'.

THE SATOR-AREPO SQUARE

[There is an extensive literature. Among the more recent discussions in English are D. Atkinson, 'The Origin and Date of the "Sator" Word-Square' in the *Journal of Ecclesiastical History* ii (1951), pp. 1-18, and H. Last, 'The Rotas-Sator Square: Present Position and Future Prospects' in *J.T.S.*, N.S. iii (1952), pp. 92-7.]

---

[1] The legendary 'Vita Abercii' was first published by J. F. Boissonade in 1838. The view of a few older scholars (G. Ficker, A. Dieterich) that the epitaph was pagan has now been generally abandoned.

Recently much ingenuity has been spent on trying to prove that the famous 'Sator square' is a Christian symbol. It is found in two forms, the second being the usual Medieval type:

```
R O T A S          S A T O R
O P E R A          A R E P O
T E N E T          T E N E T
A R E P O          O P E R A
S A T O R          R O T A S
```

Seven instances of it from Roman times are known,—two from Pompeii, one at Cirencester and four from Dura Europos. As Pompeii was destroyed by Vesuvius in A.D. 79, we have a *terminus ad quem* for its construction.[1]

It has been maintained that it was originally a secret Christian symbol, used as a passport in the early Church among the faithful. Two interpretative reconstructions of it in this sense have been propounded.

```
                A
                P
                A
                T
                E
                R
    A  PATERNOSTER  O
                O
                S
                T
                E
                R
                O
          (F. Grosser)
```

(G. de Jerphanion)

---

[1] That is, if we may dismiss the desperate expedient of supposing that it did not come from the original Pompeii, but was the work of later travellers seeking buried treasure.

The former, due to F. Grosser,[1] is at least a highly ingenious reconstruction. If the A and O can be understood of Christ as the 'Alpha' and 'Omega', it presupposes (1) That as early as A.D. 79 there was a Latin speaking Christian community at Pompeii with (apparently) a Latin text of the Lord's Prayer if not a Latin version of the Sermon on the Mount; (2) that this prayer was already well known by its title; and (3) that either the Apocalpyse or its immediate source was already written. The other interpretation, due to G. de Jerphanion,[2] rests on the observation that the letter T, which was an early Christian designation for the Cross,[3] occupies a central place in the square and that it is flanked on each occurrence by A and O ('Alpha and Omega'). But here again there is the difficulty that no other evidence is known that T was recognised as a symbol of the Crucifixion as early as A.D. 79.

Even apart from the historical improbabilities indicated, both reconstructions of the square in a Christian sense are highly artificial. They are reminiscent of Ronald Knox's demonstration that Queen Victoria wrote *In Memoriam*.[4] Besides this it is unlikely (in the absence of other evidence) that Latin Christianity had developed so early. And further there is the notable fact that in not a single case of the early occurrence of the formula is it in a Christian setting. Indeed there is no reference to it whatever in Christian literature until the 8th century.

---

[1] 'Ein neuer Vorschlag zur Deutung der Satorformel' in *Archiv für Religionswissenschaft* xxiv (1926), pp. 165-9.

[2] 'La formule magique SATOR AREPO ou ROTAS OPERA' in *Rech. S.R.* xxv (1935), pp. 188-225.

[3] Cf. Ep. Barn. ix. 8.

[4] *Essays in Satire*, pp. 220-36.

NOTE ON PATRISTIC STUDY AND BIBLIOGRAPHY

I. ORIGINAL TEXTS. With the coming of printing, the Patristic works first published were naturally those of the greatest theological or practical interest, and hence such post-Nicene writers as Augustine, Jerome, Cassian and Gregory the Great appeared before the pre-Nicenes. In the case of Greek authors, many were issued originally in Latin versions, especially at the stage when Greek founts were difficult to procure. Little importance was attached at first to securing a correct text. As next to nothing was understood of the principles of textual criticism, it was a common practice to hand to the printer an ancient manuscript to serve as his 'copy'. Even when, as sometimes happened, editions were the work of competent scholars, they were often produced with (as it seems to us) an astonishing light-heartedness and irresponsibility. On occasion a scholar like Erasmus could make highly subjective and tendencious judgements on questions of authenticity. Nevertheless, as the 16th century wore on, the standards of editing rose and the range of texts, Greek as well as Latin, which became available increased. It is of some interest to note that not a single genuine treatise of Athanasius was available in the original Greek until the very end of the 16th century, when the Commelin edition of the great Alexandrine appeared at Heidelberg (2 vols., 1600-1).

With the French Congregation of the Benedictines of St. Maur, founded in 1618, wholly new standards of editing were introduced. These devoted scholars understood the principles of textual criticism and scoured the libraries of Europe in search of manuscripts; and they also recognised the close interrelation between the problems of history and text. They were at their best on the larger canvases of the post-Nicenes and among their many great achievements were their Augustine (11 vols., 1679-1700) and Athanasius (3 vols., 1698). Of pre-Nicene texts, which came later, the Benedictine Irenaeus was issued by R. Massuet in 1710, while the deservedly celebrated Benedictine Origen (one of their last), the work of Charles de la Rue and his nephew, Charles Vincent de la Rue, appeared in four folio volumes in 1733-59. Almost all their work has stood the test of time. The range of their learning and the sureness of their judgement still command the admiration of Patristic scholars after three hundred years and for some of the Fathers their text has never been surpassed. For the greater part of Athanasius, even today the student has no better text than that of B. de Montfaucon of 1698, just referred to.

The 18th century saw a number of ambitious undertakings, though on the whole there was no advance in scholarship over the best work of the previous century. Many of the Fathers were assembled in A. Gallandi's *Bibliotheca Veterum Patrum Antiquorumque Scriptorum Ecclesiasticorum* (14 vols., Venice, 1765-81). This heralded the vast *Patrologiae* of the Abbé J. P. Migne of the middle of the 19th century. Within the space of little over twenty years, Migne produced a tool of inestimable value. In the years 1844-66 he issued a fresh edition of the whole Patristic *corpus*, Greek and Latin—the *Patrologia Latina* in 221 volumes and the *Patrologia Graeca* in 162 volumes.[1] The speed at which Migne forged ahead precluded him from aiming at a new critical text. He was content to utilise the best texts available from earlier editors. Useful aids to the Greek Migne are the Indices of F. Cavallera (Paris, 1912) and of T. Hopfner (2 vols., 1928-45).

Since the middle of the 19th century, an increasing number of the Fathers have been reissued in critical texts.

---

[1] Sets usually contain only 161 volumes, as only a very few copies of the concluding volume ('igne destructus') found their way into circulation. This volume consists mainly of a collection of miscellaneous texts omitted by oversight from their proper place in the series.

Editors have employed to an ever greater extent the new technical resources of the camera and the railway. Two important series, begun respectively by the Viennese and Prussian Academies, are still in progress. In 1866 the Vienna Academy began a series of critical texts of the Latin Fathers, the *Corpus Scriptorum Ecclesiasticorum Latinorum*. The series opened in that year with C. Halm's text of Sulpicius Severus. A notable early edition in the series was W. Hartel's text of Cyprian (3 parts, 1868-71). The complementary series of the Greek Fathers, *Die griechischen christlichen Schriftsteller der ersten drei Jahrhunderte*, in this case restricted mainly to pre-Nicene writers, was originally the work of the Kirchenväter Kommission of the Prussian Academy. This series opened in 1897 with Hippolytus' works (vol. i: Exegetical and Homiletic Writings). Its excellent texts of Origen and Hippolytus have inaugurated a new era in the study of both these Fathers. This series now includes some fifty volumes.

Of recent series, one of the best is the collection of *Sources Chrétiennes* (Paris, 1942ff.), directed by H. de Lubac, S.J., J. Daniélou, S.J., and C. Mondésert, S.J. Its volumes usually contain a critical edition of the original text with annotated French translations on the opposite page. The texts have been chosen with much imagination, though they occasionally go outside the limits of 'Patristics' in the strict sense, e.g. the titles include the Gnostic Ptolemy's Letter to Flora (No. 24) and Aelred of Rievaulx's 'When Jesus was Twelve Years Old' (No. 60). The most recent item to date is an edition of Origen's 'Discussion with Heracleides' (No. 67; 1960).

Two other important new series are the *Corpus Christianorum*, a complete new edition of the Latin Fathers in the competent hands of the Benedictines of Steenbrugge (1954ff.), and a new Supplement to Migne, ed. by A. Hamman (Turnhout, 1958ff.).

There also exists, it need hardly be added, a large number of modern editions of single texts. Many of these have already been referred to at the appropriate place in this volume.

II. MODERN TRANSLATIONS. The Fathers have been extensively rendered into modern languages. The pre-Nicene Fathers are most conveniently accessible in English translation in the *Ante-Nicene Christian Library* (24 vols., Edinburgh, 1866-72), which contains the great majority of the texts prior to A.D. 325. The translation is for the most part reasonably accurate, if not always very fluent. Another notable series is the *Library of the Fathers*, published under Tractarian influence. It opened with E. B. Pusey's translation of the *Confessions of St. Augustine*, issued in 1838. Of more modern collections, several Patristic writings have been edited in the present century by the S.P.C.K. in their 'Early Church Classics' and 'Translations of Christian Literature'. In general these have good notes and introductions, though the series makes no pretence at completeness and the method and scope of the annotation depend on the individual editor. Two other series of selected texts have been making rapid progress since the Second World War. The *Ancient Christian Writers*, published under (mainly American) Roman Catholic direction, contains several convenient and well-edited texts (about 30 vols. to date). The *Library of Christian Classics* (1953ff.) is a carefully planned selection of Christian writings in English translation from the post-Apostolic Age down to modern times in 26 volumes. The first eight volumes cover the period of the Fathers: i-ii, The Pre-Nicene Age; iii-iv, Miscellaneous post-Nicene Fathers; and vi-viii, St. Augustine. Among French translations of the Fathers, besides the somewhat eclectic choice of texts in *Sources Chrétiennes*, already referred to, there is the older series of *Textes et Documents*, ed. H. Hemmer-P. Lejay, also with text and translation on opposite pages (20 vols., Paris, 1904-12). In German a considerable range of translations is available in the various series of the *Bibliothek der Kirchenväter* (Kempten, 1869ff.). It contains certain post-Nicene texts, e.g. the writings of Epiphanius, which are not easily available, if at all, in any other modern language.

III. PATRISTIC STUDIES. An early exercise in Patristic study is Jerome's *De Viris Illustribus* (A.D. 392), which is modelled on Suetonius' work of the same title. It lists 135 Fathers and their principal writings and draws for its material extensively on Eusebius. Jerome's treatise was continued by several later writers, Gennadius of Marseilles (*c.* 480), Isidore of Seville (615-18) and Ildefons of Toledo (d. 667) from the later Patristic age among them. The growth of Church history as we know it today has developed only since the Renaissance. The earlier modern Church histories were largely polemical. A landmark on the Protestant side was the work of the Centuriators of Magdeburg which, though it saw the course of Christian history as a progressive declension from the primitive purity of the Church under the dominion of the Papacy until it was liberated from Antichrist by Luther, for the first time interpreted the course of Church history as a continuous whole. On the Catholic side, Cardinal Baronius was prompted to write his *Annales Ecclesiastici* (12 vols., fol. 1589-1607) in reply. He was spurred on by the not very difficult task of discovering errors of detail in the Centuriators though his own critical powers and wish for accuracy fell far short of his good intentions. In the next generation much was done to promote the scientific study of Church history by the Maurists. In the matter of the continuous exposition of Church history on a large scale, the work of Tillemont was epoch-making. His large quarto volumes were long under suspicion owing to their author's Jansenist sympathies, but his *Mémoires pour servir à l'Histoire ecclésiastique des six premiers Siècles* (15 vols., 1695-1707) were universally recognised as a work of immense erudition. They carried the history of the Church down to A.D. 513.

The Tübingen School of the 1840's, with its Hegelian thesis that the 'Catholic Church' was the synthesis from the conflict between 'Petrinism' (thesis) and 'Paulinism' (antithesis), led to a new interest in the first two centuries and occasioned several important monographs, such as A. Hilgenfeld's studies of Gnosticism. If their Hegelian philosophy professedly subordinated fact to theory ('If the facts don't fit the theories, so much the worse for the facts'), their speculations acted as a powerful stimulus to the study of Church history. As the 19th century advanced, the ideal of strict historical objectivity, of which an early example was Leopold von Ranke's *History of the Papacy* (orig. ed. of German, 3 vols., 1834-6), was carried over into all branches of Church history. Among German Church historians an outstanding place was occupied by Adolf Harnack with his almost unbelievable industry. In France, the brilliance of Louis Duchesne, with his keen judgement, great erudition, always lightly borne, and delicate wit, was unsurpassed. Few books can be better suited for the tyro embarking on original work in Church history as a study in method than Duchesne's edition of the *Liber Pontificalis*.

IV. CHURCH HISTORIES. Among the chief modern histories of the early Church are (1) L. Duchesne, *Histoire Ancienne de l'Église Chrétienne* (3 vols., 1906-10; Eng. tr. 1909-24); (2) A. Harnack, *Die Mission und Ausbreitung des Christentums in den ersten drei Jahrhunderten* (1902; ed. 4, much enlarged, 1924; Eng. tr. by J. Moffatt, 2 vols., 1904-5); (3) B. J. Kidd, *A History of the Church to A.D. 461* (3 vols., 1922); (4) H. Lietzmann, *Geschichte der alten Kirche* (4 vols., 1932-44; Eng. tr. under various titles, 1937-51; specially stimulating on archaeological and liturgical matters); and (5) A. Fliche-V. Martin (edd.), *Histoire de l'Église depuis les Origines jusqu'à nos jours* (1938ff.), designed to be completed in 24 vols. Vols. i-v cover the Patristic period.

V. HANDBOOKS TO PATRISTIC STUDIES. The principal guides to Patristic literature include (1) A. Harnack, *Die Geschichte der altchristlichen Literatur bis Eusebius* (2 vols. in 3, 1893-1904), monumental in its detailed learning; (2) O. Bardenhewer, *Geschichte der altkirchlichen Literatur* (5 vols., 1902-32), also a mine of information and consistently accurate, by a leading Catholic scholar; (3) B. Altaner,

Patrologie (ed. 5, 1958; Eng. tr. by H. C. Graef, 1960), with full lists of new bibliography in successive editions. It is esp. useful for its citation of items published later than the successive volumes of Bardenhewer. Smaller Patrologies are those of (4) F. Cayré, A.A. (2 vols., 1927-30; ed. 3, 3 vols., 1945; Eng. tr., 2 vols., 1936-40); (5) A. Puech (Greek Fathers only, 3 vols., Paris, 1928-30); (6) P. de Labriolle (Latin Fathers only, Paris, 1920, new ed., 1947; Eng. tr. 1924); (7) B. Steidle, O.S.B. (in Latin, Freiburg i. Br., 1937); and (8) J. Quasten (in English, Utrecht, 2 vols. to date, 1950 and 1953). On the Syriac writers I. Ortiz de Urbina, S.J., *Patrologia Syriaca*, is the most useful and most up-to-date manual (Rome, 1958). An invaluable guide to editions of the Latin Fathers is the *Clavis Patrum Latinorum* of E. Dekkers, O.S.B. (Steenbrugge, 1951; new ed. in preparation). For current bibliography the student should now consult the annual publication *Bibliographia Patristica* covering publications from 1956 onwards, ed. by W. Schneemelcher (Berlin, 1959ff.).

Among the principal collections of modern Patristic studies are *Texte und Untersuchungen zur Geschichte der altkirchlichen Literatur* (1882ff., publd. by the Berlin Academy, about 75 vols. to date); the *Cambridge Texts and Studies* (Series I, 10 vols., 1891-1952; Series II, 1953ff.); and *Studi e Testi* (Rome, 1900ff.).

Of modern dictionaries full place is given to the Fathers in the *Dictionnaire de Théologie Catholique* (15 vols., Paris, 1903-50), the *Dictionnaire d'Archéologie Chrétienne et de Liturgie* (15 vols., Paris, 1907-53) and the *Enciclopedia Cattolica* (12 vols., Rome [1949-54]). There are also many good articles on Patristic subjects in the *Dictionary of Christian Biography* (4 vols., 1877-87), though much of it is now antiquated.

Mention should also be made again (cf. p. 100) of F. van der Meer and C. Mohrmann, *Atlas of the Early Christian World* (maps and archaeological illustrations, Eng. tr. by M. F. Hedlund and H. H. Rowley, 1958).

PATRISTIC INDEX

[The principal references are given in HEAVY type]

INDEX OF POST-PATRISTIC AUTHORS

215